THE OTHER FAB FOUR

THE OTHER FAB FOUR

THE REMARKABLE TRUE STORY OF THE LIVERBIRDS, BRITAIN'S FIRST FEMALE ROCK BAND

MARY McGLORY AND SYLVIA SAUNDERS

GRAND
CENTRAL

NEW YORK   BOSTON

Grand Central Publishing
Hachette Book Group
1290 Avenue of the Americas, New York, NY 10104
grandcentralpublishing.com
@grandcentralpub

First Edition: March 2024

Grand Central Publishing is a division of Hachette Book Group, Inc. The Grand Central Publishing name and logo is a registered trademark of Hachette Book Group, Inc.

The publisher is not responsible for websites (or their content) that are not owned by the publisher.

Grand Central Publishing books may be purchased in bulk for business, educational, or promotional use. For information, please contact your local bookseller or the Hachette Book Group Special Markets Department at special.markets@hbgusa.com.

See photo credits on page 321.

Library of Congress Control Number: 2023951941

ISBNs: 9781538739969 (hardcover), 9781538739983 (ebook)

Printed in the United States of America

LSC-C

Printing 1, 2024

Contents

BOOK THREE: INDEPENDENCE

BOOK FOUR: REUNION

Prologue

It's June 6, 1964, and we're four working-class girls from Liverpool on our way to support the legendary Chuck Berry, the inventor of rock 'n' roll. We can't believe it—we only arrived in Hamburg a week ago to play a short residency at the famous Star-Club, the place where the Beatles honed their sound, and now we're going to be onstage with our idol. We've never flown before, but the four of us are on a shaky propeller plane with star bands Ian and the Zodiacs, Lee Curtis and the All-Stars, Kingsize Taylor, and the Rattles. When we take off our bass player, Mary, is so terrified she grabs hold of an All-Star, nearly scratching his arm off.

As soon as we touch down in Berlin we're taken in a limousine to the massive Deutschlandhalle, with eleven thousand people already waiting inside. There is no sound check. And then, just before going onstage, the stage manager drops a bombshell: we can't do any Chuck Berry songs. We look at each other. That's what we've spent the previous week rehearsing. How are we going to play two twenty-minute sets without a Chuck Berry?

We walk out on stage in front of the biggest audience we've ever seen. We've never played anywhere this size and as soon as we start playing "Roadrunner," we realize that the acoustics are terrible. We had no idea that everything would reverberate back so it's impossible to hear each other. After soldiering through the first set we sprint to the bar, but scarcely have time to drink a shandy before the promoter barks over the microphone, "Liverbirds, back onstage!"

We hurry back on in a panic, but the crowd are cheering. *Ah, we couldn't have been that bad.* The reaction gives Val, our normally quiet lead singer and guitarist, a burst of confidence.

"Blow it," she says, "we're doing 'Roll Over Beethoven'!"

"You can't—"

" 'Roll Over Beethoven'—one, two, three, four!"

When we launch into the song, the crowd erupts. This is what they've been waiting for. And that's when we see him—Chuck Berry himself, with his slick, pomaded hair and chiseled cheekbones, glowering at the side of the stage. As Sylvia thwacks the drums harder he starts to pace behind her, swearing and telling her to stop. The next thing we know, Berry's manager runs on stage and yells in Val's face: "STOP!"

"Fuck off," she retorts, and carries on playing. The second the song ends, Val announces: "Now, 'Johnny Be Goode.' And all the other Chuck Berry songs we can play."

By now the crowd are cheering and stomping so hard that Berry's manager melts away. At the end of the set we walk offstage, elated. We've never known a feeling like that before.

When we return to our hotel in the early hours, we find a message from our manager, Manfred Weissleder, the owner of Hamburg's Star-Club. "I'd like to speak to you girls in the morning."

Oh God, he doesn't want to manage us anymore, we've had it. After a fitful sleep, the four of us sidle into his office and sit nervously on his red velvet sofa.

"Girls. I have to talk to you."

We're about to babble our apologies—*Sorry, we'll never do it again*—when he says: "Chuck Berry's manager wants to bring you to America."

"Wha-a-t?"

"Yes. He wants to take you to America."

We love Hamburg, we're enjoying the Star-Club—but we've never been to the States before. The offer is tempting. Then Manfred shoots us a look.

"If you go to America he will take you to Las Vegas. But he wants you to play topless."

We want to go to America but don't take up the offer. Being treated as a gimmick is just one of the challenges of being girls in the rock 'n' roll world and we don't let that put us off. We've already overcome obstacles to get here, we have each other and the music we love, and we're looking forward to more adventures. We've come a long way from the Liverpool Cavern and we're still only in our teens.

BOOK ONE: LIVERPOOL

1. MARY

Dolly Dunn Always Has the Best

I remember happy times playing with other kids in bombed-out houses, what we called "the bomby." Living in Burlington Street felt cozy and safe. It was a small third-floor flat in old Victorian terraced housing near the docks, with a view of the chimneys of the Tate & Lyle sugar factory. The neighbors were close by, walking in and out of the flats, or drinking together in the Green Man pub on the corner. After last orders at ten o'clock every Friday and Saturday a crate of beer would be brought back to the flat and my uncles tinkled on the piano while Mum played the spoons and tap-danced. Everyone sang until the early hours of the morning, Cockney wartime songs such as "We'll Meet Again," or Irish and Scottish folk ditties like "Danny Boy" or "Loch Lomond." Mum was a brilliant tap dancer; when she was younger she wanted to be like Ginger Rogers and she danced at all the parties. Dad was a burly man who had a lovely big voice and in another life he would have been an opera singer. He used to sing in the bathroom, making the words up. In many ways he was misunderstood because he didn't often show his feelings—but when something did hit him he'd be in tears with emotion; he felt things deeply.

As a young child, I also loved going out with my grandma, my mum's mum, who was a fruit-seller. Dolly Dunn was short and well built, and one of my favorite things was to sit balanced on her hand-cart by the handlebars while she wheeled me up and down the Dock Road shouting "Fruit! Fruit!" It was a great feeling. People would gather around saying, "There's Dolly Dunn, let's buy our fruit, she's always got the best." She was the real money-earner in the family. From Monday to Saturday she'd get up early and go to the market to buy fruit and vegetables for the handcart, even in winter. On Sundays she sold flowers outside Ford Cemetery, keeping them in bunches in a big basket that she carried on her head. She always had the freshest blooms.

My dad's side, the McGlory family, were posh because they lived in a terraced house and always seemed to have the best food and nicest clothes. By contrast, Mum and Dad were constantly having to scrimp and save. In the winter, when it snowed, our flat was so cold that there were icicles inside the window, and we huddled round a small fireplace in the living room. Sometimes, Santa Claus didn't come at Christmas and we just had an orange and an apple each, but there was always Christmas dinner. The size of the turkey depended on how well Grandma Dunn did with her barrow. We would all stand round the table while she brought in the bird, proudly placing it in the center. It was my mum's job to pluck the feathers and get it ready. Even though we didn't get presents, this Christmas dinner made up for everything.

~

My mother, Maggie, was tall, thin and very beautiful when she was young, but she had a hard life. My grandpa James Dunn was a docker who came over to Liverpool from Tipperary in Ireland, and my maternal grandparents were from County Louth, near the Northern Irish border. Mum came from a family of ten children who lived down near Liverpool docks, only five of whom survived. In those days bad sanitation, damp housing, and poverty in general meant that many children died shortly after birth. At five o'clock every morning Mum and her siblings would go to the railway tracks to pick up coal that had fallen off the steam engines and take it home for fuel. They went to school with dusty hands and were punished for wearing dirty clothes.

The story of how my mum, Maggie Dunn, met my father, Joseph McGlory, is an unusual one. Her first love was actually Joseph's brother, Richard. At sixteen my mum worked in the British Tobacco factory, and it was there that she met twenty-six-year-old Richard McGlory. They courted and fell deeply in love, but the burgeoning relationship was interrupted by World War II, when Richard joined the merchant navy. His younger brother Joseph, my father, insisted on going with him to fight the Germans. Even though Dad was two years below the enlistment age of eighteen, he idolized his brother who arranged false papers so he could join up too. A few weeks after setting off, their ship, the steam tanker SS *British Consul*, was torpedoed in Port of Spain, Trinidad, and the crew had to stay in the Caribbean for six months while it was repaired. During that time Richard received a letter from Mum saying she was pregnant, expecting his baby.

"Oh Margaret, please arrange the wedding. As soon as I return we'll get married," he wrote back, telling her to go to his sister Julia for financial help.

But not long after his letter was sent, tragedy struck. On August 18, 1942, my dad was on the night shift but he had a high fever so Richard said, "You go to bed, I'll do your shift." Early the next morning the ship was torpedoed again, but this time it hit the engine room and two people died. My dad was rescued but his brother Richard didn't survive. Dad was haunted by memories of seeing him drown, of sitting in the lifeboat shouting, "My brother's over there!" long after Richard disappeared beneath the waves. Dad's name was on the nightshift log when the ship went down, so he was the McGlory brother reported dead. When he returned home the family was at the docks expecting to see Richard. Even though they were glad to see my dad alive, they were devastated that his older brother had died.

Despite Richard's letter to Mum before his death, the McGlory sisters pretended they knew nothing about his marriage proposal so that they could share the money that was sent to the family in compensation. Forced to have the baby alone, Mum became a single mother at seventeen, living in a poky little house by the docks while the McGlorys, a strong Catholic family, ignored her. Just three months later, baby Winifred died. On the day of the funeral Mum ran behind the glass carriage where her baby lay in a tiny white coffin. "Why doesn't anybody believe me?" she cried. "Everybody says she's dead, she's only asleep!"

Mum slowly recovered, finding work in the ammunition factory, and then on the trams as a ticket collector. My dad was on leave one day when he bumped into her.

"You'll never believe who I saw working on a tram as a clippie," Joseph said to his sister Julia.

"Who?"

"Maggie Dunn."

Julia turned to her sister Annie and said, "We've lost him. 'Cos what Maggie Dunn wants, Maggie Dunn gets."

My dad ended up marrying my mum and, even though he knew she loved him, at the back of his mind there was always the niggling thought that he'd been her second choice. I was their first child, born after the war on February 2, 1946, when much of Liverpool was still a bombsite. We had three bedrooms: Grandma Dolly shared one with my uncle, while I slept with my parents in another, and Grandpa was relegated to the box room.

Grandma was a hardworking woman who rose early with her flower cart and, like many of her friends, slept separately from her husband. People told me that my grandfather was a bit of a dandy, and may have carried on with other women. Wives might have put up with bad behavior when their children were small, but started paying their men back as they got older. My grandparents' generation didn't really get divorced, the husbands and wives would just stop sleeping together.

By the time I was born my grandfather wasn't working anymore. He used to have a job at the docks as a cocky watchman, a security guard, but after he stopped he would just hang around with his friends, and sometimes he would take me along. Many of these men had lost a limb in World War I, so as a child I assumed getting older meant that a leg or arm would drop off. Grandpa was a dandy with a hat and a blazer. He was seventy-four when he died and I always remember people saying he was still very nifty on his legs. I think he was a good catch in the day.

When I was two years old my mother had a baby, Bernadette, who died. In the Catholic Church it was considered saintly for a mother to sacrifice her life for her unborn child, and if a priest had been in the hospital that day when the baby got stuck he may have encouraged my mum to become a martyr. But a priest wasn't around so the doctor decided to save my mother, not the baby, and thank God he did. I'd have been without a mum and the rest of my brothers and sisters wouldn't have been born. She didn't tell me what happened until years later. My dad was away at sea, so a neighbor took me to visit the maternity ward, where all the mothers had babies apart from my mum. She was sitting in bed in a posh morning coat she had borrowed, and she was crying. The neighbor tried to comfort her, saying, "You'll be okay, Maggie, there'll be other ones."

Our neighbor was right—my first three siblings, Joseph, Richard, and Margarita, arrived in quick succession between 1949 and 1953. Me and my brothers slept top to toe in the big double bed with my parents, while Margarita snuggled in a cot at the foot of the bed.

Because of his job in the merchant navy my father was often away from home. It seemed that nine months after each visit there would be another brother or sister. Every time Mum wore her voluminous blouse I realized there was another baby coming. Childbirth seemed to be a magical process that happened mysteriously during the night, so when Richard was born, for instance, I remember us going to bed and when I got up next morning he was there. Now I think my mum must have gone into Grandma's room to have the baby before bringing him back to our bed.

Richard had curly blond hair and looked like an angel, but when he was a small boy neighbors in the road would complain to the parish priest, "Richard McGlory is a terrible swearer." Father Pownall from St. Philomena's church came round one day to bless Richard and put holy water on his tongue to stop him swearing. The priest tried to get Richard to talk, but he refused to speak so the priest blessed his tongue and left. After he had gone Richard turned round and said, "Who the fucking hell does he think he is?" He was so funny, he always made us laugh. He was also a fantastic footballer, winning best amateur trophies seven years in a row. But he refused offers of training with the youth teams at Everton and Liverpool because he didn't want to leave his mates.

As the family grew Mum persuaded Dad to stop going away to sea and find a job in Liverpool, so he ended up working at the power station. By the time I was seven the city was expanding with post-war reconstruction, and there was a big change when we moved to 36 Ternhall Road on the new Sparrow Hall estate. The house was just four miles north of the city center, but to us, going to the suburbs felt like moving to the country because at the end of our estate were fields with cow and sheep. When my grandma came to visit she'd sit there in the three-bedroom terrace saying, "Our poor Maggie's got to clean this great big house."

On the estate we would play in the street, tying ropes around the top of lampposts and using them to swing round and round before letting ourselves go, unraveling at speed. I would play hopscotch with my friends Maddie McKenars, Bridie Blood, and Nelly Nesbit, who lived fifteen minutes away by tram. I thought Nelly was really posh. Nelly was the youngest of a big family, and that position made a difference to their standard of living because her older siblings were already out earning money. There was also Frances Philips who lived next door and always wanted to be friends, but I was less enamored with her. When Nelly or Maddie weren't around, Mum would say, "Why don't you give Frances a try?" Frances would come round and terribly get on my nerves, so I'd say to Mum, "Sorry, she's got to go." I particularly enjoyed playing with Nelly because she had better toys and she had her own bedroom. Even after we moved to Sparrow Hall I still had to share a bed with my siblings and the family continued growing, taking up more space. I constantly had to help Mum with the younger kids, and longed for my own room.

By then I was going to the local Catholic school, St. Philomena's in Sparrow Hall, where the teachers enforced regulations through fear and suspicion. My primary school, Our Lady Immaculate (which later joined up with St. Philomena's), had also been terrifying—it was in an old Victorian building run by strict nuns, and the school priest, Father Twomey, was a canon who wore a black robe with a red belt. He would pick boys up by their ears and hit them on the knuckles with his cane. It was a system of corporal punishment that was echoed with even more severity in St. Philomena's. I was a nervy child at school and ended up being smacked every week with the cane.

I was never good at spelling but I've got a good memory, so to learn how to spell words I would have to memorize them by heart. Every Monday we would be given ten spellings for a test on Friday. All the hours spent helping Mum with housework and the children meant I didn't have time to practice at home, so when it came to Friday I never scored well in the spelling test. Accusing me of neglecting my homework, the headmaster, Mr. Naylor, would hit me with two slaps of the cane. Yes, a grown man caning an eight-year-old girl. I never told my mother because I knew that she would march up to the school and argue, and I didn't want to get her into trouble. Every Friday it was the same thing.

In 1957 my dad got a job working for the British Road Services delivering parcels to Warrington or Manchester. One of his co-workers made a profit selling items from parcels that "fell off the back of the lorry." Dad bought a few things from him, and when the management found out about the stolen goods he was reported to the police and arrested. He refused to rat on his co-workers and was sent to prison for six months, leaving my mum to look after four children alone.

A cherished present my dad bought from the lorry was a pretty watch with a leather strap. One morning before PE I had to take off my watch and give it to Miss Callaghan, a disciplinarian who later became headmistress.

"Mary McGlory," she said in front of the whole class, "That is not your watch!"

"It is my watch."

"Your family can't afford anything like that."

After the PE lesson Miss Callaghan handed back the watch with a judgmental air, scornful of Dad's attempt to buy me something nice.

She dominated the school with her strict, unforgiving approach, along with the tyrannical Mr. Naylor.

While Dad was in prison I missed him terribly—his absence was like a hole in the family. The watch reminded me of him, along with something he gave me two years earlier. When I was nine I had to go to Alder Hey children's hospital to have my appendix removed, and on the way, in the ambulance, Dad said, "What can I buy ya, girl?"

"Ah, a prayer book and a medal."

So he came to the ward the next day with a prayer book and a medal. When he was in prison those things comforted me, making him feel closer.

At that point Margarita and Colette were still very young, so it was a handful for my mum. We didn't feel judged by the neighbors—they were all struggling with big families too. Dad only served four and a half months of his sentence, but after his release it took two years for him to get a job, and that was hard. Father Pownall would come round with a donation for my mum saying, "Here, Maggie, get something for the kids." Nine months after Dad came home Christine was born on Christmas Day 1958, so that meant more kids to feed. I used to say, "I'd love a sister," but by the time my fourth sister, Sharon, arrived in 1962, I had plenty. Sharon was pretty wild and untameable as a child. I was already sixteen when she was born, and she always says that because she was such a bloody nuisance I only joined the Liverbirds to get away from her!

2. SYLVIA

Take That Monkey Away

I grew up in Cumpsty Road on a brand-new post-war housing estate in Litherland, north of the city center. I was born on October 31, 1946, and benefitted from being the youngest in my family. There was a twelve-year gap between me and my older sister Jean, who remembered the family living in a chilly house by the canal that was dripping with damp and mold. Our parents, Gertie and Christopher Saunders, didn't have a lot of money, but at that time nobody else did, and no one thought they were better than anyone else.

Jean has war memories of being evacuated to Clwyd in north Wales with Auntie Betty, who was only five years older, and staying with a mean-spirited family who lived near a railway station. She was terrified by the steam that shot up every time a train went under the bridge, and the family's two sons, "a couple of buggers," used to delight in taking Jean and Betty to the bridge and scaring them senseless. The girls had to sleep in the cellar and at night when they were asleep the sons would knock and shout through the door. Their mother took away the girls' best dresses, substituting them for dowdy old clothes.

One day my parents paid a visit and asked Jean: "What have you got on?"

"She gives us these clothes and put the others away for best."

Mum went to the woman and said straight out: "Get Jean and Betty's clothes. I'm taking them home."

"What are you doing that for?"

"You're not treating them right."

"I treat them like my daughters."

"No you don't."

And Mum took them back home, where Jean stayed for the rest of the war.

Jean and my parents spent a lot of time hiding in an air-raid shelter in the field at the back of the house. She had an identity card and a gas mask she used to sling over her shoulder and take to school. Dad was an air-raid warden with a tin hat, making sure that every night people's blackout curtains were closed. He also had a stirrup pump and water buckets to put out the incendiary bombs. After a night's bombing Jean sometimes woke up to see a huge gaping hole where a neighbor's house should be. It was very sad. She remembers the 1941 May Blitz when the German Luftwaffe bombed the Huskisson Dock and a munition ship caught fire, exploding its cargo of 1,000 tons of bombs. The explosion was heard in Southport, shattering windows for miles around. Jean saw the sulfurous flames blazing yellow and blue against the night sky, a fire that took over six days to burn out. The Luftwaffe caused a huge amount of damage, dropping more than 112,000 firebombs during the war. Outside London, Liverpool was the city worst hit, with 4,000 civilians killed and over 70,000 made homeless. No wonder there was anti-German feeling in our parents' generation that lingered long after the war.

Jean remembers they had a coal fire, and it was Dad's job to empty the ashes, build a new fire with coal and bundles of wood, before putting potato peelings on the top to seal in the heat. They burned everything; there was no rubbish and the only thing in the bin was cinders from the fire. Every bit of food that wasn't eaten would be put in a bin for the pig man, who used to collect the scraps every Friday. My dad would walk along the rail embankment with his brother, collecting coal that had fallen off the trains, and at Christmastime he would shovel snow for a few shillings. Dad also worked at the docks and ended up in Southport Infirmary when a siding train injured him, crushing his stomach. He didn't receive compensation, they just gave him a job as a crane driver, climbing lots of steps to get into the cabin and working long hours unloading and loading cargo ships.

Dad used to grow potatoes and carrots, and he kept chickens in a shed at the bottom of the garden, along with a big fat rooster. People didn't moan about the rooster because he'd give them a wake-up call up at six o'clock every morning. My great-grandma Saunders took advantage of the hens. She was a nasty old lady, a moneylender. In those days a lot of working-class families needed emergency credit, and mothers managing household expenses would be driven to borrow from pawnbrokers or moneylenders like my great-grandma, who could charge high rates of interest. As she grew older she would spend time living with different relatives, and for a while she stayed in the family house in Bark Road and took over the parlor. She claimed she was too old to get out of bed, so Mum used to cook her an egg for her breakfast. After a while, the next-door neighbor Mrs. Brondell said to my mum, "Hey, she's having you on."

"Why?"

"I've seen her in your hen pen picking the eggs up. And she has an egg when you're not there."

In the 1930s a quarter of dockers' families lived below the poverty line, and many children had to go without. Because she was born before the war, Jean missed out on the toys and treats that we had. When she was a child a visit to the doctor cost half a crown, there were no benefits and no National Health Service. Dad used to have a bad chest cold every winter, so the doctor used to make a big bottle of brown medicine and Jean would go and collect it. "There's the money," Mum would say, "and there's a shilling off what we owe him." God knows how doctors made money. Because cash was tight people would resort to home remedies, like a family friend who drank soot in his milk every day, certain that combination cured his stomach ulcer.

My mother, Gertie, was inspiring; an industrious woman who often worked several jobs. She did shifts in the Pioneer laundry steaming all the clothes, and during the war she worked in Appleby Flour Mill in Bootle. She'd come home covered in flour and say: "Jean, brush me hair." She would put her head over the kitchen sink and while Jean brushed her hair, dozens of little black flour weevils would drop out. Mum also worked in a fish-and-chip shop in Moseley Road, then a petrol station, and then she had a milk round, the first woman in the area to drive the electric Baine's Dairy milk float. She cleaned telephone boxes, taking apart the receivers to wipe away the dust and grease. She also scrubbed old people's doorsteps. There was never a moment when she wasn't working. My dad did night shifts at the docks and Mum worked during the day, so he would see us off to school before going home to bed. Then when we came home he was getting ready for his shift and Mum was back to cook dinner.

Mum was one of seven children and her family, the Hignetts, like the Saunderses on my dad's side, have been in Liverpool for generations. Granny Hignett was a cleaner at the Overhead Railway along the docks, working mostly alongside men. When they got together in the pub she would play the accordion and they'd sing along. Though Granny was musical she didn't pass that down to Mum—we had a piano in the parlor that was never touched until Uncle Tom from Salford came to visit every month and we'd listen to him play while we sang the old variety songs.

Mum could be reserved with her emotions and didn't like to pass comment. Dad, on the other hand, was easygoing and lovable, smoking Woodbines and sitting by the fire. As long as he had his fire and his Woodies he was happy. You could get round my dad, but not my mum.

~

My brother Chris was two years older than me, and a little devil. We went to Litherland council nursery, and one day he put me in the laundry basket, telling me to hide under the clothes so nobody knew where I was. *I'll get rid of her, she's always hanging round me,* he thought. They discovered me an hour later when the man came to take the laundry.

When we were a little older my brother came home after school with a bunch of flowers for our mum.

"Where d'you get those from, Chris?"

He had jumped over the cemetery wall, stolen flowers from the pots of people who had just been buried, and taken them home to her as a present. I remember our sister Jean would bring friends home from work and say, "You behave yourself, Chris." When Mum brought out fancy cakes for tea he licked his fingers, poked a cake and claimed ownership, shouting "I want that one!" Of course Jean had to give him the cake. Or sometimes Mum would go to the pantry and say: "There's a mouse been at the cheese." Because of the gap in his front teeth, she recognized Chris's toothmarks on the cheddar. Chris was always naughty, but I liked playing with him.

My sister Jean met Bob, a Royal Navy seaman, when she was fifteen. He used to walk around with me hanging on to his leg, because I was in love with him, and hoped he'd bring me something back from countries he visited. He often came with presents, like little bracelets or pajamas, and a silk bomber jacket with a dragon on the back. Once a fortnight on a Saturday night my mum and dad would go to the cinema, leaving Jean and Bob to babysit. Jean said I was a blinkin' nuisance. We were meant to go to bed at eight o'clock, but they would put the clock forward two hours and shunt us into bed at six to get more time for themselves.

Bob had a scooter and would take Jean everywhere, and much later, when he got a car, he became the Liverbirds' roadie. Jean was independent and keen to start a family—she was engaged at eighteen and got married to Bob when she was twenty-one. She gave birth to Jackie in 1959 at the age of twenty-five, and then Robert arrived two years later. Bob's family were Catholics who cooked a big family dinner every Sunday and invited their local priest. Before the priest came they liked to play cards until one of the kids watching at the window would shout, "The priest is coming!" All of a sudden the money and the cards were shoved out the way and a bottle of whisky appeared. The priest would have frowned on the gambling, but he always had a drink of whisky.

Audrey Halliwell on the corner was my friend on the street; we used to go to school together and play skipping and hopscotch. But there weren't many girls on the estate so I became a tomboy, following my brother around and trying to play football with the lads in the streets. "Here's your Syl, get rid of her," they would say. We'd swing rope around the lamppost and play hide-and-seek games like Kick the Can and Oh Sally-O. There was a wide cow field on the other side of the road, where a man we called Billy Blow Blow used to tend to the cows. We'd tease him until he chased us, even though he had a lame leg.

I was a little accident-prone. Cumpsty Road had old black fire grates and a fireguard, and one night when I was six Dad put the fireguard to the side and I sat on it, branded my bottom, and was taken yelling to the doctor with a burned behind. Then when I was eight years old I nearly poisoned myself. We would take Coca-Cola bottles to the shop to be filled with Aunt Sally, a reddish, liquid disinfectant soap, which Mum used to wash the floors. One afternoon I went to the pantry and took a bottle of Cola, thinking, *I'm going to take a swig of this, I'm thirsty.* Then I realized what I'd done.

"Oh Mum, I drank Aunt Sally!"

"You better get down to Dr. Mendix. Get to Mendix right away!"

So I ran to Dr. Mendix. "I've drunk Aunt Sally!"

"How much have you drunk?"

"Just a mouthful."

"Right just go home, and make sure the toilet is free. It'll go through you."

We started work as soon as we could, to help support the family. When he was ten years old Chris worked in the dairy with my mum, helping her to deliver milk from her electric float. To sign up new customers they would drive around the Litherland estate, knocking on doors offering people a week's free milk and a dozen eggs if they joined Baine's Dairy. The milk was bottled early every morning for deliveries, and every Friday night Mum and Chris would collect the money. Inevitably there would be some people who couldn't pay. Chris would go to a house, knock on the door, and a little boy might answer through the letterbox, "Me mum says she's not in."

We adopted cats—any that we found wandering in the street we used to pick up and put in the back kitchen. We had a ginger cat called Minnie, who disappeared one night. Dad called to her from the back door, but there was no cat, so Mum said, "Oh, she's out with a mate, so let's go to bed." Just before we went upstairs Dad opened the oven door and the cat was inside, on her last breath. He caught her in the nick of time.

We ended up adopting some strange animals. One day Chris was collecting money for the dairy and a woman said to him: "D'you want a monkey, son?"

"Oh yeah, I'll have a monkey!"

"Here take it—my husband doesn't want pets at home."

She put the dairy money in a plastic bag along with Jacko, a scrawny squirrel monkey with a long tail, wearing a tiny coat the woman had made for him. Kids nicknamed Chris the Monkey Man because he used to take Jacko to school and hide him in his desk, or ride his bike with Jacko perched on his shoulders. The monkey was a funny little thing, climbing the clothes rack in the back kitchen. He'd sit up there on a chain, and if my mum was cooking he'd come down, pinch food and scramble back to the top of the rack. It was cruel really, keeping a monkey out of its environment, but we were so fond of him.

In the summer we saw Jacko catch insects. We had an apple tree in the garden and he would go out there when it was sunny to sit on a branch and watch the leaves. If a fly or butterfly landed on a leaf, he'd grab the insect with a quickfire move—"Got ya!" He was so intelligent. Mum would say, "Take that bloody monkey away," but she also loved him, wrapping Jacko in a shawl and playing with him in the garden.

I was full of restless energy and found it hard to concentrate at Litherland primary school. I've still got all my school reports, which always say, "She needs to concentrate more." At school the only subjects that interested me were drama and sport—I excelled at sports, becoming captain of the hockey and netball teams, and I loved swimming. I was also a drama queen. My mum said she would send me to acting classes and so I started elocution lessons in town. Bob drove me to the class but when his work shifts got in the way, the lessons stopped. Mum didn't want me going on my own, so that was the end of drama.

I used to bunk off school and cut through to the park. We'd pinch apples from trees and when the park warden came round we'd run and hide in the bushes shouting, "The truant man's coming!" Sometimes I got caught and was frogmarched back to school to be admonished by the headmistress. "If you don't pass your exams you can't go to grammar school," she'd say. Because I played truant so often I did fail my eleven-plus exam, which meant I had to attend Litherland Secondary Modern, a girls' school where most of the students left at the age of fifteen and didn't go on to college.

I found the petty rules of Litherland secondary school a trial. Mrs. Anderson used to pick on me, barking "Sylvia Saunders, come here!" Even though my hair was quite short the teacher would grab it at the back and twist it into an elastic band. "Your hair is too long," she would say. There was a young hockey teacher, though, who liked my enthusiasm for sport. One day I swung the hockey stick so hard I hit her in the eye and broke her glasses. I started crying because I felt so bad, but she told me, "Don't worry, I'm fine." She was the only kind teacher I remember.

Holidays offered a sense of release and intoxicating freedom from school. We had a family caravan, and sometimes went to Rhyl, north Wales, staying in chalet huts near the beach, cooking on a small stove. I would go with my friend Kathleen Mercer to Crosby Beach, Merseyside, which was a bland expanse of sand until the sculptor Antony Gormley populated it with his beautiful, enigmatic statues. Back in 1960 it was all sand dunes and water, a place where we could wander and meet lads. Kathleen and I also went to Southport on the train to a fairground where we would get free rides, spinning on the waltzer and flirting with the gaff lads who liked to whirl the girls around at top speed. I was starting to discover freedom outside the regimented confines of school, that being a teenager in the early 1960s meant a world of fun and hedonism, with music right at the center.

3. MARY

Song of Bernadette

Starting a rock-and-roll band wasn't my first choice of profession. In fact, my initial plan had been to become a nun.

At twelve years old I was becoming aware of the wider world. Grandma took me to see *The Song of Bernadette*, a Hollywood movie starring Jennifer Jones as Bernadette Soubirous, a nineteenth-century saint who experienced eighteen visions of the Virgin Mary in a grotto near her home in Lourdes. Bernadette dug a hole where she saw the apparition, which created a bubbling, healing spring and became a place of pilgrimage for people all over the world. The film was intensely moving, particularly toward the end where Bernadette joins the Sisters of Charity, contracts TB of the bone, and despite her intense suffering, continues to pray with her rosary until her dying moment. After we came out of the cinema I thought, *I want to be like St. Bernadette*.

I went to Mass every day and prayed to become a nun. Because the Church had helped my family during difficult times I wanted to pay them back. I hated waking early, but every day I would get up in time to help Mum with the children before I went to seven o'clock Mass. Back in the 1950s you didn't hear about the child-abuse cases that were being hushed up by the Church—in fact, for me at the time, the Catholic Church was the solution to all our problems. My vocation involved more than being a nun: I believed that one day I would be a saint, working on a mission in Africa to save the babies who were dying there.

Part of me yearned to escape. I started getting bad asthma attacks in the middle of the night: we didn't have a phone so Mum or Dad had to go down to the telephone box to get the doctor. An asthma attack made me nervous and worsened the tightness in my chest, so the doctor would bring medication and stay with me until the tablets calmed me down. But partly because of my asthma and because Dad had been in prison, the council presented us with an opportunity: children from poor families were offered a week's holiday in a spacious villa in the countryside, and I was chosen. Mum was given a charity check to buy me clothes especially for the holiday. We had to buy secondhand clothes—not quite the latest fashion—and brown lace-up shoes, because I'd be going on long walks. There wasn't enough money for two pairs of shoes, so I had to take the sensible ones, along with a flowery blue chiffon dress with a voluminous bow.

I traveled with a group of girls on a coach and we stayed in Heswall, in a large Edwardian house on the Dee estuary, where there was wide open space, fresh air and views across the river to north Wales. Despite the natural beauty of the spot, I was homesick, writing letters home to family saying, "I miss you all." Being the eldest I was made head of the dormitory and put in charge of arranging activities, so at the end of the week I organized a concert. No one had musical instruments, so we sang lustily along to the record player.

When I stood up to sing I was wearing that chiffon dress with the awful bow and the terrible lace-up shoes, but even though I hated my outfit, I loved performing. I sang "Paper Roses," which in 1960 was a big hit for the Kaye Sisters, a blond female vocal trio who always wore matching dresses, and then in the 1970s became a hit song for Marie Osmond. I don't know what my version sounded like, but people were standing and clapping, and that's when I thought, *I enjoy this. Wouldn't it be great to be onstage!*

At the age of fourteen my friend Pat Clark and I had the idea of running a youth club in St. Philomena's church hall. Father Bradley was one of the nicest priests in the parish, young and good-looking, and all the girls in the school had a crush on him. He enjoyed knowing that, but he didn't exploit it—he loved his job and would have time for anyone. He was from a new generation of priests who were more informal; he mixed with the lads playing football and wore a denim jacket when he wasn't in his suit and dog collar, but he still delivered a fantastic sermon on a Sunday.

Father Bradley helped us to organize a regular youth club night saying, "If you can get a group to play I'll pay them six pounds a week." We used to see the Merseybeats in the Orrell Park Ballroom, singing Everly Brothers' songs like "Cathy's Clown" or the country classic "From a Jack to a King." Revolving around singer/bassist Billy Kinsley and Tony Crane on lead guitar, the band played well and looked cute, so I got in touch and booked them every Thursday night for the next three months. The audience consisted of kids from St. Philomena's school, while the Merseybeats were teenagers themselves. Tony and Billy were always so kind and uncomplicated—every Thursday they'd walk in, put their equipment on the stage and get ready. That's when my fascination with guitars began. They would play the same set, with maybe one new song each week, while Pat and I sold hamburgers and soft drinks. As the Merseybeats performed I'd sing along and think, I *would love to do that!* I had no idea that I would end up being in a band and performing, just like them.

4. SYLVIA

I Was a Bit of a One

As a teenager I became fashion-conscious, asking Mum if we could buy new clothes and shoes. She saved money by buying "Provvy" (Providence) checks. Moneylenders like my great-grandma had been replaced by the "tallyman," a loan system where the Providence man would come to the front door with hundred- or fifty-pound checks, which could be spent in their designated shops and repaid in weekly amounts with interest. Mum would say, "Come on, I'll buy you a pair of shoes for going out." I wanted elegant shoes with thin heels, but when we got to Blacklers, a large department store in the center of Liverpool, there wasn't much choice with Provvy checks. It wasn't like going into a high street shop and choosing anything, it had to be cheaper or older stock. I picked a smart-looking pair but Mum said, "You're not having them, they're too big. You can have these." They had Cuban heels instead of the fashionable, thin ones I liked.

"I'm not having them."

"Well, you'll have them or nothing at all."

So I had to have the dowdy ones.

I looked forward to going out to work so I could earn my own money. My brother Chris had left school at fifteen and worked in Baine's Dairy full-time, earning four pounds a week, which was a fair wage. His working conditions could be hard, however, with early-morning rounds during winter in the freezing cold, and a pea-soup smog caused by house chimneys and Liverpool factories like Johnsons Dye Works and the pungent-smelling tannery. The smog would last for hours and make work treacherous. He told Mum, "This is not going to be my life. I'm going to look for another job."

"How about where I get my hair done?" She laughed. "They're looking for an apprentice."

"A ladies' hairdresser? You're joking!" But Chris also thought to himself, *Something's got to be better than this.*

In 1959 there were very few male hairdressers in Liverpool, but the moment he walked into the salon Chris was fascinated. "I liked the atmosphere, it was a different world," he says. He was always good at art: he could draw, he liked the idea of creating hairstyles and, after a three-month trial, he was given the job. The boss, Mr. Courtney, said, "You've got the job because you're here before we open and you're here after we close, and also because your mother's a hard worker and I know that runs through families." Chris's friends teased him, but from those first few months he was hooked. He gave Jean her first perm and he loved settling the women under Eugene salon hair dryers, putting rollers in their hair, and creating beautiful sculptured finger waves.

Chris did a day-release apprenticeship at a hair academy in town, learning about biology and art, along with practical and hairdressing theory. Before they practiced on a model the tutor would tell them, "We cannot show you how to cut hair. We can show you how you use the tools." Chris understood that a good style lies in his interpretation of what the client wants. He would glimpse them in the waiting room beforehand, notice details about the way the hair grew or the shape of the face, and style the hair in a way that was flattering.

I used to model for Chris and sometimes took the day off school to go with him to competitions, where he would color my hair and put in curlers to create elaborate styles. I'd give the teacher an absence note and come back the next day with a wildly different hairdo—the cottage loaf, the DA, the victory roll, the bouffant—you name it, I had it, and that would land me in trouble.

I was a bit of a one. At fourteen I was still hanging around with Chris's friends, the lads I'd grown up with, and I dated an eighteen-year-old boy with dyed blond hair and a motorbike. Our nosy neighbor Mrs. Prince, who lived across the road, was like the Gestapo. If anybody came to the door you'd see her curtain twitch. One day when Mum was at work and Dad was in bed, the lad came to the house and offered to give me a ride around on his motorbike. I loved soaring off past the fields—it felt so grown up and adventurous. He dropped me back at the house a few hours later unscathed, but the next day Mum shouted at me, "You've been on somebody's bike!" Mrs. Prince had told her.

At that point my brother Chris was going out to gigs. He started going to the Cavern in 1959 when it was a jazz club, paying ten shillings to listen to all-night sessions with trad artists like Acker Bilk and Kenny Baker, then get a breakfast in the morning. He wore a Teddy-boy suit, a bootlace tie, and winkle-picker shoes, and was there when the jazz nights gradually changed to rock 'n' roll and blues. He remembers seeing the Blue Jeans when they were playing skiffle with a tea chest and washboard, and how the beat grew deeper and faster when they incorporated guitars and drums and became the Swinging Blue Jeans.

The Beatles' first drummer, Pete Best, had a brother, Rory, who was in the same hairdressing class, and because they were the only two guys amongst the girls Chris and Rory became friends. Every Monday afternoon they went to the hairdressing academy in town, and would go to the Cavern beforehand for a lunchtime session. Chris saw the Beatles twice, when Pete was the drummer. They had a Teddy-boy look back then, with rock-and-roll Tony Curtis-style hair-dos (what we called DAs or "duck's arse").

I finally got my freedom in 1961 when I turned fifteen, left school, and started a job as a franking-machine operator in Littlewoods, a retail and football betting company with a branch in Crosby, processing catalog orders for parcels. All the Littlewoods girls used to meet in the canteen and have a cup of tea together, enjoying the socializing and camaraderie. I hated school, so I was happy to go to work, doing my own thing and earning money. The world was suddenly filled with possibility.

5. MARY

The Squaws

If you didn't pass the eleven-plus exam to get into grammar school then there was no university. I didn't do the exam because I was terrible at writing and spelling, and didn't pay attention to history or geography because I used to think, *What's the use? I'm never going to leave Liverpool anyway.* If I'd known I was going to leave, I would have paid more attention!

Airplane travel was rare in those days—package holidays to the Mediterranean had only just started and most people couldn't afford them, so they would go to holiday camps like Butlin's or Pontin's. So I assumed I was destined to stay in Liverpool, and one day I might be lucky and find the right husband and have as many kids as my mum. Or become a nun. There were very few career opportunities for young women, other than being a nurse, a teacher, or a housewife. And it was everybody's dream to be a secretary, working in an office. Men's jobs and women's jobs used to be advertised in separate sections in the newspaper. There certainly was no expectation that girls could play music in bands—at the very best we could carve a place on the pop scene as a singer in a pretty dress.

One subject that I excelled at, however, was arithmetic, so after leaving school I went to Anfield Commercial College, studied business for a year, and became a bookkeeper in a factory. I didn't realize until later, when I became a musician, what a fantastic name it had: James Brown & Company. The factory made flour and a pastry mix that was sold in seaside resorts, restaurants, and boardinghouses around the UK. I would be typing bills for addresses in places like Torquay and Blackpool thinking, *It must be fantastic to go to all those places.*

As soon as I was earning I started going to gigs at the Cavern with my cousins Veronica and Rita, plus our friend Maggie Cuccini. One evening in 1962 we saw the Beatles. The band at this point was back from a recent trip to Hamburg; they'd just had a hit with "Love Me Do" and played with supercharged energy and striking vocal harmonies. Toward the end of a set of raucous rock-and-roll covers, John Lennon said, "This is another song that we wrote ourselves." Everybody gasped—they wrote these songs themselves! As the band ripped into "Please Please Me," the audience went into a frenzy.

After their set, Veronica, Rita, Maggie, and I enthused, "Oh, we want to do that, let's be the first girls to do it!" I noticed musicians from support band the Remo Four standing near the stage and asked them, "Where do you buy your instruments?"

"Hessy's, just round the corner from the Cavern."

So the next day we went to Hessy's on 62 Stanley Street, the music store where John Lennon had bought his Rickenbacker guitar. Hessy's had an "easy terms" hire-purchase agreement that made it possible for hundreds of aspiring local musicians to afford instruments. But faced with a shop full of guitars, drum kits, and keyboards we stood around feeling uncertain. Someone had to take charge, so I asked Veronica and Rita, "What are you going to play?"

"I'll play what Paul McCartney plays."

"I'll play the same guitar as John Lennon."

We didn't know anything about guitars, that a Gibson had a different feel to a Stratocaster, or that a Silvertone had a hollow garage sound and was much cheaper than a Les Paul. Veronica, Rita, and I bought Framus guitars and Maggie got herself a whole kit of drums. We had to pay four pounds a week each for the guitars. I only earned six pounds at the time, so most of my earnings went on my guitar—the rest I gave to Mum.

Now we had the instruments we decided to get some publicity before learning how to play. "One day we'll sit down and practice, but let's get people interested first," I said to the girls. At the Cavern we were introduced to Bill Harry, editor of the local music magazine *Mersey Beat*. He advised us to go to Harry Watmough, a photographer with a studio in Moorfields who had taken pictures of the Beatles and the Searchers, so we contacted Watmough and he agreed to do a photo shoot for us. We needed a name, and Veronica suggested "The Squaws." "We'll be the first all-female band, so let's have a name suggesting that," she said. Westerns were very popular then and Veronica was one of fourteen children, with many brothers, who loved watching westerns on TV. The Squaws is a name that no one would use now, with its nasty taste of cultural misappropriation, but then it seemed the ideal concept, so for the studio shoot we bought waistcoats in town and posed with feathers in our hair. We paid a lot for that photo shoot, because we wanted the same standard of photographs as all the big groups. We also wanted to buy our equipment from the same shop where they bought theirs. And now we had a set of striking black-and-white photos, we needed someone to write about us.

Bill Harry launched *Mersey Beat* in 1961 to cover all the new rock-and-roll beat groups in the region, tracking bands and gig listings across Widnes, St. Helens, the Wirral, and Warrington. He had been at Liverpool Art College with John Lennon and got him writing a regular column called "On the Dubious Origins of the Beatles." By 1962 *Mersey Beat* had a circulation of over 250,000 copies and was dubbed "the teenagers' Bible." We knew it was important for the Squaws to be featured in the paper, so we went to the *Mersey Beat* office, an attic room in Renshaw Street, and told Bill Harry we had formed an all-girl band. Thinking we were a working group, Harry interviewed us and we bluffed our way through it. He asked us what kind of music we were going to play and who were our favorite bands. What gave us the idea? When was our first gig? We hadn't even tried to practice, so I said: "We're in the middle of practicing, we don't want to reveal too much beforehand."

"Are you going to appear at the Cavern?"

"When we're ready."

We were so confident, we didn't think for one second this wasn't going to work out. We were convinced we would play gigs, make it and achieve success.

A week later the article was published, complete with a big picture of the brand-new Squaws. It happened so quickly. We got lots of publicity, even though we couldn't play a note.

Veronica's brother John could play guitar, so we naively thought that he would teach us. We sat down with him one day after work, but he couldn't tune the guitars very well and he could only play three chords. That was when we realized how hard this was going to be. *Oh no*, I thought, *this isn't going to work*. We didn't have any amplifiers, so while Maggie banged aimlessly on the drums we made a subdued plonking sound on our guitars. When John tried to teach me a chord all I could think about was how much the strings hurt my fingers, and my interest began to waver.

There were other distractions on the horizon at that time. Even though I still wanted to be a nun, I was becoming interested in boys.

At James Brown & Company I met a boy called Tommy Brady and went out on my very first date. He took me to the cinema to see *The Man Who Shot Liberty Valance*, a moody, monochrome western starring John Wayne and James Stewart. He kissed me and wanted more, but he wasn't getting it. I was sixteen and so nervous that my mum and dad would find out that we never went on a date again.

Then I had a crush on Billy Howard, the delivery boy at work. He was two years older than me, quite good-looking, with red-blond curly hair, and our relationship lasted about for about two weeks. We went on dates to the cinema or the pub, and we even met each other's parents. Mum and Dad didn't really want me to have a steady boyfriend because they thought I was too young. One night Billy brought me home after a date, then walked to the tram stop, but it was very foggy that night so he returned saying that the trams weren't running, and he was allowed to stay the night, sleeping on the sofa in the living room. Years later, when he became a popular comedian, one of his favorite stories onstage was about staying the night in his first girlfriend's house. Her mother locked the door so he couldn't get out of the living room, but during the night he needed the toilet, so he had to climb out of the window to go into the back garden for a wee. I think it's hilarious that my mum locked him in.

Billy liked me and was impressed that I was in the Squaws. After we'd had a few dates he said, "I'll take you down to meet some of my mates, can you bring your guitar?"

"Well, there's no use me bringing it because I can't play it yet."

"It doesn't matter, one of my friends plays guitar."

So I took my Framus down to the pub in a plastic bag, and everybody assumed I could play, but I couldn't even tune it. I was beginning to feel a little stuck, not just musically but also in terms of my budding relationship. I realized that because I intended to be a nun I wasn't going to sleep with Billy, so I told him, "You're still my boyfriend, but nothing's going to happen."

Soon after that Billy finished the relationship, and we went our separate ways.

~

After the *Mersey Beat* article was published friends were asking us, "When are you going to start playing?" We would go to the Cavern as the Squaws, holding our empty guitar cases as our ticket into the venue. The queues to the club went right down Mathew Street, but we could go straight to the door. Inside it was always packed, but as small as it was, there was always room to do the Cavern stomp, dancing in pairs with fancy footwork, turns, and jumps. We all loved doing the Stomp. Ballrooms tried to ban it, fearing the stamping and jump-ing would damage the dancefloor, shake the foundations, and make buildings collapse. Critics called it "weird and undignified" but we thought it was exciting—it was ours. Two girls would stomp together, or a boy and a girl, but strangely enough never two boys. The venue was so sweaty and hot, with a weird earthy, musky smell. They only served flat orange juice, no alcoholic drinks, and Priscilla White, who later became the pop star Cilla Black, served drinks and took your coat, if you had a coat. Cilla came from the same part of Liverpool as me, near the docks, and everybody knew her. She had the same chirpiness then as she did when she was on TV decades later, pre-senting *Blind Date*.

Our guitars were our entry ticket, signaling we were a group, so we assumed we would always be admitted free to this musical paradise. "Bob" Wooler, who was the Cavern Club compère and DJ and a very kindly man, would say, "Listen, girls, you've got to promise me your first gig will be here."

"Of course, Bob," we'd promise.

When we realized people were expecting the Squaws to perform ("It's about time now," Wooler said), we agreed that we had to stop going out with empty guitar cases and start practicing. Rehearsals became more regular, but, because it was so hard to create a satisfying sound or anything remotely tuneful, we couldn't continue and decided to stay at home for a few weeks, deliberately disappearing until people forgot about us. We had almost given up hope when help arrived from an unexpected source.

6. SYLVIA

Twist and Shout

In Liverpool, everybody wanted to be in a band. On every street corner and in every cellar there were young fellas practicing with guitars. The city was alive. Many rock-and-roll LPs came over from America via the seafarers—being a port, Liverpool heard the music first and got a head start on everybody else. There was also the influence of the Irish, with their folk songs and fiddle players, who came over from the west of Ireland to do countless pub gigs. Both John Lennon and Paul McCartney were from Irish blood; the folk melodies and harmonies are discernible in their sound. With the success of jazz and skiffle in the late 1950s, and the rock-and-roll beat boom of the early 1960s, hundreds of boys were spurred on to pick up a guitar. Our friend Tony Coates, who played guitar with Ian and the Zodiacs and Liverpool Express, says the scene was like a beehive of activity: "The 1960s was the invention of the teenager; that category didn't exist before. We wanted new clothes, our own music, it *had* to be different." We were part of a new generation born just after the Second World War, leading lives that were so different from our parents'.

At one point there were five hundred bands in the city all playing in church halls, town halls, anywhere people could gather. Boys had the freedom to do what they wanted, but it seemed there weren't the same opportunities for us girls. Our friend Beryl Marsden started singing with local group the Undertakers and remembers it as a very male-dominated world. "I didn't have a problem with that, because I was a bit of a tomboy," she says. "I was a total rebel. Nothing better for me than a big sloppy sweater and a pair of jeans. I just loved it." There were a few female singers like Beryl but it was rare to see any girls playing guitar on the new Merseybeat scene. It was inevitable that we would find each other.

While Mary and her cousin Rita invented the Squaws, in another part of town I was going to gigs with my new friend, Valerie Gell. We met at Hilltop youth club in the Girl Scouts on a party night where everyone had to come in costume as a beatnik, expressing their inner poet. I wore beads with a long black jumper and tights, and noticed Val sitting there looking good with smoldering eyes and zombie makeup, her long black hair framing her face. She was a bit older and seemed like a loner and that intrigued me. I went to the youth club with my school mates but she came from Seaforth, which was a few miles away, and coming there was a big thing for her. She was very shy, so I went over and spoke to her and we hit it off. She talked about bands in the charts like the Shadows and I discovered she had a love of music that was infectious; a passion that would lead us to the Liverbirds.

When I started going to the clubs and town halls with Val I thought, *This is great*. I wasn't musical, I didn't listen to the radio, but it was fantastic to see the bands live. We went to dances at the Jive Hive in St. Luke's, a large church hall with a wooden sprung floor that enabled jivers to bounce. At the Jive Hive there was no alcohol, just soft drinks like Coca-Cola or orange, and an easygoing atmosphere.

The first alcoholic drink we ever had was when Val bought a bottle of sherry and we drank it at her house before going out to a dance, lurching all over the place. I can remember that dizzy, woozy feeling even now—we went on to St. Luke's, but don't ask me who was playing that night. As soon as I got home I went straight to bed. Val's mother found the empty bottle in the bin and yelled at her for leading me astray. I was a year younger than Val, and we were both under the legal drinking age of eighteen, but she was determined to have fun.

The daughter of Tom and Joyce Gell, a docker and a factory worker, Val was born on August 14, 1945, and grew up an only child in a small two-bedroom house in the Liverpool suburb of Seaforth. Her parents were Unionist Protestants, and Mrs. Gell in particular was keen on the pomp and display of the Orange Order marching bands through Liverpool's city streets every summer. On July 12, otherwise known as the Twelfth or Orange Lodge day, she was there marching with baby Val in the pram, and Val remembers, as a small child, being dressed up in orange for the parades. Mrs. Gell was very aware of status and aspired to become upper class. She could also be a disciplinarian and controlling with her daughter, but early on Val found ways to rebel—making music was one of them, and making unusual friends was another.

Val left school at fifteen and did an apprenticeship in the fabrics department of the Owen Owen store in the city center. She liked the job and had a good friend there called Dave, a gay man who was openly camp and flamboyant. This stood out at a time when homosexuality was illegal and most gay men felt the pressure to hide their sexuality. Owen Owen was on Clayton Square, just five minutes from the Cavern, so Val and Dave would go there for lunchtime sessions or in the evenings, after work. Val soaked up all her musical influences, lapping up the thriving gig scene at the Cavern and at venues dotted around the city.

Every week at the Jive Hive, Val and I saw resident band, Ian and the Zodiacs, play a tuneful mix of R&B pop, with sweet-voiced Ian Edwards on lead vocals. In 1962 the Zodiacs were one of the most popular bands in Liverpool. We also saw Mark Peters & the Silhouettes, who thrashed their guitars and raced through their set of beat songs. I used to watch their every move thinking that Mark Peters was lovely. But I didn't just want him, I wanted to *be* him, thinking to myself, *I could do a bit of this...get up on that stage.*

I had no idea Val could play guitar until, six months after we met, she pulled one out of her bedroom wardrobe and started strumming the Shadows' instrumental "Apache." With their twanging guitar sound, the Shadows were at the forefront of the UK beat-group boom, inspiring a new generation of musicians.

"God, Val, you can play," I said.

"Well, yes." She was very quiet and modest and matter-of-fact. Music was in her bones. Her father, Tom, could read music and used to tinkle jazz piano in clubs, and he taught Val the guitar. She grew up watching him play and found it easy to pick out tunes on the radio.

"Will you teach me how to play, Val? I'll get a guitar."

"Come 'ere. Put your fingers there...and there." I tried to strum Val's orangey-red Vox guitar, but at just five feet one with small hands I had problems stretching my fingers along the fretboard.

"I can't reach. I'll get a kit of drums instead."

"Yeah, OK," Val enthused. "And then we'll get an all-girl band together."

We went into the city center to Rushworth & Dreaper's, an instrument shop not far from Hessy's. When we walked in I said to the manager, "I'd like a kit of drums."

"Have a look around," he replied, gesturing around the shop floor.

I noticed a black-and-white pearl set that glittered under the shop lighting. "Ooh, I like that—I'll have them."

The manager looked me up and down. "How will you pay for them?"

"I'll pay weekly."

"How old are you?"

"Sixteen."

"You can't. Your mother or father has to be a guarantor. Here are the forms, get one of them to sign."

The moment I got home I pushed the form under my mother's nose and said, "Mother, sign that."

"What now, Syl?"

"Me and Val are gonna form a group. We're going to play rock 'n' roll."

"Oh, all right."

Once I got the drum kit home from Rushworth & Dreaper's, I had to assemble it.

"Val, these drums won't stand up."

I didn't know how to adjust the height on the drum throne, or how to attach the bass drum-beater to the pedal, or how to build the high hat or place the snare on the snare basket, or work out which metal bars needed to thread into which particular holes. It was bewildering. But after trial and error we managed to assemble the kit and start playing, with the drum legs and the cymbals tottering about. Val tried a few guitar lines and I improvised a beat. There was something missing, however.

"We need some more girls," said Val. "Maybe we should advertise."

A few days later when we met to practice, Val pointed to a copy of *Mersey Beat* on the table and Bill Harry's article about the Squaws.

"Hey, look at this, there's a girl's group."

We read through the piece and noticed Mary's address was printed at the bottom of the page.

"Let's go down and see them, find out what's going on," Val said. We caught a bus over to Sparrow Hall and knocked the door of 36 Ternhall Road. Mary's mother, Maggie, opened the door.

"We've come looking for Mary McGlory. We want to start a group."

Maggie shouted upstairs and Mary came down to see us. Val stood there peering through a veil of long, dark brown hair, a serious expression on her face.

"Are you Mary McGlory?"

"Yes."

"We want to start a group and we haven't heard anything about you in the last two weeks. Have you broke up?"

"Yes." The truth was that they'd never really got started, but Veronica and Maggie had already become bored, leaving only Mary and Rita.

"Would you like to come and see us?" she said.

Mary and her cousin Rita came over to Val's tiny house in Seaforth, where I had my drums set up in the living room. They had brought their instruments, but the moment Val picked up her guitar and started playing a snappy version of "Apache" they glanced at each other and Mary said, "We've got to go now, we'll see you next week!"

We were disappointed that they disappeared so quickly. Maybe we had been a bit overpowering. Mary told us later they were afraid we'd laugh our heads off when we realized they couldn't play. Val suspected as much, but she was as patient as she was determined.

A week later Val and I went to Mary's house and knocked on the door. There was a pause, some movement inside, and then Mary appeared on the doorstep.

Val said kindly, "You can't play, can ya?"

"No."

"Well, I'll teach you. You've got the instruments, that's the good thing."

By then Rita had also had enough, saying to Mary, "I'm keeping out of this." But before she left the band she suggested a new name for the group. Rita worked in a cleaner's with a woman who said that the Squaws was a stupid name, so why not call the group the Liverbirds, after the two eighteen-foot metal birds on top of the spires of the Royal Liver Building at Pier Head on the city waterfront. Ever since the building was built in 1911, the two birds have been there, standing watch over the city and the sea. According to local legend, if the birds were to fly away the city would cease to exist.

"With a name like the Liverbirds, everyone will know right away that you're from Liverpool, and that you're female," reasoned Rita.

Once Rita departed we needed a new bass player, so another cousin of Mary's called Sheila McGlory stepped in. Val was decisive, suggesting that Sheila should play rhythm, and she would teach Mary the bass. From that moment, the Liverbirds were born.

There was a little opposition at first from Mrs. Gell. Val told us later that her mother was angry about her being in a band with Mary and Sheila.

"That's two Catholics you've got in your group," she said. By contrast, I wasn't from a religious family. Nominally I was a Protestant and when I was ten I went to Sunday School, but only because I wanted to be confirmed and wear a white dress. After that I lost interest. For Mary and Sheila, though, it was a different matter, because they came from strong Catholic families.

There has long been a large immigrant Irish community in Liverpool, and in the 1960s sectarianism was rife, sometimes with street clashes between Catholics and Protestants on St. Patrick's Day, or during the parade season in June and July. But we were part of a new generation who believed in unity—to us, those religious divisions didn't make any sense. What was important was our friendship and playing together in the band. Despite Mrs. Gell's objections, Val made it clear to her that she didn't have any choice—nobody else could take Mary and Sheila's place.

With the name the Liverbirds we gained a solid identity as a group. Gradually, we got better on our instruments, more confident about what we were doing. I took drum lessons with a teacher in Birkenhead, who showed me the rudiments, and then I began developing my own style. And for Mary, all that time picking out notes with the Squaws wasn't lost—she had been learning how to listen and familiarize herself with the bass guitar. "So that when I was ready I picked it up really quickly. That's what gave me the determination to do it, like learning a language," she says.

At this point I had started seeing my first boyfriend, a mechanic named Freddy whom I met on the Sand Hills in Crosby. Me and my good friend Kathleen were sitting in the sun and watching the waves when Freddy and his mate Stan Jones walked past.

"You're all right?"

"Oh, yes," we replied.

They sat down with us and by the end of the afternoon she was with Stan and I got together with his friend Freddy. That's how it started.

For a while it was serious, he wasn't a "sort of" boyfriend like the one who took me out on his bike. Freddy didn't live far from me; he was a lovely fella and we were courting for six months. His father wasn't around so to earn some extra money, his mother sold clothes through a catalog. One day I was flipping through the pages and spotted an elegant dress with a big beige fur collar. It had an old film-star look, the kind of tailored dress Katharine Hepburn might have worn.

"Oh, isn't that lovely? Isn't that beautiful?" I said, then turned the page and forgot about it.

I enjoyed hanging around with Freddy, but there just wasn't any passion. As my attention was taken up by the Liverbirds I became less interested and that gave me a good excuse to say to him one day, "Oh, we can't have boyfriends now."

"Well, you don't need to tell anybody," he said.

"No, we've got to finish."

A week later Freddy came to the house and knocked on the door with a parcel for me. Inside was the beautiful catalog dress with the fur collar. He'd only gone and bought it for me!

I felt really bad. "Oh, take it back, tell your mom to send it back."

"But it's for you."

"No, please."

So Freddy did take it back, and I never saw him again.

The band had become the most important thing to us. Every day after work we would take it in turns to practice—one week at Mary's in Sparrow Hall, then over to my house in Litherland the next, where I kept the drum kit assembled in the parlor. I would find the rhythm of what we were doing in rehearsals at Mary's and then at my house we'd pull it all together. Sometimes I would just bring the snare drum over to Sparrow Hall on the bus, and sometimes my brother-in-law Bob would drive us from one place to another in his Ford estate. I was in the parlor with the drum kit, and the first song I learned was the theme to the TV comedy series *Steptoe & Son*. After a while we became more musically confident and as we rehearsed the local kids gathered outside the front door, sitting on the wall, shouting and clapping.

We still went out to gigs to see other bands play and learn from them. Mary told us, "I know Bob Wooler and how to get into the Cavern without having to queue and pay. I just carry my guitar case and say, 'We're an all-female group and we promise the first place we play will be here.'"

But by then Wooler was getting wise to us.

"OK, girls, when are you going to start?" he asked one day.

"We're getting there."

He paused for a second and then said, "Would you like to come and meet the boys?"

That day the Beatles were playing, all kitted out in black ties, white shirts, and black trousers. It was so hot and crowded in the Cavern that, as usual, sweat was dripping off the ceiling, but we didn't mind. The Beatles' rhythm and harmonies were so tight and focused that we couldn't stop dancing. They played covers of Barrett Strong originals, like "Some Other Guy" and "Money." They did a raucous version of "Twist and Shout," and wild rock-and-roll songs like Chuck Berry's "Roll Over Beethoven" and Little Richard's saucy "Long Tall Sally." More than ever, we wanted to be up onstage like them, playing our guitars and making the crowd rock.

After the set Wooler said, "Come on, I'll take you to meet the lads." It was so exciting. He grabbed us and we threaded through the audience backstage where George Harrison was standing in the corridor talking to a very good-looking blond girl. He was wearing a fantastic black leather coat, and later walked out of the Cavern with her, already like a rock star. In the dressing room John Lennon and Paul McCartney were in their undies, getting changed. They were drying themselves with towels because they had just come offstage and were dripping with sweat. They were very handsome. Apart from our brothers, we'd never seen men in underpants before, so us four teenage girls just stood there staring at them.

They were very down to earth, and Paul was particularly kind. "Hiya, girls, y'all right?" he said, while John sat there looking at us in a way that was direct and penetrating.

Bob Wooler told them, "This is the Liverbirds, they're gonna be the first all-girl group."

"What a great idea," said Paul, but Lennon was sarcastic. "Girls don't play guitars," he said.

After we left the dressing room we huffed, "The cheek of it! We're going to prove him wrong." Years later we found out more about Lennon, that although he often made sardonic comments he was also sensitive and intelligent, an artist who regretted his disdainful treatment of women in his early career. "We can't have a revolution that doesn't involve and liberate women. It's so subtle the way you're taught male superiority," he said in 1971, in an interview with Tariq Ali and Robin Blackburn for the underground paper *Red Mole*. It's clear his feelings about women evolved, but we also wonder if what he said that day in the Cavern dressing room was meant to test us, provoke us into making a success of the band. If so, it certainly worked.

Our friend Lee Curtis, one of the first singers on the Merseybeat scene to go to Hamburg, remembers the Beatles as being in a world of their own. Nobody ever controlled them, they were a law unto themselves. He says:

> It's very strange, but the one who stood out was Pete Best. If you could have blue plus yellow makes green, then Paul, John and George made green. But Paul, John, George with Pete made a kind of off-green. Even though he's my mate and a lovely lad, Pete wasn't there with them all the way. He was a different shade, he didn't have the same energy. He was too cool-looking for them, he didn't join in with their surrealist messing around.

Lee also thinks that Pete Best was sacked in a roundabout way because of his mother, Mona, a domineering woman who helped to sort out bookings for the band. She started the Casbah Club as a coffee bar in her house, so the band could rehearse and play to an audience.

Local boy Brian Epstein then took charge; he had been doing RADA training and he had them wearing smart suits and giving a collective bow on stage. One day he said to Lee's brother and manager, "I'm having trouble with Pete's mum, she keeps interfering."

"Sack her."

"That's not easy—what about Pete?"

"If she won't go, sack Pete. There's no reason for him to stay."

After Pete Best was sacked we went along to demonstrations in Liverpool, which showed how popular he was. Fans nearly turned the Cavern upside down with fighting and Ringo ended up with a broken nose. Best then joined Lee Curtis and the All-Stars—a band that was aptly named. As well as Best, the line-up included guitarist Tony Waddington and bassist Wayne Bickerton, who ended up becoming a hit songwriting/production team for 1970s acts like the Rubettes, and Mac & Katie Kissoon. The Beatles were so important to our generation; they represented the start of a new era where we were living our lives in our own way. At that point they were still part of the scene, hanging out with other bands in the Kardomah coffee bar before playing at the Cavern. As the Beatles became famous, they spearheaded this fantastic thing going on in Liverpool and their success gave us hope that even if you were from a poor home you could have a different life.

At the end of 1962 Mary's priest, Father Bradley, told us: "When you're ready to perform I'll let you play at St. Philly's [Philomena's] for the old-age pensioners." We were so excited to have our first gig. Father Bradley helped set up our equipment, which wasn't too taxing since we only had little amplifiers and no microphones because we didn't sing. That night after the bingo we stood in the corner of the hall (there was no stage) and performed for the pensioners while they drank cups of tea. We didn't feel nervous, just glad to experience the novelty of an audience listening to our four instrumentals including "Apache," the theme tune to *Steptoe and Son*, and a Jewish celebration song called "Hava Nagila." None of us was Jewish, but the latter was commonly played at gigs. The pensioners showed their appreciation with clapping and cheering, and we joked that the positive reaction was because they didn't have their hearing aids in.

The second gig we played was in Chester, in a popular club in a beautiful part of the old town. By then we organized our own stage wear—each of the major bands on Merseyside had a readily identifiable image, and we knew it was important to look like a group. Val's cousin was a tailor, so he made us bright red corduroy trousers and waistcoats, which we wore over black shirts embroidered with two Liverbirds on the collar. We thought it would be clever to echo the uniform of the city bus conductors, who wore black shirts emblazoned with Liverbird motifs.

Val's cousin was late getting our clothes ready, so we didn't have time to try them on before going onstage. We stood there playing and it was only afterward that we realized how terrible we looked. Thick red corduroy makes you appear larger than you really are, so we resembled four fat little Father Christmases. After that night we never wore the costume again, opting for lurex skirts with a denim blouse instead.

Our third gig was at the Cavern, the point when we really gelled as a band. Many of the musicians who had been skeptical about us, who just knew us as the girls who blagged their way in with empty guitar cases, could see we were serious about our music. We had developed our set since that first gig with the pensioners, and played a few more songs. We were still without a singer, concentrating on instrumentals because Val could play Shadows songs and "Peter Gunn," Mancini's theme for the eponymous private-eye TV series. We were terrified because the Cavern crowd had never seen a girl group and we didn't know how they were going to react. Bob Wooler introduced us that night, saying, "Listen, these are our own Liverpool girls, something to be proud of—the first all-girl band here."

When we started playing I was struck by how echoey it was, but the place was tightly packed and close-knit so you could hear everything clearly. The stage was so small that we could touch each other, and the crowd was right there in front of our eyes. Once we started playing they were positive and friendly, shouting, "Come on, girls, you're doin' great!" Their enthusiasm meant that after our first song, "Apache," we loosened up, lost our nervousness and just enjoyed the gig. Afterward, when everyone was clapping and cheering, Wooler bounded onstage again. "Isn't this amazing? Another great thing that's come from Liverpool!"

He'd stuck by us, even when we were going down to the Cavern with empty guitar cases. We were kids, but he saw something in us and liked us. We couldn't hide our excitement at being part of this Cavern family—finally we were onstage, making the audience dance and cheer. As Mary said, "When we first played the Cavern I thought it was like a fairy tale, with me as Cinderella for a night." From that moment we wanted to keep going, give up our day jobs, and become professional as soon as we could.

7. MARY

Future in Cold Meats

By early 1963 we were rehearsing every day and getting more and more gigs. We played the Cavern six times. Family would come to see us—my cousins, and Sylvia's brother Chris, of course, with all his mates. My brother Joseph was so inspired he bought himself a guitar and learned to play it. He was always very fashionable, cutting the collars off our coats so they looked like Beatles jackets, or putting a pudding basin on my siblings' heads and cutting round it, Beatles style. We all had curly hair so it didn't work out, but he tried.

The atmosphere at the Cavern crackled, musicians were always willing to help, and we struck up enduring friendships. The Dennisons, who were signed to Decca Records, gave advice, helped set up equipment, and practiced with us. We also loved the smartly dressed Mark Peters & the Silhouettes, and cool movers Earl Preston & the TTs, who were supportive anytime we shared the bill. One of our best gigs at the Cavern was with electric blues musician Alexis Korner, and Derry Wilkie & the Seniors. Derry was a gutsy, warm-hearted R&B singer, a great mover on stage and, along with the Chants, one of the few black artists on the Merseybeat scene. Apparently he was turned down by Decca because he wouldn't keep still in front of the microphone and kept climbing up the curtains. He also did a stint as a Savage in Screamin' Lord Sutch's band, being killed every night by Sutch as part of his "Jack the Ripper" shock-rock song. He was such a wild performer.

We used to hang out in the *Mersey Beat* office, chatting with Bill Harry and his wife, Virginia. He wrote another article about us for the magazine, which attracted the attention of booking agent Mick Lowe, who called and met with us after he read the feature. A man in his forties with long, grayish hair, he ran a toy store in Birkenhead market with his girlfriend, Thelma, as well as booking bands. "How much do you earn?" he asked.

At that point I was earning six pounds a week working in the bookkeeping department at Hunters, a cold-meat factory in Child-wall that made pâté and Spam, and Sylvia took home a seven-pound wage from Littlewoods.

"I'll give you all, guaranteed, seven pounds a week. Pack in your jobs and I'll get you the gigs."

Mick started coming to watch us practice and he would say, "You've got to be good, gotta be serious about it. When you're ready to play I'll start getting you gigs."

We practiced every night for four months, keeping the weekends free to go to the Cavern and check out what was happening. Val taught me and Sheila guitar, and we topped that up with lessons every Sunday in a studio flat in Bold Street with Bob Hobbs, a really proficient teacher who wrote a guitar column for *Mersey Beat*. He was serious about his lessons, teaching us chord structures and what was meant by augmented and minor and diminished chords. As a band we practiced so much that we complained of calluses and blisters. Val would say to me, "Mary, you've got to keep playing. If you stop playing and the blisters go, then you have to go through the whole process again." Val did all the tuning for us because we couldn't tune ourselves.

Even though we practiced five nights a week and must have made an awful racket, the neighbors never banged on the wall. We plowed away, just focusing on instrumentals, and didn't think about a singer. I bought an amplifier for my guitar, but because we weren't doing many gigs yet, I couldn't keep up with the payments. One day we were practicing in Ternhall Road when there was a knock at the door and two burly bailiffs walked in, unceremoniously unplugged my bass and took the amp away. When I started crying, Val said, "Don't mind, Mar, I'll plug you in with me," and she connected me to her Vox amp. I thought that was so nice of her.

Mick noted that we needed better costumes for our photo shoots, so for a feature in the *Liverpool Echo* we wore ski trousers, mod-style tops with three buttons, and ballerina shoes or Chelsea boots. The only problem was that I couldn't afford boots, so Mick told me to wear his. I'm a size four and he was size eight. I found the photo shoot so embarrassing—stupid me, I had feet like a clown.

Mick booked us onto *Scene at 6:30*, a popular Granada TV show that featured all the local northern bands. The Beatles were regular guests, and presenters included people like Michael Parkinson and Mike Scott, who later became famous with their own prime-time shows. This was our big break. We were so excited at the thought of being on TV, but for some reason the rambling journey with Mick, from Birkenhead to Manchester, took us six hours. We still don't know why the trip took so long—it was like he drove via Wales to get to Manchester. As a result we arrived at the studio just ten minutes before the program started. We were wearing our ski trousers along with the special polo shirts and thought we looked good. Everybody on the TV crew said, "Would you like to get changed?"

"We are already changed!"

With no vocalist we wanted to make our set interesting, so we told Sylvia to stand up at the end of "Hava Nagila" and shout, "Yay!" We had no time to rehearse, so when we performed the song and Sylvia yelled, all the cameramen stopped filming. They thought something had gone wrong.

Our parents were delighted to see us on the TV, and any reservations they might have felt vanished. At first Mrs. Gell had been disapproving about me and Sheila being in the band, but now she could see that the Liverbirds were becoming successful. Our mums and dads were so supportive of us, glad that we might be able to turn our hobby into a profession, making sure that we had enough to eat and drink when we were practicing or on the road. One Friday after a gig, for instance, we came back to Sylvia's house. Usually, on a Friday night, Mrs. Saunders made us cups of tea and ham sandwiches. That evening she had busily prepared everything ahead of time, and, once we were drinking our tea, she offered around a plate.

"Mike, have a ham sandwich."

"No, I'm sorry, guys. I'm Jewish, I don't eat ham."

"Oh." Then she offered the plate to me.

"I'm awful sorry, I'm Catholic, I can't eat meat on a Friday." I was still pretty devout at the time.

"Bloomin' heck. He can't cos he's Jewish, she can't cos she's a Catholic. Who's next?"

We all came from similar backgrounds, where money was tight. My mum would always make the band feel welcome—every time the girls came round to practice she'd pop her head round the door and say, "Hello, gals, you all right? Have a cup of tea."

"Oh, thanks, Mrs. McGlory," they'd say.

Sylvia remembers my house with chipped cups, a fire burning in the hearth, and a fireguard draped with countless drying nappies.

She went home to her mum one day saying, "Mrs. McGlory's got all them children, all the kids are running around, and the cups have got cracks in them."

"Oh, love!"

For the next rehearsal Mrs. Saunders sent Sylvia round with three new mugs. We were delighted and didn't see this as charity; we were just grateful to have mugs without cracks.

After our appearance on *Scene at 6:30* Mick said that we needed to get a singer, so we placed an advert in the *Liverpool Echo* and there were a few replies. We held auditions at Sylvia's house, but the first two girls either sang too quietly or too loud and out of tune. Then a pretty girl called Irene Green walked in, with dark hair and a cool beat style. We started playing Shirelles songs and she sang "Will You Still Love Me Tomorrow" in a strong, soulful voice. We liked Irene's confidence so we chose her right away. With her we were able to expand our set, practicing daily to push our band to the next level. Mick started booking more gigs, getting us ten-day tours out of town, and suddenly our horizons broadened. Now we were going to travel and experience other places, it felt like the right time to leave our jobs.

Nervous about telling the boss of Hunter's meat factory that I wanted to leave, I sent my dad instead. When he came back, Dad told me, "You'll never guess what they said, Mary. They think you're making a big mistake. They said you've got a great future ahead of you!"

"A big future in cold meats?"

"Sure you're doing the right thing, girl?"

My future was definitely not in cold meats. I was convinced that the best way to help my family would be to go professional with the band, and then later become a nun and offer them spiritual support.

When we first started touring we were elated that we were able to make a living from music. Sylvia's brother Chris and brother-in-law Bob became our roadies, and we traveled up and down the country— whether it was driving through thick fog to a scout hall in Wigan or playing the club canteen in Warton Aerodrome, near Freckleton in Lancashire. I shared a bed with my sisters Margarita and Colette, and when I came back home in the early hours after a long journey in a cold van I was freezing, so I'd insist on wriggling in the middle to warm myself up. When they protested I'd say, "Don't moan, you'll be OK in a minute." I was earning the money after all, and they were like my giant hot water bottles.

One of the highlights was performing with the Rolling Stones in November 1963 at the Co-Op Ballroom in Nuneaton. The band weren't yet big stars. They had just released their second single, "I Wanna Be Your Man," which was steadily moving up the charts. Their manager, Andrew Loog Oldham, was trying to push the band as threatening and animalistic, a complete contrast to the Beatles, and there were sensational headlines in the press like "Would You Let Your Daughter Marry a Rolling Stone?"

We found them to be friendly, easygoing London lads who were into the blues and Chuck Berry. Keith Richards was just nineteen years old and Mick Jagger was twenty. Our show in Nuneaton wasn't a very rock 'n' roll gig. We played two sets, including a junior session that was packed with small children throwing cream buns. The Rolling Stones were able to dodge most of the missiles, but Charlie Watts had to stay perched on his drum stool so by the end of the show he was covered in cream. The second set was a learning process for us. Nobody sound-checked in those days—we just tuned our guitars and went onstage. Halfway through "Johnny Be Goode" my bass string broke and I started crying. I knew that the strings of a harp could break, but I thought the bass was indestructible. Val glanced over at me, looking concerned, and Sylvia mouthed from the back, "What's wrong?" At that point the Rolling Stones' bassist, Bill Wyman, clambered onstage and swapped my guitar for his. While we finished the song he threaded a string on my bass, tuned it, and then handed it back. What a gentleman.

After the gig we sat in the dressing room and talked. Mick Jagger and Brian Jones had a kind of innocence. They were fascinated with the fact that we were a female group. They had never heard of that before.

"What's it like, girls?" they asked. "D'you enjoy playing music? What are the audience like with you?"

"We thought it would be terrible because girls usually scream for the fellas. But the girls are fantastic, they shout for us as well."

We had been afraid that girls would be jealous of us stepping on their territory with lad bands, so we were surprised by the way they clustered at the front of every gig and yelled with enthusiasm. We never had any problem, because they liked the fact that women were up onstage. There were so few girl groups in those days, we'd like to think some female fans felt inspired to pick up an instrument and play.

The Stones were a huge influence on us—once we played with them we realized we wanted to go more in that grittier, bluesy direction. We were doing Beatles songs with Irene (and changing the gender in the lyrics), numbers like "I Saw Him Standing There," and girl group stuff like the Shirelles' "Da Doo Ron Ron" but we suddenly had a fervent desire to perform darker R&B. We didn't yet know who wrote those songs or how we were going to do it, but it became our secret ambition.

Ten days after the Nuneaton gig we stopped at the Blue Boar, the service station at Watford Gap between Junction 16 and 17 on the M1 motorway. We went into the coffee bar to have a snack and saw the Rolling Stones leaving. Brian Jones shouted, "Look, there's the Liverbirds!" and they came and sat with us for a coffee—we were traveling back to Liverpool while they were on their way down to London. That service station at Watford Gap was a major stop-off point for all the touring bands hacking up and down between London and the north. Dicky Tarrach, for instance, drummer with German band the Rattles, remembers the Blue Boar with affection. "When we played England, every night we would stop on the M1 at the Blue Boar services and meet other bands there. We never had that in Germany because the country was too big. The stretch of motorway between Hamburg and Munich, for instance, was nearly four hundred miles," he told us. The M1 was the *only* motorway, and on weekends nearby hotels would be booked up by forty or fifty girls hoping to meet their favorite musician at Watford Gap.

There is only one bum note to this story. The Stones were ever so nice to us at the time, but in 2012 Keith Richards told their biographer, Stanley Booth, that we were like a novelty female Beatles and "real slags." We were young and innocent, anything but slags in those days. Our new singer, Irene, was trying to get off with Mick Jagger, but that was just flirtation. We realize that being in a 1960s all-girl band means that we have sometimes been written about as a gimmick. But to call a woman a slag is a huge insult. Perhaps Keith Richards was just being careless with his words, but if we ever meet him he will have some explaining to do—we'd ask: Could you elaborate on the word "slag"? What does a slag mean in this context, please?

Mostly, however, there was a strong camaraderie between musicians. We were happy to be part of that, meeting other bands and swapping tips and stories. We knew that the Beatles had found success at a place called the Star-Club in Hamburg, and news filtered through about an amazing scene. Our friend Roy Dyke, who played with the Remo Four, says: "Everyone was going to the Star-Club. Along with Rory Storm and the Hurricanes, the Beatles were the band we kept track of, they were the lodestar."

Irene was dating Keith Karlson, the bass player from bluesy beat group the Mojos, when the band was doing a six-week residency at the Star-Club. She read us the long letters he sent from Hamburg and it sounded so fun, with all the musicians hanging out together. "We go to the Seaman's Mission every day and have our chop and chips," he wrote. He also talked about recording a song in a church in Hamburg, a cool bluesy holler called "Everything's All Right" that in 1963 became their second single and the Mojos' biggest hit in the UK. Their lead singer, Stu James, said later the song sounded really different on the radio, like it was "plucked from the heavens." Bands would come back from Hamburg sounding different, stronger, more confident, and that planted the idea in the back of our minds that this was the place for us.

But after four months on tour, tensions began to surface. We were staying at a B & B hotel in Edinburgh when a reporter came to do an interview. He took a photograph and Irene posed at the front in a way that suggested her idea all along was to be billed as Irene Green and the Liverbirds, with us as the backing band. She was pretty, but she didn't really fit in, and promoting herself as frontwoman didn't gel with us. Besides, Sylvia's brother Chris had styled our hair in big bouffant beehives and we thought we were lovely as well. Realizing that she wasn't going to get star billing, soon after the Edinburgh date Irene announced that she planned to go solo and abruptly left the band mid-tour, changing her name to Tiffany. We had a laugh when Sylvia grabbed the newspaper photo and drew a cartoon mustache on Irene's face, but her departure left us with a problem because we had to get a new lead singer, fast.

Irene's last Liverbirds date was the Club a'Gogo in Newcastle, a mod mecca where local stars the Animals played their own brand of fiery, gritty R&B. It was that night we found our next lead singer, and it was also the night we found out that our manager Mick was outrageously exploiting us. A band had failed to appear and Mick wasn't there, so the promoter said to Bob, one of our roadies, "The next band has let me down. The girls are going down great, will they do another spot?"

"OK, but you'll have to pay them, and more than we're getting now. I'll go and ask them."

Bob told us, "They're desperate, will you do it?"

"Yeah, we'll have to play the same songs."

"That's all right."

"And we want paying in cash."

We played a second set to a rocking crowd. Then, when the promoter gave us the cash, we couldn't believe the amount—sixty pounds in notes. We said, "Mick, the bloody sod. He's getting all this money for gigs and paying us just seven pounds a week. That's it, he's going."

It was a night of changes for us as a band. We shared the bill with Birmingham group the Rockin' Berries and got chatting in the dressing room, telling them we needed a new vocalist. They recommended a young singer called Heather who worked at Club a'Gogo and was just starting out, so we did an impromptu audition with her just before the show. She had a bob haircut and wanted to be like Cilla Black, who had now graduated from cloakroom attendant at the Cavern to the pop charts with her debut single "Love of the Loved," a song written by her friends Lennon and McCartney.

We put the record on the turntable for Heather and she stood onstage, singing along with Cilla Black, her voice slightly drowned by the brass trumpets. We couldn't really hear her singing, but were impressed by her confidence and her energy. "OK, we'll take her," we agreed afterward. The only problem was that she lived in Newcastle so we suggested she stay at Sylvie's house so she could practice with us. She was keen and willing, bringing a couple of suitcases crammed with clothes down on the train. Rehearsals had a whole new energy and the Liverbirds felt like a band again, rather than Irene's backing musicians.

The next person we had to sort out was Mick Lowe. We called a meeting with him, told him we knew he was underpaying us and said, "You're not our manager anymore."

"Your parents have signed a contract and you can't get out of it because you're underage," he retorted.

We found a solicitor to check the supposed contract and discovered our parents hadn't signed Mick's piece of paper, and because we were so young it was invalid. We were free. Bob got in touch with Roy Tempest, a theater impresario and booking agent who lived in Upper Wimpole Street in London, a fancy address just up the road from where Paul McCartney had moved in with Jane Asher and her family. Tempest took us on, renegotiating the rest of the gigs on our itinerary. As the weeks went by we were gradually getting a little more savvy.

We made sure that we were the first to hear news of upcoming auditions or gigs. There was a café in Bold Street where people would go to swap information about gigs, instruments, or band vacancies. Or we went to the Mycroft Hotel where all the Cavern groups stayed and sat for hours chatting with the landlady, or spent time in the Searchers' office talking to their lead singer/manager, Mike Pender, and his wife, May. The Searchers were big stars at that point, hitting number one in 1963 with "Sweets for My Sweet," a Merseybeat version of the Drifters' original, and then number two with the follow-up "Sugar and Spice." Our parents would say to us: "Where have you been today?"

"Sitting in the Searchers' office."

"What were you doing there, girl?"

"We sat there and spoke to May."

Four sixteen-year-old girls talking to a man and wife all day—no wonder our parents asked questions. But it was worth all those hours and all those conversations because we were the first to hear about opportunities—like the morning in early December when Bill Harry said, "By the way, girls, there's a fella coming this week doing auditions for the Star-Club in Hamburg."

We gasped, realizing this was our chance. An agent called Henry Henroid was running auditions in the Rialto, an old 1920s cinema in Toxteth. We went along the following Saturday, bringing our own guitars and drum kit. A lot of bands at the audition still had day jobs, but because we had given up work to focus on music we knew we had the edge. We were on at three in the afternoon, the last ones to audition that day, and we played six songs, keen to impress Henroid. Everybody assumed that because of his surname he was German, but it was his real name and he was a Londoner with the strongest Cockney accent you could imagine. After we finished the audition Henroid said, "Well, girls, I'm sure Manfred will like you."

Exuding a gentlemanly charisma, Henroid was part of the generation who helped to promote rock 'n' roll in Britain. In the late 1950s he used to go to the 2is coffee bar in London's Old Compton Street, where he met the producer Mickie Most and impresario Don Arden. He then became Arden's assistant, working with Chas Chandler from the Animals to bring top American acts, like Jerry Lee Lewis and Little Richard, over to the UK. By the time we met him Henroid had approached Manfred Weissleder, who ran the Star-Club in Hamburg, saying, "*I'll* get you the groups." He was true to his word, auditioning countless bands. At the Star-Club there would be four groups a night on weekdays and six at weekends, so he needed to draw from a constant supply. In Liverpool, especially, there were dozens to choose from.

By then all eyes were on Liverpool because of the Beatles' meteoric success. Earlier that year, when "She Loves You" had just been released, Sylvia's brother Chris and his girlfriend Val went to the Odeon Cinema in Southport to see them and the whole venue was packed with screaming girls. George Harrison had said in an interview that jelly babies were his favorite sweet, so girls threw a hailstorm of jelly babies onto the stage until they swamped the stage. The Beatles had reached stardom, but there were a lot of good groups competing for attention, like Kingsize Taylor, Farron's Flamingos, Ricky and the Red Streaks, the Escorts, and the Merseybeats. Every promoter wanted a band from Liverpool, and every musician wanted to go to Hamburg. According to our friend Roy Dyke: "We were young and open, we didn't have any cares or responsibilities. We just wanted to play music and travel. I was born in Liverpool just after the war and there wasn't much to do, it was a bombed-out city. It was a struggle for everyone because we didn't come from rich families." When the Remo Four were offered a month at the Star-Club they didn't hesitate, saying, "Let's take a crack at that!"

So we were delighted when Henroid said: "Yes, we want you. You will be going to Hamburg. Because Sylvia is underage we just have to sort some documents first." We were even more excited when he wanted us to meet a group from Hamburg who were playing a special gig at the Cavern that night.

He took us in his van from the Rialto to the Mycroft Hotel and introduced us to the Rattles, an early line-up with Achim Reichel on vocals, Hans Kreutzfeld on guitar, bassist Herbert Hildebrandt, and drummer Dicky Tarrach. Playing fast, loud beat rock, they were one of the first German bands to tour the UK. When they stood onstage at the Cavern the Rattles seemed very exotic with their black leather jackets. They looked so good. People in the crowd exclaimed, "Wow, they're *Germans*," and girls were screaming for them just like they did with the Beatles. Older British people may have been hostile toward Germans, but our generation felt differently because nearly twenty years had elapsed since VE Day in 1945. When we went to the Cavern that night we felt so proud because we had come in with the band. We became friends and still are—the band was to play a big part in our lives.

A month before their Cavern slot, the Rattles had been on a five-week tour around the country opening for Little Richard, the Everly

THE OTHER FAB FOUR

Brothers, Bo Diddley, and the Rolling Stones. Their drummer, Dicky, couldn't believe that as a young lad from Hamburg he was playing the Hammersmith Odeon with Little Richard and Bo Diddley, the absolute gods of American rock 'n' roll. It was an intensively competitive tour, with Little Richard stretching out his set so the younger bands were forced to cut their songs short. On the first night Dicky was shaking and nervous. Their songs were only two and a half minutes long, but he had the feeling that the curtain was deliberately slow to open. They performed "Zip-a-Dee Doo-Dah," which had been a big hit for Bob B. Soxx & the Blue Jeans, and "The Stomp," which would get the crowd dancing.

The Everly Brothers traveled separately in a Rolls-Royce, but the Rattles were on a bus with all the other acts. Every morning Little Richard would get on the bus last, sashaying into his seat and saying, "I look so beautiful today!" He would sit behind the driver while his manager read to him a positive review of the previous night's gig. "We never realized, because he was so powerful onstage, that this man was gay. No idea," recalls Dicky.

Life on the road could be stringent, certainly when they were starting out. Dicky says they were given a measly five pounds a day to pay for food and hotels. In every town the coach driver stopped at a swanky hotel and Little Richard would say, "See you later, boys!" The Rattles then had to find their own B & B, usually the cheapest and worst imaginable. But they survived, and on returning to Hamburg said to Manfred: "Next time we go to England it's only first-class hotels."

On that first tour in 1963 the Rattles picked up stellar techniques and rhythms. "I learned a lot from just being around blues star Bo Diddley," says Dicky. "At first I thought, *The man is playing the same two-measure, syncopated pattern and it's kind of boring.* I noticed the Stones spent a lot of time with him, sitting together, working and listening." The next single the Stones released was "Not Fade Away," with harmonica, handclaps, and a speedy Bo Diddley beat right up front in the mix. The song became their first Top Ten hit, shooting to number three in the UK charts. Everyone learned from each other on that tour, like it was a supreme master class.

~

After the auditions with Henroid at the Rialto cinema we dashed home to our parents saying, "We're going to be the female Beatles!"

"Are you?" asked my mum.

"Henry said we could go and play in Hamburg!"

Our parents were supportive and excited for us. However, as soon as we solved one problem, another reared its head. Heather was a dynamic lead singer, but her enthusiasm didn't last much longer than the remaining six dates of our tour. She became very homesick, and it became harder and harder to talk to her because she was so miserable and reluctant to perform.

At the same time, we weren't too sure about my cousin Sheila on rhythm guitar. She was a lovely person but shy onstage, strumming the chords with a lackluster energy. We were improving as a group and becoming better known as we toured the country, but we realized Sheila had to go.

8. SYLVIA

The Final Piece in the Jigsaw

Matters came to a head a few months later on February 21, 1964, when we were booked to play the Mersey View in Frodsham with a new band called the Kinks, who played American-influenced R&B. This was four months before they had a number-one hit with "You Really Got Me." Later they would develop their style with touches of folk and English psychedelia, but that night frontman Ray Davies, along with his brother Dave on lead guitar, drummer Mick Avory, and bassist Peter Quaife, played an electric set of straight covers with some of their own songs. Ray was obviously attracted to Val, flirting with her after the show and complimenting her guitar-playing. He wasn't sure about Sheila, however. When she was out of earshot he said, "You know, girls, it's not going to work out. She's got to go."

"We know ourselves. But it's difficult because she is Mary's cousin," I countered.

"There's a girl here tonight you should meet. She comes from Liverpool and she plays guitar."

The Kinks had performed a session at the Cavern earlier that day, bringing the girl with her, and they offered to give us a lift back to Liverpool in their van. As we clambered in the back we were introduced to a tall blond girl wearing a black cap, striped jacket, and Chelsea boots.

"This is Pam."

"Hello," she said with a smile. "I can play guitar."

"Would you like to come over tomorrow and we'll give it a go?"

Pam agreed, then spent the rest of the journey back to Liverpool kissing and cuddling with Ray Davies. They weren't in a relationship, but, as we were to discover about Pam, she could have pretty much any man she wanted, and that night she had him.

We made arrangements for Pam to meet us at my house, without Sheila. It was obvious from the moment she walked into the rehearsal that Pam was the right fit. The way she looked, the way she played— that was what we wanted. She had great style with a leather coat and her hair in two sleek, immaculate bunches, and she was very knowledgeable about music, enthusing about the bands she'd seen at the Cavern. She also had a great record collection, which included rare R&B and rock 'n' roll, and we realized that she was going to be the person to steer us into the right direction, more like the Stones than girly pop. When we met Pam we truly became the Liverbirds. Her arrival was like the final piece in a jigsaw puzzle.

Giving Sheila the news she was no longer wanted was one of the most difficult things we had to do as a band. We had to tell her in a way that didn't involve Mary, so Val was the one to say, "Look, Sheila, I don't think you're really enjoying the music, you're not fitting in." Sheila sat there quietly, she didn't rant or rave like one of us would have done, saying, "I don't think that's bloody fair!" She just accepted it, said, "OK," and cried. Then she went home to her father, Mary's uncle Johnny, who was naturally dismayed and very protective. He and Mary's dad fell out over it and stopped speaking to each other for over ten years, until Johnny, chronically sick with diabetes, said, "It's terrible what happened to our Sheila, but I think it's about time we made up." Years later, when Mary saw her at a family party, Sheila admitted she had been broken-hearted, but she did realize that things wouldn't have happened for us without Pam. When she came into our lives Pam brought star quality, opening up opportunities for Hamburg and the Star-Club and a whole new world for the band.

Pamela Ann Birch was born on August 9, 1944, in Kirkdale, Liverpool, the eldest of four girls. Her parents, Alma and George, met when they were teenagers and used to busk in an area of Liverpool called Broadway, playing guitar and singing folk harmonies. George's mother was a tiny Welsh lady from Bangor who moved to Norris Green. When we were young we'd often hear the joke that Liverpool was the capital of Wales, because it was less than an hour's drive to the border and so many Welsh families settled in the city. Mr. and Mrs. Birch were both in the armed forces, and got married in their uniforms at the start of the Second World War. Soon after Pam was born her father had to go fight in India and Burma, and her first six months were spent with just her mother and grandma, Annie Percy. Mrs. Birch trained as a cook in the ATS, the women's branch of the British army, dividing her time between auxiliary work and looking after Pam.

When Mr. Birch came back the family moved to Speke, and he worked at the Ford factory. He rarely spoke about his war experiences, apart from one chilling story. He told Pam and her sisters that one day, after a bombing in the jungle, he went into a camp where he found a pair of boots. That didn't sound like anything traumatic until the gruesome punchline, "The feet were still in them." While he was in Burma he also became very ill with malaria and dysentery, but he referred to this in an offhand way, as if it were a joke. Years later, we thought, *Goodness, what else must he have seen that he didn't talk about?* Maybe war experience meant that Mr. Birch felt it wasn't worth getting distressed about small things.

When Pam's sister Jennifer arrived in 1947, Pam found it hard to adjust, and there was friction between them that remained throughout their lives. But Pam doted on her younger sisters—Dyan, who was born in 1949, and Glynne, who arrived much later in 1957. Most of the sisters were redheads, taking after their father's side of the family, but Pam inherited her mother Alma's blond hair and the dimple on her chin. Glynne said to us later, "She would peacock it and prance about with her blond hair. She made the most of everything."

Headstrong and bossy, Pam liked to guide Dyan, coaching her as a singer. The two of them entered talent contests when the family went on resort holidays to the Isle of Man or south Wales, and often won them singing folk and blues covers of songs by Joan Baez and Bob Dylan. When we met Pam she was performing pub gigs with her sister, and later Dyan built on that with a successful career in the soul band Kokomo. Pam liked to say that Dyan was her project.

Pam always craved attention and wanted to be center stage. In her early teens her father bought her a cheap guitar and she taught herself to play. A young lad called Geoff Nugent, who lived two doors down, also had a guitar, and sometimes they would pair up and play together, teaching each other notes and strumming chords. Before they could afford more expensive instruments they would also go to Hessy's music shop in town and test out the guitars. By the time Pam joined the Liverbirds, Geoff was already performing with the Undertakers, a hard-rocking beat group in tall black hats whose gimmick was to take a coffin onstage.

Pam inherited artistic flair and instinctive fashion sense from her mum and grandma. Both were good seamstresses, scouring jumble sales to find clothes they could recycle, and Pam also had this knack for customizing clothes, always looking for bargains and ways to create a signature style. She wore different kinds of hats, like a bright cerise-pink velvet hat little Glynne found in a jumble sale for a few pennies and sent to Pam after the Liverbirds went to Hamburg. Pam loved it so much she wore it onstage, telling everyone it came from Harrods. In return, whenever Pam came home she lavished attention on Glynne, dressing her up like a cute pet and taking pictures of her posing with a guitar and teddy bear.

Pam also liked to style her father. Mr. Birch had a typical 1950s quiff slicked back with Brylcreem. She would laugh at him, saying, "You can't have that hair, it's too old-fashioned. You should be like the Beatles, grow it at the back and have a proper haircut." He resisted until the day Glynne came home from school to find him pinned to the stairs with Jennifer and Dyan holding him down, and Pam at his head hacking off his quiff. "He was screaming, but I think he appreciated it in the end," Glynne told us.

Pam and her father had a combative relationship. In the early 1960s, when record players became very popular, he bought one of the first stereos. He placed it in the dining room, and every evening after school Pam would fold down the table, put on records, and dance on the linoleum floor. She loved that stereo and hogged it so much that Mr. Birch took the needle out of the arm of the record player so she couldn't use it. But then he caught Pam trying to stick a drawing pin to the arm—a makeshift attempt at a replacement needle, but something that would have completely destroyed the vinyl!

At Speke Comprehensive school Pam had met Dave Brown, her first long-term boyfriend. Sometimes we speculate about how if she had stayed with him she would have had such a different life. He was a lovely guy, good-looking like Buddy Holly, and he wore the same kind of nerdy glasses. Everybody loved him. Her dad loved him. Her grandma loved him. When he went to study at Sheffield University, Pam would visit him every week in his uni halls, bringing with her the latest single she had picked up. In his letters he would say, "The guys in halls are really jealous because you always bring the best records with you." They shared a taste in music and were together for three years before she went to Hamburg, but she didn't want the life that clearly he was heading for. Pam knew she was going in a different direction. He wanted to settle down and in those days once you got married there was a pressure to start a family. She was very ambitious for her music, and not ready to settle down at all.

Pam left school at sixteen and worked as a typist, spending her paycheck on clothes and records, each week building up her collection of R&B, blues, and American imports. Her job as a secretary in Liverpool city center meant she spent most lunchtimes at the Cavern, avidly following local bands. For a while she was a proud, self-confessed groupie, skilled at attaching herself to musicians, maybe hoping some of their artistry would rub off on her. After the Rolling Stones played the Cavern in 1963 Pam had put the band up for the night. Pam's sisters came downstairs in their school uniforms to find a Rolling Stone in the living room. "I was in primary school and didn't realize who it was, other than he had a London accent," Glynne told us. "He said, 'All right there, kid?' and ruffled my hair while Pam made him bacon butties. I found out later that was Charlie Watts."

Pam apparently had a fling with Mick Jagger. She knew how to handle men, whereas we were still learning, and sometimes it took a while to realize when musicians we knew were just being sleazy. One afternoon, for instance, Mary and I got talking to Deek Rivers and the Big Sound, a group from Manchester who were sound-checking at the Cavern. They had a few hours to kill before the gig, so I suggested, "Why don't you come back to my house and I'll ask my mum to give you some sandwiches?"

They agreed and arrived at my house in a battered old van. Mum took one look out of the window at their shaggy hair and scruffy clothes and said to my sister Jean, "Quick, put the china cups away! Get the best towels out of the bathroom!" Deek Rivers devoured the sandwiches and drank gallons of tea before going back to play the gig. Afterward they invited me and Mary back to Manchester to stay the night, so, thinking it would be fun, we joined them in the van. When we arrived at a poky, terraced house on the outskirts of Manchester we saw unsavory bunk beds upstairs and young girls sitting submissively in a queue waiting for their turn. We exchanged glances, made our excuses, saying, "Oh oh, we'd better get back quick," and got to the station as soon as we could. Back home in Liverpool my mum asked, "I thought you were staying at Mary's?"

"No, I just decided to come home."

"Did you fall out?"

"No, I just thought I'd go home."

Mary told her mother the same story, and embellished it, saying that Deek Rivers was a religious band, like gospel ministers. We'd made a lucky escape and were glad to be out of there.

Pam may have been interested in the male musicians but that wasn't her prime focus. Looking for a chance to shine, she jumped at the opportunity to front the Liverbirds as lead singer. Once she came along, playing robust rhythm guitar and singing with a confident rocking style, the band gelled immediately. She encouraged Val to sing too, saying, "You have a deep talking voice, I'm sure you could sing." Val had never considered vocals but once she started singing, a powerful voice emerged, one that sounded husky and soulful like Helen Shapiro, a jazzy pop singer from east London who had a number-one hit in 1961 with "Walking Back to Happiness."

Pam's and Val's vocal harmonies blended well, and Val took on most of the arrangements, doing what we called "the fiddly bits." We would create our own fiddly bits too. While they concentrated on melody and lyrics, we kept the bass and drums locked in synch. We soon realized that in a strong band all four elements work seamlessly together. There were no stage monitors at the Cavern and half the time I couldn't hear what Pam and Val were singing, so I just kept to the beat and hoped for the best. It usually worked because we could draw a crowd and we'd have girls in the audience yelling at the front of the stage, absolutely made up and great in the way only Liverpool girls can be, proud that women from their hometown were onstage. We thought we were moving into a different league, but we still had to fight through many obstacles to get the recognition we craved and to make it big as a band.

9. MARY

You Really Got Me

The last time we played the Cavern in 1964 we loaded the van near the venue, with all the equipment inside, and went for a cup of coffee. When we got back the van door was loose and all the guitars had been stolen. We were gutted. Despite having a few bookings, we were still without a manager after leaving Mick Lowe and we weren't making much money. My mum said, "Go tell Auntie Chrissie." My aunt was from a famous Liverpool barrow family, selling fruit and flowers on an estate with a lot of rogues and criminals. We went to her complaining, "We've lost our manager, we've got no money, we've lost band members, our instruments have been stolen, all these things have been happening."

"Leave it with me."

Two days later Auntie Chrissie said to us, "Your guitars are in my house. Come and pick them up, but don't ask how I got them."

We were just grateful to get them back.

Now we had the guitars back, we had to find a new manager. Our parents were beginning to worry about us and whether there was a future for the band. They introduced an element of doubt, saying, "You're only teenagers, maybe you should go back to your office jobs." We knew something had to happen quickly. Pam was always ready for an adventure, so she suggested, "Let's go to London and get Brian Epstein to be our manager." We had his West End address— 13 Monmouth Street, Seven Dials—where he had just set up his NEMS Enterprises management company with the Beatles, Gerry and the Pacemakers, and Cilla Black. By then the Beatles were dominating the charts, Gerry and the Pacemakers had scored number one with their first three singles, and Cilla Black's song "Anyone Who Had a Heart" had just gone into the Top Ten. Mr. Epstein obviously had strong instincts and would be a good manager—and he was from Liverpool.

We bought one-way tickets, the most we could afford, and set off one morning from Liverpool. Stopping everywhere, the train journey took an interminable eight hours, and we didn't pull into Euston Station until six o'clock in the evening. London was buzzing with people rushing up and down escalators on the Underground. We headed for Piccadilly Circus, working out that we had enough spare change to buy a drink in a coffee bar. We were sitting there nursing a few coffees and gazing out of the window when Pam exclaimed: "There's Brian Epstein!"

"Oh, give over."

"It is!"

"My God, it is him."

We put two shillings on the table and dashed out into the street calling after him. Because the four of us were wearing duffel coats with hoods, he must have thought we were mad Beatles fans and made a run for it toward the Underground. When we caught up with him, Pam said, breathless, "You're Brian Epstein!"

He looked around nervously.

"No, I'm not him."

"Brian, we're not Beatles fans, we're a girl group and we want you to be our manager."

He visibly relaxed. "Listen, girls," he said, reaching into his jacket pocket, "here's my card. Come into the office tomorrow and we'll talk about it."

After he disappeared we stood there wondering what to do, because we had no money for a hotel. Pam, however, was very resourceful and knew her way around the city because she had been there already with the Kinks and the Rolling Stones. We were just following her— she was in charge. She led us down Piccadilly to Green Park near Buckingham Palace, where tall plane trees and black poplars stood in rows. Even though it was February, we found a couple of benches and spent the night there, sleeping in pairs with one head on one lap, then swapping around. We managed to sleep even though it was cold and we didn't think about being harassed because we had Pam and Val, who seemed fearless. It would have been different had we been on our own. God knows what we looked like the next day—we didn't have a mirror and had nowhere to wash or put on lipstick. Still, we tidied our hair and made it to the NEMS headquarters in Monmouth Street by ten o'clock.

"Mr. Epstein is expecting us," we said to the secretary.

After a short wait Epstein appeared from behind a door and ushered us into his office.

"Come on in, girls."

We told him our story, how we were a girl group looking for a manager, how we had done an audition for Henry Henroid and been offered a residency at the Star-Club. We also told him about how our instruments had been stolen, our first manager had exploited us, and there had been disruption with changes in the band lineup but that we were determined to carry on playing. He listened patiently.

"OK, I'll arrange for you to play and I'll come and see you, otherwise I can't make a decision. How can I contact you?"

Pam gave him her parents' phone number, and told him that we had no return ticket. Epstein dialed through to his secretary.

"Can you please get the girls four train tickets to Liverpool?"

A few days after we returned home we were given an audition appointment in London, added to the bill on a gig with several up-and-coming bands. Sylvia's brother-in-law Bob drove us down, and because it was a Sunday we had to stop off halfway down so I could go to church. I was still planning to become a nun, after all. "We might be famous tomorrow, but I have to find a church today," I said, and located somewhere to attend Mass before driving on to London. After the gig a man walked into the dressing room and said briskly, "Mr. Epstein couldn't come today, but he's sent me. I think you're very good and I'm sure he'll be interested." We thought, *He can't be very interested; otherwise he would have come himself.* It wasn't until later that we realized the man was Peter Brown, his right-hand man.

We decided not to pin all our hopes on Brian Epstein and kept looking for other options. We came down to London again in March, because the Kinks had invited us to visit their recording session in Dean Street studios and Ray Davies told us to bring our guitars in case there was time to audition for their manager, Larry Page. Their first single, a cover of the Little Richard song "Long Tall Sally," had been released the previous month but had stalled at number forty-two in the charts, so they were recording demos for new songs, still finding their style. We got the money together to get a train down to Euston Station, where Ray and David Davies picked us up and took us to a grand old hotel near Russell Square. By then the band had a deal with Pye Records, so Larry Page booked and paid for our rooms—with beds that were much more comfortable than benches in Green Park!

After we arrived we sat awkwardly in the foyer. We'd never been in a hotel that big, and it felt very old, almost spooky. We were all sitting talking when Val and David went off, walking around the hotel, arm in arm. They vanished for a while and I don't know where they went. Years later I met Ray Davies again and he told me that he really fancied Val. He was disappointed that she obviously liked David, and he even said that it was the resemblance to Val that attracted him to Chrissie Hynde.

Ray and David told us to bring our guitars, so that came in useful the next morning when we arrived at Dean Street Studios and Larry Page rushed out to say that their guitars had been stolen from the van parked outside.

"Look, you can use ours," we enthused.

"Thanks so much!"

Inside the studio Ray was busy setting up. Until then the Kinks had focused on covers, but now they were experimenting with a new song. "I wrote this myself," he said while they were tuning up. Then they launched into "You Really Got Me." Amazed by the deep bluesy sound of the opening riffs, we had no inkling that when it was released four months later the song would become one of the Kinks' biggest hits. Not only that, it would change the course of guitar pop and form the basis for heavy metal. They stumbled on that fuzzy, distorted sound by accident, telling us they'd put their guitars through an old radiogram at home because they didn't have proper amplifiers, and they liked the effect. We were just pleased they could use our guitars for their demo.

The Kinks had nearly finished recording when Mick Jagger and Ian Stewart wandered in to say hello, because the Stones were booked into the next session.

"Have we got time to let the girls have a go?" David said to Page.

"Yes, but just one!"

This was our chance to impress Page, so we played our jubilant version of the Chuck Berry song "Reelin' and Rockin'" and everyone joined in, with Ray and David on backing vocals, Mick Jagger shaking the maracas, and Ian Stewart doing boogie-woogie piano. It was the first time that we'd heard ourselves on big speakers in the studio and were absolutely knocked out, especially with the additional backing. We felt we had arrived.

Page's office faced the studio, so we went in there afterward for a chat and he said, "Leave it with me, I'll get back in touch." Page was tall, commanding, and straightforward. Even though he had been a pop singer in the 1950s, known as Larry Page the Teenage Rage, he was more like a besuited manager type than a musician. The Kinks, by contrast, were art-school weird, wearing striped jackets and colorful strangely patterned shirts—their image was already distinct from the Beatles'.

After the studio session Ray and David took us to a music shop on Denmark Street where they bought their guitars. Pam wanted a Cadillac-green Gretch like Brian Jones, so she was delighted when she found one, loving its crunchy, dirty tones when she played rhythm. Val also loved scouring the guitar shops—her favorite model was a Vox, with its crystal-clear twang, and later she bought the Jaguar, which had an even richer sound. We then wandered around Carnaby Street and bought Beatles-style Chelsea boots in Anello & Davide in Covent Garden. The Kinks' song "Dedicated Follower of Fashion" didn't come out until 1966, but when we hung out with them that spring of 1964, London boutiques had quirky clothes inspired by designers like Mary Quant and Kiki Byrne, and the Kinks were already getting into that psychedelic style.

We returned to Liverpool that night talking excitedly about our meeting with Larry Page, but soon after we got back we became distracted: things started happening with our plans for Hamburg.

Because Sylvia was only seventeen years old she needed permission via a court order from Bow Street Magistrates' Court before she could work in Hamburg, and Henry's friend Mickie Most, the record producer, was going to act as her guarantor. While we were waiting for permission Henry had us booked into the Aaland Hotel, near Russell Square in London. The hotel was where artists stayed before they went on TV shows like *Ready Steady Go!* and *Top of the Pops*, and it was also the base for artists to make a quick getaway for Hamburg once all the forms had been signed.

That's when Brian Epstein got in touch, saying he would like to be our manager. We realized, *Oh my God, he did mean it!* But by then we were so set on going to Hamburg that we put him off, saying, "We're going to the Star-Club and when we come back we'll talk about it."

"I know Manfred. If you go to the Star-Club you'll never come back," he replied.

Henry Henroid had advised us to go for six weeks. When you are young that amount of time seems like forever. We didn't know what would happen after those six weeks, but we knew the money was good—four hundred Deutschmarks a week, which was about thirty pounds each. It was a lot of money in those days—and a lot more than the seven pounds a week we'd started with.

We also had an offer of management from the Kinks' manager, Larry Page, but put him off, convinced that we would come back from Germany a stronger band and in a better negotiating position for either Brian Epstein or Page. Over in Hamburg the owner of the Star-Club, Manfred Weissleder, had already strung a flag across the road outside the Star-Club announcing us as a featured attraction. People were expecting us.

Now we just needed to wait to begin our new lives in Hamburg. What was originally going to be one week in London turned into six. Manfred might have been paying for our room but that didn't include food, so we had to eke out our pennies by staying in to save money. We had no money to buy new clothes, so washed our underwear in the sink and draped it round the bedroom to dry. We would get very bored, and sometimes just sat in reception people-watching. One day a beautiful woman with long blond hair came in, a good-looking beau on her arm. Pam recognized them immediately.

"My God, that's Astrid Kirchherr and Gibson Kemp. God, she looks fantastic, doesn't she?"

They had just got together, an amazingly gorgeous couple. He had been the drummer for bands like Kingsize Taylor and Rory Storm and the Hurricanes before he joined psychedelic rock group the Eyes. Kirchherr was the German photographer who took pictures of the Beatles during their early days in Hamburg. She had a relationship with their first bass guitarist, Stu Sutcliffe, before he died tragically of a brain tumor in 1962, and at that point she was still very close to the Beatles. She had captivating, ice-blue eyes and was strong and willowy like Jean Seberg, the icon of French new-wave cinema. Men were drawn to her—as Bill Harry told Beatles biographer Bob Spitz: "The minute she walked into a room all heads immediately turned her way. She was in full control of that room." She had an untouchable beauty that we were in awe of. We had no idea that soon she would be working with us, helping to create the Liverbirds' style.

Seeing Astrid and Gibson was one of the high points of our stay. Pam and Val had brought portable record players, so sometimes we listened to Chuck Berry records in the hotel bedroom, thinking of ways to expand our set in preparation for Hamburg. We'd listen to songs like "Johnny Be Goode" and "Maybelline," and Pam would write down the words while Val worked out the chords. When we weren't doing that we whiled away the hours talking to Hannah, the hotel groupie, a stylish girl with a round, jolly face. Every evening Hannah sat in the basement kitchen with us, recounting tales of sex with musicians. As she talked we would respond nonchalantly, saying, "Oh, really…?" acting like we knew what she was referring to, though (apart from Pam) we were still virgins and sexually innocent at the time.

"This fella was here today, he was nice so I gave him a blow job," she would say. Afterward we privately compared notes.

"What's a blow job? What's a back passage?"

We were fascinated by her. Poor Hannah, she was our entertainment, part of an illicit grown-up world that we found intriguing but also slightly scary. Being in a girl group gave us protection and mutual support, and we didn't realize how vulnerable girls like Hannah really were.

In the same hotel we stayed in, the Aaland, the DJ and presenter Jimmy Savile rented a permanent room all kitted out with a pink bedspread and frills. At that point Savile already had his eccentric long blond hair and a cigar permanently clamped in his mouth. He was a DJ for Radio Luxembourg, and on New Year's Day 1964 he presented the first edition of a new BBC music chart show, *Top of the Pops*. A regular co-host at the annual *New Musical Express* Poll-Winners' Concert in Wembley Stadium, Savile was at the center of the music industry and a very influential man. Many years later, after his death in 2011, Scotland Yard launched a criminal investigation into allegations of child sex abuse spanning six decades with three hundred potential victims, concluding that he was a "predatory sex offender."

In 1964, however, nobody suspected him of wrongdoing, even though there was something odd about his energy. He used to say, "Everybody knows I have a house in Salford, but I need a room in the hotel to keep in contact with the groups." The real reason was a bit different. We would see young girls go into his room with their uniforms on, straight from school, and we'd say, "Hey, Jimmy, what are those girls going into your room for?"

"They just like to tidy and clean for me . . . for a bit of pocket money."

We didn't think anything of it until we saw the headlines in 2011, and we shuddered, remembering one afternoon in particular.

We had been in the Aaland Hotel for six weeks, getting our parents to send postal orders for food, and they were worried.

"You've got to come back now, girls," they said. "It's taking too long."

One day, sensing that something was wrong, Savile invited us into his room. He was already in bed, and got the four of us to sit on top of the covers, two each side, while he talked to us.

"Come on, girls, tell us your problems."

"Our parents say we've got to go home if this isn't sorted."

"Listen, girls, I've got an idea. If I arrange for you to do an interview with a newspaper and you get a bit of money, will you do it?"

"Yes, of course!" we chorused.

He arranged it all—the photographer came from *The Sunday People* to take a picture of us. We were sitting on the stairs of the Aaland Hotel and he gave us directions: "Look happy. Look sad. Jump up in the air. Hold your guitars." We did all that and Savile arranged for us to be paid a hundred pounds for the interview, which was a lot of money in those days. We thought it was great. Then Sunday came and we dashed to the newsagents. *The Sunday People* featured a photograph of us on the stairs looking downcast. "Mothers, Don't Let This Happen to Your Girls!" barked the headline. The feature claimed that we were being exploited by a music-industry sweat shop. Our parents were on the phone, crying, "Get home tomorrow!" But that was the day the court granted permission for us to go to Hamburg, and Mickie Most, Henry's record-producer friend, swiftly picked us up and took us to Liverpool Street Station before our parents could fetch us.

It seemed that we had escaped Jimmy Savile's predatory attention, but then we look at the picture of the four of us with him outside the hotel and he's just wearing a tiny pair of silky shorts, which looks a bit odd and over-revealing. Though it didn't enter our heads then, we realize now he must have been titillated when we sat with him on the bed. What Savile was doing with those young schoolgirls, we didn't know things like that existed. Savile was already becoming part of the establishment and committing his crimes in plain sight. In those days, if we'd written to our parents saying "Jimmy Savile's taking care of us" they would have assumed we were in good hands.

BOOK TWO: HAMBURG

10. SYLVIA

Swinging the Lights

On May 28, 1964, Henry rang the Aaland Hotel and spoke to Pam. "The court hearing was this morning—Sylvia has permission to go and Mickie Most has signed the guarantee form. We'll be there in two hours, so pack your bags!" We screamed with excitement. After six weeks of killing time, we were finally going to Hamburg. We bustled around, fussing over guitars and hair and stuffing damp undies into our little travel cases.

Henroid and Mickie Most arrived at the hotel and took us in a taxi to Liverpool Street Station and we got there at the last minute, running down the platform with our little zip cases in one hand and guitars in the other. They more or less threw us on the train, where we found spare seats and sat there for a moment laughing and catching our breath. The train took us to Harwich on the Essex coast, where we got an overnight ferry to the Hook of Holland, dozing on uncomfortable chairs, too excited to sleep.

From there it was a nine-hour journey on the train to Hamburg. Sitting in a carriage by ourselves gave us an ideal opportunity to practice the songs we'd been listening to in the Aaland Hotel, the girls playing their guitars while I beat a rhythm on the seats and walls with my drumsticks. Val had figured out the chords in arrangements she taught Mary and Pam, while Pam had memorized most of the lyrics, glancing down to her notebook every so often if she forgot a phrase. She would work on the vocal harmonies and lead melody lines. As the train threaded its way through Holland and northern Germany via Rotterdam, Munster, and Bremen, we rehearsed Chuck Berry songs we had never performed live before, nervous with anticipation. Every so often we would look out the window at a landscape that was so different from England—wide open fields and plains dotted with timber-framed farmhouses and chalets with pointed roofs. Even the sky seemed different, wider, more blue and expansive. Before this the farthest we'd been from home was London and Edinburgh, so it was a thrill to be in mainland Europe for the first time.

It was evening by the time we arrived at Hamburg Central Station. We bundled our cases and instruments through the barrier and were met by Manfred's right-hand man, a tall blond guy called Hans Bunkenburg. He drove us in his car to the Hotel Pacific and said, "Girls, you have half an hour to get ready, and then we go to the Star-Club." We ran upstairs through this completely basic three-star hotel and thought we were in Hollywood. We had arrived! Mary and I shared one room, while Val and Pam settled in the other. It was natural to pair off that way because of our roles in the band— Mary and I keeping in synch with the rhythm, while Val and Pam led the melodies and the tune. There wasn't much time to change, but thankfully we already had our outfits worked out—smart white shirts, trousers, and boots. Pam was clear about that. Back home in Liverpool, within weeks of her joining us we had done a photo shoot by the Liver Building wearing dresses, neat shoes, and demure stockings under our duffel coats. Pam had turned up in jeans, a cap, and a leather jacket like the one George Harrison wore. During the shoot she said, "Listen, girls, this isn't me at all," and after that she forbade any dresses or chiffon.

Once we were changed, guitars at the ready, Hans took us to the Star-Club, which wasn't very far from the hotel. He parked his car down a side road so it wasn't until we walked around the corner that we saw all the red lights and got the shock of our lives. The club was surrounded by porn parlors, striptease clubs, and brothels. We thought, *Oh my God—what if our parents see this?* But then Mary noticed a Catholic church right next to the Star-Club. To her that was a reassuring safe haven, somewhere she could go to Mass every Sunday and pray.

We had never been anywhere like this before and were trying to take it all in, while Hans briefed us about the Star-Club. He said that the barmaids were all gorgeous and it was very important that they liked us. Musicians back in Liverpool had also warned, "The barmaids are the stars, they're so important. They're beautiful and they've got everything under control. If they don't like you, you've had it." There were lights hanging on chains above the bar, and if they liked a band the barmaids would hit the lights until they swung.

On entering the club, the first thing that struck us was how large and cavernous it was, with a very high ceiling. The place was crowded, with a busy bar to the left and another one on the right, and round the dancefloor were boxes where people sat, drank, and watched the action while waiters moved deftly from table to table, taking orders. As we walked through to get to the backstage dressing room, people were touching us and saying, "They're really here! They do exist!" The Liverbirds had been a featured attraction for a month on the banner outside, and people were wondering if we would ever arrive. We paid close attention to the barmaids, hoping that they would like us. Before we went onstage we wished each other luck.

The curtains opened and we looked out at the 2,000-strong crowd. The Star-Club was one of the biggest places we'd played and it seemed absolutely massive to us. It felt like the other girls were miles away from me, and at first we were terrified. I was at the back so I could almost hide away. We played our first song, but nothing happened. Then when we launched into "Roadrunner," people started to move and right there at the front fellas and girls were hollering and screaming for us, and that buoyed us up. It was like something ignited and the audience went wild. "Oh my God! They're swinging the lights!" Pam shouted. That spurred us on. Our set wasn't note perfect; we played the songs we had rehearsed on the train, which meant we'd never heard them over an amplifier. We stumbled in a few places, but by the time we reached our ballad "Love Hurts" everybody was swinging the lights like mad and the crowd were swaying back and forth. It felt like we had passed a test. We'd been worried that the barmaids might be jealous or afraid we would take their boys, but that didn't happen. We knew we were accepted.

As we finished playing one of the barmen came onstage with a large silver ice bucket, a bottle of champagne, and four glasses. All the music stopped while he poured the drink and handed a glass to each of us. We said, "What's this? What's happened?"

"Those girls, there…" He pointed to four ladies sitting at a long table. "They've sent you a drink."

"Oh, isn't that nice!"

"Be careful, girls, they're lesbians."

"Oh," said Mary. "Where's that?"

The lesbians had been waiting for a month since the announcement of our concerts, and we made their night because there weren't many women on that scene. Beryl Marsden and a Scottish singer called Isobel Bond were the only solo singers performing at the club, and all-girl bands were as rare as UFOs. When we went backstage to the dressing room musicians from other bands came up and said, "Girls, that was great! We thought you were just going to be a gimmick, but you're really good and you've got your own sound!"

Our set that night was forty-five minutes. Just after the lesbians sent the champagne a bell rang over the Tannoy and Manfred announced, "All people under the age of eighteen must leave the club NOW!" Police entered the club with torches to check identity cards, and I noticed the German kids didn't argue—because with German parents they would get into a lot of trouble. I was still seventeen so it was a condition of my work permit that I had to leave the club before ten o'clock and take a taxi back to the Hotel Pacific. It was hard to tear myself away, so about ten minutes after I arrived at the hotel I went straight back to the Star-Club and snuck in backstage.

This happened every night that week, and for the next five months, until my eighteenth birthday on October 31. Beryl Marsden was performing the same time as us, and she was also underage, six months younger than me. We would leave the Star-Club together every night before ten, and sometimes sneak back in after the police had left—particularly if famous artists were playing, like the Walker Brothers or Ben E. King. We were closely monitored, and every four weeks we had to get a new stamp in our passport to say we were playing the Star-Club. The German authorities were very strict—that's why an underage George Harrison got deported when the Beatles first came to Hamburg.

Playing every night at nine o'clock we soon became tight as musicians, honing our stagecraft to keep the crowd dancing. When the Beatles played the Star-Club the fans would shout, "*Mache show! Mache show!*" because they wanted them to put on a show. So we thought, we need to provide something special. We focused on covers and started doing more R&B songs like "Can't Judge a Book" or "Before You Accuse Me" and "Diddley Daddy." Once the curtains opened we'd start with "Roadrunner" and as part of the performance Mary and Pam would run up to each other and run back. Charging toward Mary with her hair down, Pam looked like a big glamorous cavewoman.

I'd thrash the drums, smiling and nodding my head to the beat, and when we played "Money" Pam and Mary would turn around and wiggle their behinds while the audience threw money onstage. The routine looked comical with Val singing in the middle, little Mary on one side and big Pam on the other, waggling their hips. Although the Star-Club had a demanding audience we knew it was working for us when the whole place was full with two thousand people dancing, and the moment we went offstage the dancefloor was half-full again.

After we had played there for a week things were progressing well and we were improving quickly as musicians, so Manfred called us into his office, a large, high-ceilinged room above the club that looked directly onto Grosse Freiheit ("the Great Freedom"), a cross-street to the north of the Reeperbahn. In a room at the back was his book-keeper, the cigar-smoking Mr. Anderson, who had only one arm. Mr. Anderson was Manfred's right-hand man, only he didn't have a right hand! We perched nervously on the red velvety embroidered sofa opposite his desk.

"I'd like to be your manager," he said. "You girls are going down very well here."

As soon as he said that we knew that was what we wanted—we loved the atmosphere in Hamburg, and we were happy for him to be our manager. As young as we were, we didn't realize that meant not going back to England.

"I want to see how you go down in other parts of Germany," said Manfred. "So would you like to play in Berlin this weekend with Chuck Berry?"

Chuck Berry was a god—a phenomenal singer/guitarist, the inventor of rock 'n' roll, and a major influence on the Beatles and the Rolling Stones. Of course we would like to perform with him!

Playing that gig in Berlin's Deutschlandhalle with other Star-Club bands like Kingsize Taylor and the Dominoes, and the Big Six was such an awe-inspiring experience. We learned so much, and grew in confidence overnight, especially when we were onstage and Chuck Berry's manager tried to stop us playing "Roll Over Beethoven." In those days Val hardly ever swore, but that night she pushed him away and shouted, "Now you, fuck off!" When she did that the audience went wild and started smashing the chairs.

All the bands got the crowd going, but when Chuck Berry finally hit the stage he took over with an elemental, primal force and a driving rhythm. He had a perfectly manicured image with coiffed, oiled hair, eye makeup, and a tiny, sculpted mustache. Back home in St. Louis he had trained as a beautician at a college founded by the famous inventor of African-American cosmetics, Annie Turnbo Malone, and you could see he had used that training to refine his visual style, along with his black suit, bootlace tie, and shiny, pointed shoes. He had a strangely formal pronunciation, especially when he was introducing "Roll Over Beethoven." Just in that title, with its mix of rock and classical language, Berry was breaking down the division between high- and low-brow music.

"This is a song about a man who had a lot to do with music. A good musician, might I say so. This man was called…" he said with a dramatic pause, "…Beet-*ho*ven. Ladies and gentlemen, I ask him to forgive us. Roll over and listen to this." Constantly crossing the stage with his frenetic duck-walk dance, Chuck Berry strummed hard on his Gibson guitar, propelling the band through all his rock-and-roll classics from "Maybellene" and "Rock and Roll Music" to "Johnny B. Goode." He also sang a new song, "No Particular Place to Go," that had a strange underlying aimlessness. He had just served time in an American jail for transporting a fourteen-year-old girl across state lines and his popularity there had been on the wane. Now his career was being revitalized with the British Invasion and the release of a new album called *St. Louis to Liverpool*. He happily name-checked Liverpool, but was furious that we dared to perform his songs before his set. We didn't worry about the fact that we'd broken protocol—we were young and just having too much fun.

Manfred had booked all the musicians into a hotel with a rambling garden, so the day after the gig we all sat in deckchairs, laughing about the night before. We were then taken on a coach trip to Checkpoint Charlie, the heavily armed crossing point between West and East Berlin. The Berlin Wall had been built just a few years before, and was a scary reminder that we were in the middle of a Cold War with Soviet Russia. As a coach party we were allowed to walk through and get a brief glimpse of "the other side," and we saw old buildings still riddled with bullet holes from the war. It was like going back in time.

When we got back to Hamburg to find Manfred's message summoning us into his office, we were convinced he would fire us. But instead Chuck Berry's manager was offering to take us to Las Vegas. With one proviso: "He wants you to play topless."

"What? Topless?"

"Yes."

"Me, playing topless? Shaking everything? I can't play like that. No, Manfred, we're staying here," I said.

"Girls, I'm not trying to persuade you..."

"No Manfred, we're staying here."

Later we realized Manfred didn't want to lose one of his star attractions—the club was crowded every night—so he'd added the topless part of the performance to discourage us from leaving for Las Vegas. We were still very naive about the music business. Manfred was a dynamic promoter, a diehard music fan who went out of his way to book American stars, yet also knew how to make a good deal. Chuck Berry had played the Star-Club the night before the Berlin show and did the trick he was well known for, which was refusing to go onstage until he got more money. I'm sure Manfred expected this and offered him less at first! He had secured the franchise for Star-Clubs dotted across Germany, in cities like Bremen or Kiel. Although he was an imposing guy and made a lot of money, he made sure to look after his artists, so ensuring our loyalty.

We became friendly with the other musicians, and one group in particular who paid us attention were Screamin' Lord Sutch and his backing band the Savages, which included the rock guitarist Richie Blackmore, who later went on to play with Deep Purple. David Sutch was a singer from Harrow who was so inspired by voodoo blues star Screaming Jay Hawkins that he changed his name to Screamin' Lord Sutch, Third Earl of Harrow (even though he didn't have one noble connection). In the 1980s he went on to form the Monster Raving Loony Party, standing as a political candidate in many British elections, but in the early 1960s he was just a garage-rock musician. Sutch's horror-themed set began every night with him leaping out of a black coffin, wearing a cape and a battered top hat. As he waved around his prop knives and daggers, girls would scream with delighted fright. Despite his threatening appearance he was very friendly to us backstage, and we ended up being wooed by a couple of his Savages.

In those early weeks Mary and I were fairly well-behaved because I had my nightly ten-o'clock curfew and she was still determined to be a nun. Even though sexual activity was all around us in the form of strip clubs and brothels and groupies, we made a pact to keep our virginity and not be led astray. One night in the Hotel Pacific we were settling down to bed with our hair rollers and nighties when there was a loud knock on the door.

"It's me, girls," said Pam through the bedroom door. "I've got two Savages and they wanna meet ya."

We opened it to find two band members standing there, smiling expectantly. They wanted to get cuddly with us, but all we let them do was sit on the bed and hold our hands.

Manfred rented out the whole fourth floor of the Hotel Pacific for

Star-Club musicians, and we soon became used to communal living, making adjustments as we went along. We settled into a daily
routine. We usually went to bed very late, about three or four in the
morning, and got up around midday. There were no cooking facili-
ties in the room, not even a kettle for tea, so we usually went to the
Seaman's Mission, a cheap restaurant near the port, for breakfast.
We'd get a good meal there of eggs, chips, and beans. Then we'd go
back to our rooms to work on songs and music, or book rehearsal
space at the Star-Club. The four of us were very close and never went
anywhere separately. Our main meal was back at the Seaman's Mission around 5 p.m., often tasty chicken with soya sauce—we lived
on chicken. Then we'd go back to the hotel to get ready, and have a
drink around seven before going to the Star-Club next door at eight
thirty. We'd hover backstage feeling nervous. I was always apprehen-
sive about getting my drumming timing and breaks right, but the
moment we were onstage the adrenaline kicked in and the set would
pass in a rush.

The Liverbirds were together twenty-four hours a day, so every
time Val and Pam started to get on each other's nerves we swapped
around rooms to stop them falling out. Val and Pam had a very
strange relationship, sometimes arguing like cat and dog. Maybe
because they steered the songs and arrangements, they sometimes
became locked in a kind of creative rivalry. Whenever that happened,
Mary or I would be the peacemakers.

Hotel Pacific was painted bright white inside, with one shared
bathroom and two separate toilets on each floor, for both men and
women. In each room was a double bed joined together with two
mattresses, a settee, and a sink in the corner. On entering the hotel
we would walk in the glass lift and press the button for the fourth
floor. It always stopped at first floor reception so the concierge, a big
fat man called Herr Waldt, could check who was in the lift. Musicians

weren't allowed to take people upstairs, but then we discovered that if we got out of the lift at reception and asked for chocolate then Herr Waldt had to walk down the corridor. As soon as his back was turned everybody legged it upstairs with their friends. That's how we smuggled them into the hotel.

Herr Waldt was a dirty old man, but we didn't realize it at the time. He used to say to us, "Listen, girls, I've got this fantastic bubble bath, so if you ever want to have a bath, just let me know and I'll give you some bubbles."

Every so often we would run a bath and say, "Mr. Waldt, we're gonna have a bath now." When the bath was ready, all foaming up, he would hang around near the door and we'd say innocently, "Mr. Waldt, can you leave now?"

I don't know what he was expecting, but there was no way we were going to get undressed in front of him. For a long time we used his bubble bath, without further incident, especially Pam—she loved it.

Back home in Liverpool on July 10, 1964, not long after our arrival in Hamburg, Pam's seven-year-old sister Glynne took the day off school and went with their mother, Alma, to join the crowd at Speke airport waving the Beatles home from America. Over 200,000 fans lined the streets to welcome them back for the northern premiere of their film *Hard Day's Night*. The Beatles were the big success story, but it wasn't just about them—every group that came back from Hamburg played with greater volume, attitude, and energy. Beryl Marsden says, "Bands would come back to Britain more confident and all leathered up, with leather trousers or jackets. There was a change. Because you worked hard out there." The six weeks we were originally booked for at the Star-Club stretched into months.

Performing at the Star-Club was like rehearsing for hours every day. The sound came out of a house cinema PA that had originally been used for films. Everybody had to play through that PA, and sitting at the back as a drummer I couldn't hear anything, so I'd say to the girls, "When you're ready to stop the song just turn around." We had to use such basic equipment it's amazing that we still played in time. It was the same everywhere. The Beatles had no monitor in Shea Stadium, but Ringo still kept time with his drumming. I don't know how he did it. The Star-Club was hot and I played so fiercely that I began to get blisters and had to wear gloves as I drummed because my hands were so sore.

I played straight and loud, hitting the bass drum hard and pushing the rhythm forward. As I played, the drums would move away from me so the stage manager had to put bricks in front of the drum legs so they would stay in one place. I used to hit a lot of rim shots because that made a good, heavy sound. We were like the fellas, we could talk about drumming, talk about the music. The musicians didn't think, *Oh, we have to be careful around the girls.* Dicky from the Rattles told me, "When we heard a girl band from Liverpool were coming to the Star-Club everyone was interested. I saw you the first evening when the curtain opened and you started to play. It was unexpected, you were working like hell. I'd never seen this before, a girl playing drums with that power. Your whole band had a good groove." Bands often shared instruments, and I would bring my own cymbals and snare. If I borrowed the bass drum I'd end up paying the owner because I had broken it with a kick. When I perform, my whole body moves— I can't help it.

I phoned my mum every Friday night from Hamburg around eight o'clock—that was a condition of me going—and I sent regular postcards, scrawling a few lines to Cumpsty Road between rehearsals. My first postcard home read: "Dear Mum and Dad. Arrived safe. Everything OK. Just going out to the Star-Club, love Sylvia." And after a few days there was more: "Dear Mum and Dad. I'm in East Berlin over the wall for a few hours, so keep this card if it reaches you, love Sylvia." The postcards became like little news bulletins, a vital connection home.

Every night had a different energy. Fifty Russian sailors might come pouring in at eight o'clock, and an hour later the crowd could be full of teenage hipsters and totally different. The place was always heaving and always crowded backstage with musicians. We weren't competitive with each other—if somebody broke a string there would always be someone to help out. The jealousy arrived later, with all the money and status that comes with fame and success.

As we grew more accomplished it was time to work on our image. The Liverbirds were classified as one of the lads, which worked in our favor in that we were accepted by the male musicians, but Manfred thought we could be a little more stylish. We had been through various looks—from the horrible red corduroy trousers, the ski outfits, the black chiffon dresses that Pam hated, to blue lurex skirts and denim shirts with "Liverbirds" motifs sewn on the collar. When we first came to Hamburg our zippered travel cases had room for only a few clothes, and our onstage makeup was restricted to a bit of mascara and faint lipstick. The minute we were paid by the Star-Club we went to the Western Store on the Reeperbahn to buy smart black bell-bottom trousers. We wanted to have our own distinctive look, so Manfred got in touch with Astrid Kirchherr, the Beatles photographer we had once seen in the Aaland Hotel back in London, when we were waiting to come to Hamburg. He asked her: "Can you work with these girls? They need some advice; they need to change their image."

We were so excited to work with Astrid. The first time we went to her apartment at 45a Eimsbütteler Strasse it was like entering a special, sparkling world. There were ornate candlestick holders and silver foil smoothed onto the walls like pretty, shiny wallpaper. No one had apartments like that. Her mother lived downstairs while she and her boyfriend, the cool Liverpool musician Gibson Kemp, had the upper floor and an attic with a sloping roof. She had converted the attic into her studio.

"Would you like a drink?" she said.

"Yes."

She brought out a bottle of pink champagne.

"Would you like pink?"

"Yes…er, what's that?"

We didn't even drink white champagne!

Manfred had flown in the famous German photographer and promoter Hansi Hoffman to take shots, and Astrid picked out our clothes, giving us frilly white shirts and Beatles-style jackets with Nehru collars. She dyed a small section of my hair blond so it stood out in a patch at the front, two-tone style. Pam took one look at me and said, "You look like a bird shat on your head."

But aside from that, we liked the pictures from that session so much that afterward Astrid became our regular stylist. She was very gorgeous and sophisticated. Her father was a salesman for the German arm of Ford Motor Company, and her mother, Nielsa, was an heiress from the family jukebox-manufacturing firm. In the mid-1950s Astrid enrolled in Hamburg's Meisterschule to study fashion design, but soon switched courses to photography. A student of Reinhart Wolf, the groundbreaking German photographer who built his own studio in Kleine Kielort, she evolved her own style, experimenting with light and shade. Working with a Rolleicord camera she would use exposure to create atmospheric portraits. Astrid took hundreds of band photos, but she told us her favorite was of a Liverpool street boy smoking a cigarette. She had been in the city one day, scouting locations for the Beatles, when she saw kids playing on a bombsite and asked them: "Can I take a photo?"

"Give us a ciggie, miss," said the boy. He was about nine years old.

Another photo she loved was of three kids in the road with a large tire, their sparky energy contrasting with the drab, gray streets.

Astrid and her art-school friends were part of the European existentialist movement, what we used to call "Exies." Val and I had dressed up as Exies in black tights and beads for that youth-club party, but Astrid was the real thing. She said later that she was inspired by French artists and writers like Jean-Paul Sartre, because England and America seemed so far away and France was the neighboring country. "We got all our information from France and tried to dress like the French existentialists. We wanted to be free... to be different... to be cool," she told Spencer Leigh for BBC Radio Merseyside's *On the Beat* program in 1995.

One night in 1960 she went with photographer Jürgen Vollmer and musician Klaus Voorman, her boyfriend at the time, to see the Beatles at the Kaiserkeller. Blown away by the band's rock 'n' roll harmonies, they returned every night, sitting at a table near the stage. She fell in love with their bassist, Stu Sutcliffe, and became very close to the band. Though credited with inventing the Beatles "moptop" haircut, Astrid said later that lots of German art-school boys had that haircut and Stu asked her to style his hair in a similar way. He used to borrow her clothes, her leather pants or collarless jackets or oversize shirts, and that look became part of the Beatles style. Although they got engaged, Stu tragically died of a brain hemorrhage in 1962. When we met her she was still friends with the Beatles and still working as a freelance photographer.

As we got to know Astrid we spent more time in that attic room with the sloping roof. She was fascinated by the spirit world and would do psychic seances and sessions with a Ouija board, trying to communicate with the dead. Even though she later married Gibson she never forgot Stu. One night John Lennon came to visit her and she used a teddy bear that Stu had given her to spell out words on the Ouija board. When the teddy moved of its own accord Lennon leapt up in terror, shouting, "That's it! I'm never touching a Ouija board again!"

Gibson was a lucky guy. In Liverpool we remembered him as a pimply young drummer playing with Kingsize Taylor at the Iron Door Club. His mother was a pianist who led a band in the war called Betty Daily's Rhythm Boys, and she frequently played Litherland town hall. She also played piano at my brother Chris's wedding. By the time Gibson got to Hamburg at the age of seventeen the pimples had disappeared and he was very good-looking. He had something about him. We were a bit frightened to talk to Gibson because he could be a little standoffish and belonged to Astrid and Klaus Voorman's clique—the three of them were always together. After a few months, however, we bonded, and I would get up and jam with Gibson at the end of a night in the Star-Club. He was such an expert at drumming, and we had a connection as drummers. They had a particular booth near the stage and when we weren't working we sometimes all sat together. We all liked each other. It felt as though we were part of a team.

~

Even though Mary and I vowed to remain virgins until we got married, we soon changed our minds, and I was the first to fall. In December 1964 I went to bed with my first love, Klaus Voorman. I'd point him out to the girls, a great-looking fella with black hair, and say, "He's gorgeous, look at him, he's lovely." After weeks of flirting he asked me out for a drink and we went to a local bar, talking nonstop about bands and music. As he escorted me back to the Hotel Pacific I felt a little in awe, thinking, *What's it going to be like?* I'd never been with a fella, but he was too gorgeous to pass up. *God, he wants to have sex with me!* I thought. *He's the one.*

But going to bed with him was an anticlimax. Everybody says the first time just hurts, and it did. I thought, *Oh, is that what it was all about?* Then Mary opened the door to see my knickers on the floor and Klaus's head peeping over the covers.

"Oh, Sylvia, you haven't! You promised you wouldn't! You've let me down."

I had broken our pact. But after that first night there was no follow-up date and I was upset that nothing more happened. I thought, *Was that it?* and just got back into playing the music. I'm sure Klaus was never in love with me. I thought he was handsome and I was flattered he wanted me. Perhaps it was unfair to think this, but for a long time I worried that he just had a bet with the lads—that someone said, "I bet you can't get off with one of the Liverbirds because they are all virgins."

A couple of years later, in 1966, a mutual friend told me that Klaus had offers to work as a musician with the Hollies, the Moody Blues, and Manfred Mann, but needed a work permit to play in Britain. "What if you married Klaus?" the friend suggested, only half-joking. "You don't have to live together, just get married on paper." I told him to get lost. Klaus gave me one and then buggered off, so why should I do him a favor?

Klaus joined Manfred Mann for a while, and he designed the album cover for the Beatles' *Revolver*, illustrating it in the style of Victorian artist Aubrey Beardsley. He ended up marrying Christine Hargreaves, a Manchester actress who was friends with Shelagh Delaney. We used to see her every week on the TV soap opera *Coronation Street*, playing a young independent woman called Christine Hardman. I was very glad Klaus married her and not me...I found out many years later that he liked me and had fond memories of our fling, which was nice, but I was meant for someone else entirely.

11. MARY

I Pick My Nose in Spanish Harlem

When Gibson first took Astrid home to Liverpool to meet the parents his mum said, "What are you doin'? She's German! Don't you remember the war, don't you remember your grandad putting out incendiary bombs with his hat?" In the early 1960s the memory of the Second World War was still raw for many people, particularly of our parents' generation, and German friends were treated with suspicion. The Rattles' drummer Dicky Tarrach remembers how people would stare at him.

"What are you looking at?"

"I just wanted to see what a Nazi looks like."

Another time the band came out of a gig to find the words "NAZIS GO HOME" daubed on the windows of their van.

But we were a younger generation, breaking down barriers, trying to dissolve the resentment and divisions that were a hangover from the war. Every night in the Star-Club 2,000 German fans and British musicians onstage built a bridge without anyone realizing what was going on. In that sense, our music was part of healing rifts that went deep into society.

Liverpool and Hamburg were two cities badly bombed during the war. Rosi Heitmann, one of the key barmaids at the Star-Club, had strong memories as a toddler of a terrible bomb firestorm that obliterated large parts of Hamburg, particularly areas where wooden houses were built close together. "We all cowered in the bunker and when we came out our whole house was gone," recalls Rosi. They went to live with her mother's family in the country and returned in 1947 but by then her mother had died of tuberculosis. When the family came back to Hamburg her father brought up Rosi and her sisters alone. He had a day job working in the shipyard, and when he came home at five o'clock she had potatoes bubbling in a saucepan on the hob, so he could eat something before working the night shift as a waiter in a bierkeller in the Reeperbahn, in a pub featuring Bavarian folk musicians. Everyone was poor. Waiters had to wear a black suit with a white shirt, so Rosi would iron the parts that were visible, just the collars and cuffs. He also had to wear black shoes, but as there were no black shoes to be had anywhere he slipped black socks on top of his shoes instead.

At sixteen years old Rosi was a jive boogie-woogie dancer, working as a waitress in the bierkeller. Musicians would come in to play blues or boogie piano in the bar, ragtime songs like "When the Saints Go Marching In." She learned that musicians are the same everywhere, no matter what they play. Whether it was the Beatles or a Bavarian folk group, she says that musicians always loved to drink. Rosi worked all night and was getting ready to close up at 7:30 a.m. one morning when a wild man in lederhosen staggered into the bar.

"What's the matter?"

"Rosi, give me one beer! I just need a beer!"

She also knew a very large man in a Bavarian band who played clarinet, who was a "quiet" drunk. One night he took a stick and walked around the bar silently conducting to some imaginary music. "He didn't say a fucking word! I liked that man," she fondly recalls.

By the age of nineteen she was working at the Kaiserkeller, a music club on the Grosse Freiheit, and she used to sing along with the juke-box to her favorite artists, such as gospel star Mahalia Jackson. In 1960 a young rock-and-roller from Norfolk called Tony Sheridan appeared there, singing and playing guitar, and Rosi was smitten. Within a month of his arrival the place was crowded and people were queuing down the street to hear him play. A young group called the Beatles also showed up, and the manager said to her, "Rosi, there's a new band, you serve them." They performed at a nearby strip club called the Indra, playing half-hour sets in between the striptease acts. The Beatles would chat with Sheridan during their breaks, admiring his style and musicianship, and he loved them too. He and Rosi got together and he became so possessive that he wouldn't let anyone near her. One night a man was talking to her during a gig so he jumped offstage and broke his guitar over the man's head.

At that time the red-light district, St. Pauli, was rough and edgy, with strip clubs, brothels, and the first Chinatown area in Germany. Rosi can remember when the Chinese laundries there also sold opium. The war had destroyed the city's drainage system, so rebuilding and reconstruction went on for years. Some areas of Hamburg stank and musicians even talked about stepping over dead bodies on the way to work. There were well-known local characters such as Pico, who was born in St. Pauli before the end of the war, a little child running around ruined buildings. He survived and became good friends with all the English bands, charming everybody. Musicians lived alongside pimps and petty criminals, and a drug trade started at the same time as rock-and-roll music, thriving in bomb-damaged areas. Along the Grosse Freiheit, for instance, there were Chinese people working in a laundry and selling opium at the back. Rosi remembers sharing a flat there with Sheridan. They had a baby together, but had to be careful because even though she was twenty-one, being unmarried meant the social services could take her child.

That first night when they swung the lights, we saw the Star-Club barmaids as all-powerful, like goddesses. But getting to know women like Rosi gave us a glimpse into their lives and their struggles. They were trying to make a living, just like anyone else.

We were friendly with some of the English rock-and-rollers like north Londoner Johnny Kidd, who sang "Shakin' All Over," and Vince Taylor, who wrote the rockabilly song "Brand New Cadillac," later covered by the Clash. He took too much amphetamine, which led to a mental breakdown and delusions that he was Jesus. Then in the 1970s he became the inspiration for David Bowie's Ziggy Stardust persona. We also liked Kingsize Taylor and the Dominoes, who were fronted by Ted "Kingsize" Taylor, a tall, magnetic singer/guitarist who wore vivid jackets and had a deep feel for rock 'n' roll. He and second vocalist Bobby Thompson would sing "Mashed Potatoes and Hot Pastrami" as a frenzied call and response.

Gibson Kemp joined Kingsize Taylor and the Dominoes in Hamburg as a drummer when he was seventeen, and they had a neat arrangement when the police came in at ten o'clock to check ID cards. There was a false back to the stage and behind it a ladder going up to the ceiling. If Kingsize was playing a fast song like "Johnny Be Goode" as the police walked in, they would abruptly tune into a ballad so there was no need for drums, allowing time for Gibson to disappear up the ladder and hide until the police left. Then he would return to the stage, and do another set with them at four in the morning. It was never the same musicians each week. Manfred was inundated with

American agents, so he would mix guest headliners like Little Richard and Jerry Lee Lewis with a regular supply of British beat bands. The Ray Charles Orchestra was the most he paid for anyone.

Manfred also knew how to protect himself, a stark reality that Gibson noted one morning on Grosse Freiheit. Unlike many musicians, Gibson didn't start drinking until he was twenty-one, and he was an early riser. Every now and then he would see Manfred in the coffee shop going for breakfast, and the club owner would have boiled egg, toast, and tea. He'd sit and talk in a broken English that was very exact, and he always had a bag full of money on the chair beside him. The banks opened at nine thirty and Manfred timed his breakfast perfectly so he could eat and then deposit the money. One morning he unzipped the bag to pay the waitress, took out a gun and put it on the table. In the coffee shop. "They knew him, they didn't mind, but I was shocked," recalls Gibson. "Then Manfred got his ten marks out. Manfred would pay for everything. I was the only one who ever paid him back, which he never forgot. There weren't many musicians who got up at nine o'clock in the morning."

Manfred was always being threatened with closure. The chief of police was a man called Mr. Falk whose main aim in life was to get the Star-Club shut down, making a habit of coming into the venue at 10 p.m. to check all the young people had gone. One night he reckoned that too many had been admitted so they closed the club for a few days. We all demonstrated outside, creating headline news as far away as England. There was even a photograph of Sylvia in a German newspaper under the heading, "This Is What Pills Do to You!" Mr. Falk would tip off journalists, trying to imply that the Star-Club was an underage drug haven. He tried for years to get Manfred out, but in the end he had to give up.

As the weeks went on, we got to know Manfred better. Everybody loved him but you didn't mess with him. He wasn't a gangster, but he had power in the gangster fraternity and he knew all the villains. Over six feet tall, he was a big man in deed and word as well as size, and people listened when he spoke. He was a goodie because he also took care of us and was like a father figure—people found that hard to believe, but he knew how to keep us happy. Even though we settled in well, sometimes we needed to go back home to Liverpool to visit family. I would cry and get homesick because I'd never been so far from my family before.

I'd go into Manfred's office and say, "I'm missing Mam, my dad, and the kids."

"You girls, you drive me crazy. Mr. Anderson, four plane tickets for the girls, they're homesick again."

~

That first year we went back home three times, and would stay for a week or so to catch up with family or to go to someone's party or a wedding. The whole family was so proud of me being in the papers and on TV, saying, "That's our Mary, she's going to be famous and rich." When I started earning money I liked to buy clothes for myself—no more secondhand cast-offs and sensible shoes. I also enjoyed buying clothes for my sisters, and whenever I came back from Hamburg I always bought presents. German children dressed well, with high-quality clothes. One of the Rattles' wives had a seven-year-old girl, so she would give me really good stuff to take home to Christine and Sharon. It gave me a thrill to be able to support my family.

When I left for Hamburg my twelve-year-old sister Margarita had to take over, looking after the kids when she came home from school so my mum could do cooking or washing. When she started working a few years later, half her wages went to Mum and the rest was pocket money for the smaller children. She had a heart of gold. Margarita was very shy, in contrast to Colette, who seemed tough, but both of them could have done with more attention. Later, when people looked at family photos from the time they would point to Margarita and Colette and say, "You can tell they're the sandwich children"—the ones who were overlooked.

There were some key differences between the British and German bands. Dicky from the Rattles, for instance, remembers the Beatles' witty nonchalance onstage. "They had a cool patter between songs. German groups would announce each song very seriously, whereas John Lennon would tell jokes." There was a lot of pressure for young German people to get responsible jobs, and playing rock music was seen as a hobby rather than a career. The Rattles' sound was supercharged rock 'n' roll, Chuck Berry with the right lyrics. They also had the right image, looking raunchy in leather. This was new for Germany, where so many bands wore formal jackets and narrow ties. As Sylvia says, "A lot of German bands, like the Lords, looked good but had no oomph. The Rattles did."

At school Dicky was the best in English because he liked American rock 'n' roll—to him the language and the songs sounded exotic and so exciting. Despite his passion for music he started working as a civil servant when he left school because his dad said, "If you do this, when you are fifty-five you'll be in a good position." Playing in small bands as an amateur drummer, Dicky soon realized that the civil service wasn't for him. By the time Dicky was eighteen Dicky's father had passed away and he had to tell his mother that he wanted to be a pro musician, not a civil servant like his dad.

"Reinhard, you'll give up your nice pension," she said.

For German musicians under twenty-one, their parents had to sign a business contract for them to work the clubs, and Dicky's dad would never have allowed it. Once his mother signed a contract with

Manfred, the fun started. Dicky's first wage at the Star-Club was just twenty marks (two pounds) a week, sometimes only ten ("You come in tomorrow and I'll give you ten more," Manfred would say). Things improved and soon he was earning a decent living, playing Cliff Richard songs in a cover band before joining the Rattles.

Most of us played cover versions of pop hits. To get the lyrics we'd play a record and write down the words, stopping and going back until we had them exact. English musicians would write out song lyrics for the German bands, and for fun they would jot down utter rubbish. So instead of "I picked a rose in Spanish Harlem" it would be "I pick my nose in Spanish Harlem." And when they did a version of the Sonics' "Walkin' the Dog" instead of "Baby's back, all dressed in black" it was "Paper bag, dressed in black."

It was a challenge learning so many songs so quickly, but we loved it and we enjoyed mucking in with the bands. However, we did draw the line when it came to getting changed. Backstage there was just one room, so we usually changed in club toilets because the ones in the dressing room weren't very nice for ladies. That was often the case, wherever we played—no separate space for women. The Star-Club dressing room was small and stinky, so they made another one for big fancy American artists like Chuck Berry, but after a month it looked and smelled just like the other one.

By the spring of 1965 we were thoroughly settled in Hamburg and had regular haunts, like the Monckebergstrasse, a big shopping street that had more clothing stores than Liverpool. As well as the Seaman's Mission, where you could get egg and chips, there was a pub two doors down from the Star-Club that British musicians nicknamed the Beer Shop. That's when we first had a drink, and where the bands would congregate in a special corner or play raucous games of table football, with the English groups pitted against the Germans. Even the Beatles went to the Beer Shop. There's the story that later, when Paul McCartney was in Wings, he went back into the Beer Shop and said, "I owe you twenty marks."

One of the favorites was Granny's café, which Lee Curtis from the All-Stars discovered by accident one night when he was walking down Grosse Freiheit during a break. He saw a flight of steps leading up to a cozy café with four tables and an old lady behind the counter busy making sandwiches. A TV in the corner blared out *Coronation Street*, with gossipy lead character Ena Sharples dubbed into German. *Bloody hell*, he thought.

"Young man, what do you want?" said the old lady.

Lee ordered a delicious pork chop with egg and chips and as soon as he'd finished his meal, he went back to the Star-Club and said to the lads, "Hey, fellas, I've found a great place to eat." Once the All-Stars began eating there, word spread. Their guitarist, Paul Pilnick, christened her Granny, and the café soon became as popular as the Star-Club and the pub. Granny made beautiful sausages, and we liked her so much we brought her back to Liverpool with us for a holiday, because she had never been to England. She'd never flown before and she didn't speak any English, and we planted her in Sylvia's house with her mother. There they gabbed away, even though one didn't understand a word the other said. Granny loved it.

That first year we rehearsed more frequently, slowly improving as a band. We became louder onstage and more confident as players. There was more rhythm to my bass-playing, so I was in synch with Val and Pam, risking a few adventurous notes and getting into a groove. Pam became skilled as a singer, projecting a sensuous stage presence, while Val, who was initially wary of her own voice, sang out and tackled the vocal harmonies with the same strength and imagination as her guitar riffs.

As a girl band we didn't have much competition apart from a four-piece from New York City called Goldie and the Gingerbreads. Featuring lead singer Goldie (aka Genya Ravan), guitarist Carol MacDonald, drummer Ginger Bianco, and a fantastic Hammond organ player called Margo Lewis, the band was well connected. They played a party for Warhol superstar fashion icon Baby Jane Holzer and were invited by the Animals and Rolling Stones to tour the UK. While they were waiting for British work permits to come through, they stopped off for a month at the Star-Club. Like us, the band was sometimes not taken seriously and treated like a novelty act. Carol MacDonald said later to Emily Agustin from Chicago's Chirp Radio blog: "We didn't care. We were happy because we were knocking the socks off most of the male bands. And the guys couldn't believe it. They'd start off laughing, and then they'd walk out crying."

The band was very slick, with crisp, soulful harmonies, and we admired the way Goldie casually threw her tambourine from hand to hand. She used to leave it on the organ; the weight of it was unbelievable. Even though Goldie and the Gingerbreads was a girl band, we didn't see them as rivals because their music was so different from ours. They had a bombastic power pop sound that wasn't very rock 'n' roll, and although they were a vibrant group, the Star-Club crowd didn't take to them as much. We became friends and Goldie had a relationship with our road manager, who was younger than her. The band had a song called "Little Boy," which Goldie would sing for him, introducing it by saying, "I'm doing this for my fancy boy."

After a four-week residency the girls headed for London, where they found a pop manager and became close friends with Dusty Springfield and Madeline Bell. They did better there. I think our German fans considered them rivals. The fans used to call us the

Little Beatles or the Female Beatles, which would irritate Pam. We had more freedom in Germany than if we had stayed in England, where girls had to fit into the music-business mold and be marketed in pretty dresses. In Germany we didn't feel discriminated against because we were female—if anything, they wanted to book us more. In the sixties it was rare to have four girl musicians together. You might get lineups like the Honeycombs where one woman played with three guys, but when we were touring, we never met another all-girl rock-and-roll band at all.

As Lee Curtis says, "Goldie and the Gingerbreads were amazing, but they didn't affect the audience in the same way as the Liverbirds. You were younger and had your own style. People came to see you."

We played the music that people wanted to hear. Even though the Beatles became huge worldwide, many in the Star-Club crowd preferred bands like the Big Three or Johnny Kidd and the Pirates. Our friend Tony Coates says: "They would listen to the Beach Boys and the Four Seasons, but if you played full-out rock 'n' roll the Hamburg crowd would go berserk. That's why the Liverbirds did so well. You just played rock 'n' roll and the Germans loved you for it."

12. SYLVIA

Miss Karin Wants You Tonight

When we first arrived in Hamburg and were driven by taxi down the Reeperbahn, we saw lights flashing everywhere. *What's this*, we thought, *it's like a circus!* The strip clubs and brothels were crammed into just a few streets and seemed like a very adult world. We'd seen lights in Blackpool, but not like this. Overnight it changed our attitude; we were young and adventurous and it was exciting. It could have been scary but with all the musicians roomed together on the top floor of the Hotel Pacific we felt safe, like one big family. We quickly realized that we were in the right hands.

At the back of the Star-Club was a yard with places where you could get yourself a man or a woman or both, whatever you wanted. Our parents didn't know the full extent of it. When they visited us a few years later we walked down the Herbertstrasse, one of the most famous streets in St. Pauli, where the sex workers sat in the windows. My dad kept looking at them, his eyes wide. He had been a sailor, so he should have known. "Chris, stop looking!" my mum hissed. Then she turned to me. "If I'd have known you were coming to a place like this you would never have gone."

Mary's dad tried to act as if he had seen it all. Along the Reeperbahn a doorman outside a strip club grabbed her mother by the arm.

"Come inside. Live intercourse onstage!"

"Oh God bless, no!"

We both blackmailed our mothers, the bosses in our families, before we first went to Germany. I would say, "Mary's mum is letting her go to Hamburg, you've got to let me go," and vice versa, until they gave us permission.

Not even in Soho, the red-light district of London, was there anything like this. In the Star-Club the stage manager Hilda, a butch lesbian with thick trousers and men's shoes, looked after the bands. She did a remarkable job, organizing the schedule and making sure each group was in the right spot at the right time, managing bands from six o'clock at night to six in the morning.

We hung out with the barmaids and learned about their money-making tricks—how they would doctor the shots, for instance. In a one-liter bottle of spirits there were fifty shots, each costing two marks, so one bottle was worth a hundred, and fifty bottles were worth five thousand. We had one type of gin and one type of vodka. Management knew how much money should go over the counter for each bottle, but the barmaids would put chewing gum at the bottom of a measure, with a coin on top, so punters didn't get the full amount. Doing this they could squeeze out more measures, even of schnapps, and pocket the extra money for themselves. With good tips, the barmaids could earn more than the musicians or the owner! They were the stars.

Sometimes barmaids would give musicians free beers and put it on a sailor's bill. Maybe a female fan couldn't afford a Coca-Cola, so the barmaid would say to a sailor, "You like the musician? You buy that girl a drink." Whalers would go to sea for three months and spend half their cash in the bar. Splashing it around freely added to the carnival atmosphere. The older barmaids also looked after the younger girls. They noticed if a man was buying drinks to get a girl drunk, so they would say, "Give me twenty marks and I'll order her a taxi home. She's too drunk to go on the underground train."

It was all interconnected, with a network of support. Many bands came over from Britain who weren't at the Star-Club, instead playing dingy places where they never got paid, so the sex workers would look after them, buying drinks and meals. They also befriended us because Manfred was our manager, and we were young girls they wanted to mother, in the same way they looked after the musicians playing in grotty clubs for nothing.

Though it was a precarious life for sex workers in Hamburg, they seemed happy and were, to a certain extent, looked after by the government. In 1963 prostitution was legalized in Germany: sex workers had regular health checks and if they had any STDs they weren't allowed to work. The top-class girls had rooms and a lot of control, though there were plenty of girls on street corners too and I don't know how well they were treated. The sex workers I befriended were great. I got to know them because I was curious. In an earlier life I think I'd have been the madam of a brothel, like in the Wild West, organizing all the girls.

I became friends with one in particular, called Karin, who was stunning, with beautiful red hair. She looked like Ursula Andress, who in the James Bond film *Dr. No* emerges statuesque from the sea in her famous wet bikini. As a person Karin was very bubbly, though she wasn't friendly with everybody. She liked the scene at the Star-Club, walking in there with her bodyguard after she finished work. She'd be wearing a mink stole and have champagne on the table. After watching the groups for a while she would whisper something to her bodyguard, and he would go up to a musician, saying, "Miss Karin wants you tonight." I don't think anybody said no.

I used to go down with her to Herbertstrasse. Sex workers would sit on stools in the neon, red-lit windows all along the street, scantily dressed in bra and panties or tiny negligees, enticing clients and flirting with passersby. One night Karin said, "Come and sit in the window, Sylvia."

"I'm not doing that!"

"Oh yes, just for a laugh."

"I'm not getting undressed."

"Just go as you are."

"Oh, all right."

I had just come offstage and was wearing bell-bottom jeans and a top, nothing particularly sexy. I perched in the window and four lads came past.

"Hey, look at this one. She's got her clothes on!" they said, in strong Liverpool accents. "Hey, how much are you?"

"Too much for you, lad!"

"God, she's a Scouser as well."

I jumped away from the window, saying, "Karin, I'm not sitting there!"

I was often propositioned in Herbertstrasse, but I didn't take it seriously. And I was fascinated by how much freedom Karin had. She was the best sex worker in Hamburg, a dominatrix who earned more money than anyone else, the Queen of St. Pauli.

There was solidarity between the musicians, barmaids, sex workers, and female fans. A lot of drag queens, lesbians, and trans people would go to the clubs in St. Pauli because they felt accepted and protected. In the outside world many led unhappy, closeted lives—during the Second World War thousands of homosexuals were persecuted and interned in concentration camps, and male homosexuality in West Germany was criminalized until 1969. The sixties was heralded as a time of licentious freedom and exploration, but there was still a lot of ignorance about sex.

Rosi, the Star-Club barmaid, told us that when she and Tony Sheridan shared a flat with the Beatles, it was in a spirit of innocence. "We were sleeping in dirty bunk beds in a hole of Calcutta flat. We all slept in the one room—Pete Best on one bed, Cynthia and John Lennon in the bunk under George, and me and Tony in another bed." When we were young many thought you could get pregnant from a kiss and that if boys masturbated they would go mad. Girls wouldn't even think about it. "Girls now discover themselves at the age of thirteen or fourteen, but for us it was absolutely taboo," says Rosi. "We didn't know about sex in the beginning, but that changed very quickly." Another gorgeous barmaid, called Ruth, the daughter of a Protestant minister, rebelled against her religious upbringing. Her father had no idea that she worked in the red-light district. "I would go out to work in modest clothes," she recalls, "then glam up for the Star-Club, and take off my lipstick and change my clothes before going home!"

We grew from being foreigners in this circus to feeling very much at home. Many musicians never went further than St. Pauli, and that, along with the Hotel Pacific, became our world. We would go from the hotel to the club to Granny's or the Beer Shop, and hang out the whole night, either playing or drinking until we could do it no more and then we'd stagger back to the hotel and sleep.

This environment was not always glamorous. Many musicians came from working-class Liverpool and remembered the gangs, but in Hamburg the *zuhälter*, or pimps, were even more aggressive. We knew that if we didn't interfere they never did us any harm; Star-Club musicians were protected because Manfred had his eye on everybody. The doormen for the Freiheit clubs could also be hard sometimes, but when they got to know you they were friendly. "Hi, d'you want to see a show? Just come in and I'll give you a beer," they would say.

They knew that musicians brought in the punters, so we were accepted by the staff, the waiters, and anybody who was in the business, because we were the lifeblood. Manfred booked the biggest and the best rock-and-rollers, and even though artists came in with hit records, the real focus was on the live performance. He made sure the venue was a fun place to work. One Christmas, for instance, the Star-Club did a special show. They bought twenty giant Christmas trees and the Hi-Fis sang German hymns with Beach-Boys-style harmonies while all the Christmas crowd joined in.

We knew to never get involved in the *zuhälters'* affairs or mess with the doormen. I remember sitting with friends at a long table in a pub near the Reeperbahn, laughing, joking, and drinking beers, when two drunken men leered up, wanting to dance with us. They were refusing to take "No" for an answer. A sex-worker friend fetched the doorman, who came striding into the bar, his face set. "What's going on?" With a swift movement he punched one man into the jukebox, then grabbed the other one and smacked him to the floor. We sat there in shock. The drunken men didn't get up again, and we paid and left the bar, surprised but grateful. It was helpful sometimes to have the protection of the right people.

Another night I went for a drink with Lee Curtis, Pam, and a few friends, and I noticed German sailors making fun of someone, pouring beer over him. I thought, *How can I sit and watch that?*

"Stop doing that, it's not right!" I said, and got punched in the face. Lee quickly picked me up.

"Come on, Syl, are you all right?"

"Yes," I said, bleary and unsteady. It's true what they say about seeing stars, I actually saw stars circling in front of my eyes. My friends wanted to call the police, but in the end the bouncers threw out the offending sailors. People say you should never hit a woman, but clearly some men weren't bothered by that.

One of the musicians who looked after me was Roy Dyke from the Remo Four, the best drummer on the Hamburg scene. People would come from all over Germany to see his drum solos. He became a member of Ashton, Gardner and Dyke, the seventies trio who had a huge hit in 1971 with "Resurrection Shuffle." In 1964, though, he had just arrived with the Remo Four for a month's residency at the Star-Club. We remembered them from auditions at the Rialto in Liverpool with Henry Henroid. "Before I left Liverpool I heard you were doing well in Germany as a girl band. I had the impression you knew everything," Roy recalls. "You spoke great German, you knew where everything was: if you want something to eat you go to Granny's; if you want a beer, go to the Beer Shop."

I loved Roy. I went up to him after a show and said, "You're a really good drummer, can you give me some lessons?" We would sit and play together, and after a while we played a little bit more than the drums. It was fun and romantic. We were enjoying ourselves doing exactly what we wanted: playing music, working, meeting different artists from all over the world. As Roy says: "We were doing more than you could ever wish for if you stayed in Liverpool. We were mixing with bands from all over the UK. Some just came for a short stay, some you'd forget. There was a rapid turnover. We were playing every day so our chops were good. It was exactly our time."

13. MARY

Please God, Forgive Pam

It was never Our Father, always Hail Mary. The Virgin was like a role model to me, and sometimes I felt a connection with being in an all-girl band. I don't quite know why, maybe it was about being in a single-sex group, dedicating myself to music.

I also loved to watch films about nuns in convents, the special atmosphere that was created when praying and singing together—it sounded so pure. In 1965, when I came back to Liverpool for a visit, I took my grandma to the Odeon cinema to see *The Sound of Music*. Grandma was over eighty at the time, and during the scene where Mother Abbess sings "Climb Every Mountain" we were both crying our eyes out. I thought it would be a noble thing to wander around the Alps, devoting myself to God.

I was lying in bed one morning at the Hotel Pacific when Anka, the receptionist, rang my room.

"Mary, there's a man here to see you."

There had been a wild party the night before, and the whole floor was heaving with musicians from the Star-Club.

"OK, Anka, send him up."

"Maybe, but I don't think that's a good idea."

"Why not?"

"He's a priest."

I came bounding down to reception to find Father Bradley, my priest from Liverpool, all dressed in his formal suit and dog collar. He'd come to pay a visit, to see how I was getting on, so we went for breakfast in the restaurant downstairs and I told him all about my life with the Liverbirds. He said he was only in Hamburg for a few hours and he'd love to see the Star-Club. We were practicing that afternoon so he came to see us practice and went home quite happy. Father Bradley must have seen all the strip clubs but he didn't say anything—he was very broad-minded and he could see that we were safe—though he did say, "Mary, I don't think you want to be a nun anymore." He then went back to Liverpool and told my mum that I was OK. "She's in good hands and there's a church next door. It's a beautiful church, Maggie!"

Built in the early eighteenth century, St. Joseph's was a solemn, sacred baroque building right in the heart of Grosse Freiheit and historically it was always surrounded by drinking places and brothels. The church was in a special zone of free trade and freedom of religion in the old city of Altona, and the oldest Catholic community in northern Germany. In 1823 it was very nearly dismantled and built somewhere else when the church council complained that it was sited "in the most ill-reputed quarter of the city…a place for pleasure-seeking public," where policemen would keep order with loaded pistols. But in the end the church stayed put, probably because it offered refuge and a chance for sexual sinners to repent.

For me it was a peaceful place amid the noise and chaos of St. Pauli. During Mass every Sunday, I would look up at its vaulted ceiling and pray for the band or my family back home. The Mass was in Latin, so I could follow it, and if the service was at ten o'clock in the morning sometimes I didn't sleep and went straight to the church, enjoying the beautiful surroundings and the ethereal choir. I didn't see any contradiction with being in the Liverbirds and having a vocation to be a nun. I would kneel by my bedside every night, wearing, pinned to my vest, religious medals that Grandma had sent. Val used to laugh at me. "Look at Mary with her medals. Let's say a few Hail Marys!"

I had a rosary with five decades, ten beads on each row, so that was fifty Hail Marys. Reciting those with the rosary would take me half an hour each night, along with prayers like, "Please God, forgive Pam. She's OK really, even though she sleeps with men."

There were always a clique of girls standing in a corner of the Star-Club by the stage, the same ones who every month would make a selection on band changeover night—"I'll take the drummer! The guitarist looks good." They would pair up with their chosen musician for the month and the night before he left would cry in the Beer Shop, "Oh, Mary, Sylvia, he's going home. He was the love of my life, what am I going to do without him?"

"He'll probably write to you, don't worry."

Then a new band would arrive and they'd hook up with a new musician and fall in love all over again. We were like their big sisters. A few German girls had babies with musicians who were friends of ours, and the musicians didn't even know. Roadies would call the groupies horrible names, labeling them "the slit corner," but they were proper music fans. Some sex workers were fans too, working the rooms in St. Pauli during the day, and coming to the Star-Club at night to relax and hang out with musicians. As I got to know them I began to understand their lifestyle, and see them as people rather than just being sinners or fallen women.

Being in a band granted us power because we were considered part of the gang as musicians, but after a while we began to find romance and do more of our own thing. Pam was the most adventurous, but she was a risk-taker and that's why I prayed for her. The first time I realized she slept with men was when we were in London and she brought a man called Ray (not Ray Davies) back to the Aaland Hotel.

"He's great," she said, "but he smokes a lot of weed."

We didn't know what she meant.

"When he smokes, he goes limp."

She told us once that she lost her virginity when she was twelve on a school camping trip. Everybody was sleeping in tents, and there was one fella whom everybody wanted. All the girls queued up outside the tent for him, and Pam was first in the queue. She needed to be able to say, "I've had him." She wanted to be the one in control.

The first time we played Hamburg, the All-Stars were performing. Pam said, "Oh my God, that horrible Lee Curtis is on tonight as well." One of our friends was mad about Lee and although he was tall and good-looking with a compelling rock-and-roll voice, Pam thought he was terrible. Lee had a bad reputation with women, but that didn't bother her as much as his Teddy-boy haircut and the way he sang, Elvis style. It was amazing to see how gradually, over two weeks, she stopped saying nasty things about him until one day she declared, "You know, I can't believe it but I think I fancy him!"

She completely fell for him. At twenty-six he was seven years older than her and already had four children. He was a Catholic, and he and his wife were at school together and very young when they married. He was attractive to many women, but Pam was his favorite. As time went on she lavished attention on him, styling his hair and making him wear shirts we had custom-made. Lee was born Peter Flannery, but chose his stage name by inverting the moniker of American doo-wop singer and soul balladeer Curtis Edwin Lee. With his resonant voice Lee could have been a big star, but never had the Top Ten hit he needed to break through. Pam, however, believed in Lee, seeing him as someone who was as musically ambitious as her.

Years later Lee had fond memories of Pam, saying: "She had more ideas than a prime minister, more style than a Rolls-Royce. She dressed like nobody else. She could educate you, in more ways than one. She had a mind of her own, a will of her own. She had style and brains, and her hair was always immaculate." However, he was reluctant to acknowledge their romance. "I was a married man with a couple of kids. I wanted to enjoy myself, I was a man with sexual desires like anybody else, but I wasn't jumping into any bed," he claimed. "I was trying to keep my nose clean and be selective."

The longer we stayed in Hamburg, the deeper Pam fell for Lee, though after a while she realized that he wouldn't leave his wife back home. In many ways it was up to her to make the changes and to leave him, but it would take years before she could accept that. We knew German men who used to come round trying to court her. She could have easily found somebody else and settled down.

But she managed to find a creative outlet for the pain that her relationship with Lee caused her. "Leave All Your Loves in the Past" was the first song that Pam wrote with us, and it summed up what we were all thinking. It emerged during rehearsals at the Star-Club. All the bands wanted to practice, so we had to put our name on a list to reserve a time slot. I remember the day we got there and started rehearsing, and Pam came in with three chords.

"I've just written a song," she said.

When we hear it now, we feel sad. With Val's beautiful chiming guitar, it sounds so mournful. The lyrics are about how Lee left her when she needed him, about the tears she cried and the pain she felt. Pam really loved Lee and it hurt her that he would always go back to his wife. There is sorrow when we think about the star she could have become.

We all sat together and each contributed to the arrangement. Nowadays we would have gotten a co-credit, but back then it was just Pam. It's not that she meant to harm us, that's the way everybody did it, and that's why so many sixties-era musicians spent subsequent decades chasing money for songs they had co-written. Just being in that environment inspired Pam to write, and although she had composed two songs with her sister Dyan before she joined the group, the four she wrote with us were in a different league.

Manfred made sure that our efforts ended up on vinyl. In December 1964, six months after we arrived in Germany, we went into a studio in Munich to record our debut album *Star-Club Show 4*— so-called because ours was the fourth album on Manfred's fledgling Star-Club label. He had struck a deal with Phillips Germany, to create something that captured the energy happening live onstage. Along with the Searchers, the Rattles, and Lee Curtis and the All-Stars, we were among their first single releases. They also licensed big American hits like Little Richard's "Whole Lotta Shakin' Goin' On" and James Brown's "Out of Sight." Right from the start the label made an impact.

Our debut single from the album was the Smokey Robinson/Berry Gordy song "Shop Around," which had been Motown's first million-selling single in 1961. Our version, backed by Pam's song "It's Got to Be You," didn't make the charts when it was released at the end of 1964 but we were still thrilled to have a record out. Manfred called us to the office and said, "Come and pick the single up, it's arrived today." We ran back to the hotel with it and played it on Val's record player, dancing around the room and screaming, "The Liverbirds have done a song!" It was something very special in those days to make a record. We used to go to a record shop next to the Star-Club and the girl who ran it would put our music on the loudspeaker. She was a Star-Club regular, working the record shop in the daytime and the club at night. We'd also go to a store in the Colonnaden, a shopping street in the Neustadt quarter, where they sold hi-fis and TVs and had booths in which you could listen to the latest singles, and they would put us on the loudspeaker there.

Our second single, Bo Diddley's chuntering, bluesy "Diddley Daddy," shot into the German Top Five the following April, and we were delighted when we had a hit. Once we were in the charts it meant we were touring more, and it made a big difference to our lives. Our booking fee doubled—on the first tour the band got a thousand marks a gig, but after our Top Five hit we received over two and a half thousand, and Manfred would get 10 percent.

Our first album was recorded quickly on a basic two-track tape over two full days and was produced by Hans Beierlein, a top impresario who'd brought artists like Petula Clark and Françoise Hardy to the German market. He was very easygoing, encouraging us to play as if we were doing a live show. We had our own stage set in the studio and were tight and rehearsed; we didn't waste a moment. Some tracks were challenging to record, like "Talking About You," which features a speedy bass part. Feeling the pressure to display virtuoso technique, that song always made me nervous.

However we all loved doing the Willie Dixon song "You Can't Judge a Book by the Cover," which was made famous by Bo Diddley with his howling rock-and-roll blues. Val sang it with a cool vocal delivery and Pam joined her on the chorus, their voices linked together in a sassy call and response. It was an unusual rhythm for Sylvia because she doesn't see herself as a technical drummer. "I more or less taught myself. I had drum lessons and hated doing rolls. I was frightened about getting those stops in the song right. Afterward I felt a real sense of achievement, thinking, *Great, smashing, I've done it!*" she recalls.

By then we had been playing live every night, with Sylvia at the back of the stage listening out so she could get the stops bang on. Being in the studio was a new experience because we could hear ourselves through the monitors and it gave us a fresh perspective on our music. We thought, *Wow, is this what we really sound like?* We cried when Hans played back the songs and we realized how far we'd come. We thought back to those early days in my front room in Liverpool, plodding through *Steptoe and Son.*

Another Bo Diddley song we loved was "Before You Accuse Me." When we were recording it Val's bluesy voice seemed to come up from the depths, flowing with her inventive guitar lines and the loaded beat Sylvia and I provided on bass and drums. I remember the Rolling Stones singing this song when we toured with them in 1963, and it was the same gig where Bill Wyman put the string on my bass—afterward, in the dressing room, he taught me to how to play the bass riff. "Before You Accuse Me" was one of the songs we rehearsed on the train coming to Hamburg.

It's hard to pick songs we didn't like, but we were less fond of "Love Hurts," which has a more laconic feel, sounding like the downtempo garage sound of New York band Velvet Underground and Nico. It was first recorded in 1960 by the Everly Brothers, and in the seventies Scottish hard rock band Nazareth made it a big hit. Our version needed more instrumentation, and Pam sang in a way that was strained and guarded, out of her comfort zone, trying to sound sweet.

"Talking About You" was another challenging song, led by syncopated bass and Val's rock-and-roll guitar break. It was a hard one for me to perform on bass and I used to put the girls through torture before I would play it. "Can we play it now?" they would say in rehearsals, after hours of procrastination. I had to psych myself up to get in the flow, and with hindsight, we would have miked up the instruments differently.

Working with a two-track tape could be so restrictive. Nowadays we would have gone for a second take, but back then we only had two days to record everything and Hans caught that raw, spontaneous Star-Club feel, which led to people in later years calling us a proto-punk band. The Bo Diddley song "Roadrunner," for instance, sounds like a trashy, punky party. People loved it and would shout along while Pam hollered the tune, Val played shredding guitar up and down the frets, and Sylvia hit the drums hard. The whole *Star-Club Show 4* album is a snapshot of our energy at the time. When we hear those songs we can still feel the connection, and what was special about the band. We still wish that Pam and Val were both here with us now.

I was determined to remain a virgin, still pursuing my vocation to be a nun. I used to perform with my holy medals pinned to my jacket and they'd be jingling onstage. I continued going to Mass every Sunday and saying my nightly prayers, but as the months went on my feelings began to change. I started focusing on boys and had a crush on Pat McCann, the pretty lead singer from eight-piece Irish showband the Crickets. Hailing from Dublin, the band was inspired by early rock-and-rollers like Buddy Holly and Bill Haley, and fifties soul group the Platters, singing songs like "Rave On" or "The Great Pretender." With a full brass section they really filled the stage and Pat, sporting a black quiff and bootlace tie, had a striking style. He could do any Elvis Presley song and sound like Elvis. They began performing at the Star-Club the same time as us, so we became friends, and even though Pat had a girlfriend at home in Ireland I hoped he would notice me. My love of Pat was unrequited, but Val started having a relationship with their guitarist, a short, sensitive guy called Shay McCarthy who was a master at playing John Lennon riffs.

I was pining after Pat one night when Pam pointed out to me a tall, dark-haired man in the crowd.

"He looks like Bob Dylan," she said.

His name was Frank Dostal and I noticed he came back again the next night, standing close to the stage while we played. At first I wasn't attracted to him because I was stuck on Pat from the Crickets, but then on December 15, the day before his birthday, we met and started talking and he asked me for a dance.

Frank was very easygoing and totally dedicated to music. He was nineteen and still at school when we met, but wanted to be a rock singer. He fronted an amateur band called the Faces (long before Rod Stewart's band) and one of the first things he said to me was, "I'm a singer. And I play maracas." Initially he had eyes for Val, but that first night we ended up finding a bar and talking until we kissed. We saw each other every day after that, and when we had been going out for six weeks we decided that my nineteenth birthday—February 2, 1965—was the best day to have sex for the first time. By then my thoughts of a chaste, religious life were receding, and it helped a lot that Sylvia lost her virginity first, so I didn't feel guilty. Having sex was a nice way to celebrate my birthday, and the experience was not a let-down. When I told Pam about it she said, "Did he wrap it up for you?" Pam used to wrap Lee's thing up in a bow.

After Frank and I had sex I was afraid of getting pregnant, so I went to the doctor and he offered me the pill. The contraceptive pill had just arrived on the market and I was wary about taking it because there were rumors it would make you infertile. The doctor's only question was, "How old are you?" I used precautions but didn't take the pill until 1974, after my son Benny was born and I knew I didn't want any more children. Even though a lot of us at the time were experimenting with sexual freedom I was very worried about my mother finding out that I slept with Frank. She was a religious woman and I thought she would react negatively. She became pregnant when she was eighteen, and I was nineteen when I started having sex.

I still wanted to be a nun until I met Frank. It seemed to just wear off the longer I was with him, and the more I got to know the groupies and the sex workers in the Reeperbahn, I realized it doesn't make someone a bad person if they have sex before marriage. I stopped going to Mass about a year after I met Frank, finally admitting to myself that I wasn't cut out to be a nun. I also realized there was no proof that God exists. According to the Catholic Church the Pope couldn't make mistakes, but I thought that was ridiculous, he's only a human being. In his gentle way Frank didn't try to influence me, but always stressed the importance of believing in evidence not faith. Looking back, I can see that my vocation was good for a while, helping me through a traumatic time when Dad had just come out of prison.

As for Frank, he was so swept up by the scene at the Star-Club he left school before taking his *abitur* (the final high-school exams) so he could focus on being a musician. We went to see his band, the Faces, a few times and liked them. They were very soulful, covering poignant songs like Arthur Alexander's "You Better Move On." The Star-Club had an annual beat competition and the Faces won it in 1965, the year we met. Frank was a very cool performer, with fluid moves and his own style—he was one of the first musicians in Hamburg to have bushy sideburns.

One person who was very disappointed when I got together with Frank was the singer Paul Raven. Fronting a group called the Boston International Showband, he had been hanging around the music scene for a while, and although he was in his twenties he'd already been through several record deals and seemed much older. We'd say, "Look at that old man onstage." He was an odd person. He used to wear a lot of makeup, and a curly wig because he was balding. After gigs he wouldn't join in the banter or socialize, he just disappeared offstage and you never saw where he went. The lads would say, "You having a drink?" after they had finished, but not Paul. He had a weak spot for me, flirting with me in the Star-Club dressing room. Not long after Frank and I had got together we were lying in bed one night at the Hotel Pacific and there was a loud knocking at the door. Paul Raven shouted through the door: "Mary, get rid of that bloody German and give me a chance. I'm a lot better than he is!"

We thought he was a bit of a pest and didn't pay him much attention, so we were very surprised, seven years later, when he changed his name and became Gary Glitter, one of the biggest glam rock stars of the 1970s. In Hamburg I assumed he was fifteen years older than me, but when he became Gary Glitter, all of a sudden he was younger than me. It was rumored that he lied about his age, so when he was having those big hits in the 1970s he could have been at least forty.

Despite selling millions of records, his career came to a spectacular halt in 2006 when he was convicted in Thailand of child sexual abuse, and then after returning to Britain he was imprisoned in 2015 for sexual offenses including attempted rape. Like Jimmy Savile, Gary Glitter was a pedophile attracted to the rock-and-roll world because he thought it would give him easy access to young girls. Thank God we all protected each other—being an all-girl band meant there was safety in numbers.

14. SYLVIA

Ask the Girls

By 1965 we were touring a lot around Austria and Germany, using the Star-Club as our base. We'd pack our estate car full of equipment and I automatically went in the back seat because when we traveled to a gig Pam always sat in the front next to Oskar, our road manager. "I'm the biggest," she would announce as she clambered in. The drums, amps, and guitars had to fit in the back with us. We wanted a front seat but being the smallest, Mary and I didn't stand a chance, and though Val was nearly as tall as Pam, she didn't get one either.

We were often on the same bill as the Rattles because we had the same manager, so we would set off at the same time as them and overtake each other on the motorway, waving through the windows. Every time we passed the Rattles' car Pam would have something in her hand or mouth or a different hat on. She made everybody laugh.

Sometimes our booking agent, Henry Henroid, would come on tour with us around Germany. One time, when he was driving us down the long road along the Rhine to our next venue, we spotted a fella on a jetty up ahead, about to start his speedboat.

"I'd love to go on one of them," said Pam, gazing out of the car window.

Henry slammed on the brakes, pulled over to the jetty, jumped out and asked the man, "Can you give these four girls a ride in your speedboat?"

The man obliged. Nobody ever said no to Henry because he was so polite and seemed so harmless. He was also spontaneously witty. He'd say, "Tell you what. I don't believe in this Jesus fella. But if he comes down I'll be the first to book him!"

After a while I found a way to tour in style—going out with boyfriends who had smart cars. "What kind of a car have you got?" I'd ask. "All right, I'll let you drive me." There was a man from Cologne called Dieter, a fan with a smashing red Mercedes who flirted with me and offered to drive me to gigs. Because we were always shoved in the back of our car, I opted to travel in luxury with Dieter. The only problem was that he fell for me, giving me a ring and asking me to get engaged. I said yes, but added, "Don't tell the girls. I'll wear the ring around my neck."

He bought me a gold chain and for two or three months I pretended to be involved because I wanted to go to gigs in the car. It was shameless, really—we were such heartbreakers back then!

The singer Drafi Deutscher had a fabulous car as well. I met Drafi backstage on tour during the summer of 1965. He was nineteen years old and of Sinti Romani gypsy heritage, with smoldering dark eyes and a manly cleft chin. Drafi came from West Berlin and was well known—he'd already had a few big Top Ten hits with sweet, sentimental *schlager* pop tunes that went down well in Germany at the time. He started driving me on tour dates up and down the country. One night we stayed in a lovely hotel room, but the next morning, while he was in the shower and I was making the bed, I got the shock of my life. Under his pillow was a gun. *Oh my God*, I thought, *I'm afraid here. I don't know what's going on.* When he came out of the bathroom I pointed to the gun.

"What's this?"

"I've got to have it for protection."

"What…a gun?"

"There's always people after me. In this business you've got to be careful."

"Well, I don't want to see you again."

I was terrified. At that point Drafi drank too much, paranoid as he was about his fame and stardom. It made for such an uncomfortable journey back to Hamburg because he was passionate about me and didn't want to let me go.

The following week we flew back to Liverpool for Pam's twenty-first birthday. Her party was in the Blue Angel, the place everybody went to after the Cavern closed at night. A former jazz club in the 1950s, it became one of the main venues for the beat sound and many bands played there, including the Beatles, the Rolling Stones, and a young Bob Dylan. In fact, that was where drummer Pete Best auditioned for the Beatles. Old friends crowded around to celebrate Pam's birthday, making a fuss of us, elated at our success. A fella came up to me.

"Sylvia, there's a phone call from your mother."

I hurried to the Blue Angel office, mystified as to why she had rung me so late.

"You'd better come home quick," she whispered urgently.

"Why, what's happened?"

"There's a Daffy Duck here!"

"Daffy Duck? Do you mean Drafi Deutscher?"

"Yes, that's it. He's come here to marry you! He's brought me a pair of slippers!"

One of the girls must have given him my address. I still don't know whether it was Mary, Val, or Pam, but one of them did because that is how he ended up at my house.

"Oh, Mother, get rid of him."

"I'm not getting rid of him."

"Don't tell him where I am, Mother. Please."

"You get yourself out of this. I don't know what he's doing here."

So she told him where I was and within half an hour Drafi appeared in the Blue Angel. I was furious. "What are you doing here?"

He insisted on getting up to sing, and Mary's Frank said, "Oh my God, don't let him get onstage." In the end Drafi gave a loud, dramatic rendition of "Roll Over Beethoven." After he had finished he tried to get amorous with me, but I waved him away, saying, "I don't want anything more to do with you, just forget it. Go and stay in a hotel."

And with that he disappeared. Two months later he had a massive hit with "Marble Breaks and Iron Bends," an epic song about enduring love. It went to number one in Germany and sold 800,000 copies, and the following year he released an English-language version that was even a hit in America, selling a million worldwide. Despite all his success I didn't regret my decision to send him packing. In 1967 he was convicted for public indecency, for urinating drunk in front of a group of schoolchildren. I still remember that gun, and how much his paranoia frightened me.

Another strange character we toured with was Freddie Starr. Nobody could manage Freddie. He started his career imitating Elvis Presley and Eddie Cochran, singing with Merseybeat groups like Derry and the Seniors, and later the Midniters. As a teenager he had been in *Violent Playground*, a fifties B-movie set in a Liverpool police department with the tag line "Every city has its dangerous youth." The role was appropriate for Freddie, who seemed permanently on edge. It wasn't drugs, he was just outrageous. One night he invited us out to an Italian restaurant, where he ordered spaghetti bolognese. The next thing he emptied the spag bol all over his head.

"I vill haff banana fritter," he said to the waiter in a mock-German accent. The banana fritter came and he pushed it into his ear. Then he paid for the meal, for all of us.

We did a few more tour dates at Star-Clubs around Germany and one night we came into the dressing room to see he had drawn a huge penis on the wall. Underneath he'd written: "Hi Liverbirds. Have a suck on this."

In the 1970s he became a stand-up comedian and impressionist, and his humor was often rude. We understood him a bit more when his autobiography, *Unwrapped*, came out in 2001, and he wrote about how his dad, a bare-knuckle boxer who drank too much, beat Starr as a child. Once he even broke both of his son's legs. After that Starr was taken into care and remained a teetotaler all his life.

One of our favorite people was the American R&B singer Ben E. King, who sang and co-wrote that moving soul classic "Stand by Me." He played with us at the Star-Club and we had a party in the Hotel Pacific afterward. In the middle of festivities he remarked, "Oh, I'm going to Berlin in the morning. I'm playing at a big American base. Why don't you come there?"

"Yeah, OK, let's do that!"

Mary, Frank, Pam, Lee, and I booked a flight from Hamburg to Berlin to see Ben E. King's show at the U.S. Air Force base. We stayed in a hotel close by and the next morning, while walking around the base, we saw a huge secondhand American Cadillac for sale. It cost two thousand marks, which was a lot of money in those days, but its shiny cream chassis glowed in the sun. Pam was so entranced she bought the Cadillac outright, and got Lee to drive us back because she didn't have a driving license. On the way out of Berlin the East German police stopped us on suspicion of hiding drugs in the car and had us searched by a policewoman. She was unnervingly thorough, even looking between the cheeks of our behinds, but luckily found nothing.

After Lee drove Pam's Cadillac back to Hamburg we had fun with it all summer. When the weather was warm we'd pile into the car and go to a nearby beach, or straight after work drive an hour away down to Timmendorfer Strand, a beautiful shore on the Baltic Sea, just north of Lübeck. We would change into bikinis, sit in the sun and relax, lounging on large wicker baskets. It was like a long lazy party, a welcome break from the frenzied activity of Hamburg, where our day was structured with a strict work rota.

The Hotel Pacific was our base for over two years, ever since our first night in Hamburg. Because we were there on a long-term basis, it was like we became the unofficial collective boss. Everybody would say, "Ask the girls." We would help other musicians, and even babysit for them. One time Ian Edwards from Ian and the Zodiacs brought his wife to stay, and Irene, the wife of guitarist Tony Coates, came over with their seven-month-old baby, Kevin. Tony had been so busy touring it was the first time he had clapped eyes on his son. Irene originally planned to come for a fortnight so Tony could see his son, but she and the baby ended up staying in the hotel annex for three months.

Irene and Tony were a lovely couple, teenage sweethearts who met when he was seventeen and she was sixteen. She lived next door to the toy factory in Liverpool where Meccano and Dinky toys were made. "I used to jump over the fence and rob all the spare parts from the skips to make new little customized cars," she told us. In the hotel annex she cooked food on a small electric hob hot plate and stank the place out. She had a Pedigree pram in the hall, and would go out with Kevin in the pram because she didn't want to be stuck in that room all day.

One night Tony was playing with the Zodiacs at the Star Palast in Kiel, sharing the bill with Paul Raven (aka Gary Glitter). After he left for the gig Pam said to Irene: "You need a night out. Find somebody to mind the baby and we'll go."

Pam dressed Irene in skintight bell-bottom trousers, a flowing cape, and a flamboyant hat. Mary looked after the baby while the pair of them hitched in all that gear from Hamburg to Kiel, which was sixty miles away. Tony couldn't believe it when they walked into the venue. "Pam in a great big cape and ruffles and Irene standing next to her, like it was the most natural thing," Tony recalls. Pam could be a pain in the arse at times, but she was so daring that people didn't mind being swept along.

We also had raucous parties in the annex with the Chants, an all-black doo-wop act from Liverpool, whose specialty was singing R&B songs by the Drifters and the Coasters. After they made their debut at the Cavern in November 1962, backed by the Beatles, Paul McCartney became an ardent fan. Through the sixties they had record deals with Pye and Fontana, releasing a series of singles, but without Top Ten success. They were best as a live act, and captivating singers. When they stayed in the Hotel Pacific we partied long after the Star-Club closed, and the band became friends of ours, particularly Nat Smeda, whom Mary had a crush on because he was so good-looking. We stayed in touch with the Chants when we came back from Hamburg, and they made us feel welcome when we visited them in Liverpool 8, where there is a strong black community. The Chants' lead singer/songwriter Eddie Amoo ended up in the 1970s soul band the Real Thing, and had a lot of success with big hits like "You to Me Are Everything" and "Can You Feel the Force."

The Hamburg scene was a crucible of creativity for so many of us. It was also where each of us found love and grew up as women, learning so much about life's challenges in the process.

15. MARY

Rome Is Perfect
for Shopping

One by one we paired up with boyfriends. Val had unusual taste and would sometimes go for guys with obvious flaws. She could also be unpredictable. People were sometimes alarmed by her sarcasm, but that was really just her strange sense of humor. Friends used to say, "How the hell can you have a conversation with her?" because she could be so monosyllabic. In the band Val was the hardest one to communicate with, and she kept to herself, yet we really did have good conversations one-to-one. She didn't have a big friendship circle, but she liked people she could trust and with us she was fine.

Every so often she would do something completely out of character. One night we were at the Hotel Pacific, ironing our shirts to get ready to go on at the Star-Club. We were listening to music and having a few drinks and in a good mood, maybe even a little bit tipsy. Then we slipped our shirts on hangers and walked over to the taxi stand near the hotel. Normally Pam got in the front, but for some reason on this night she got in the back with me and Sylvia, and Val sat next to the driver. He seemed like a really old man to us—maybe he was sixty years old—but before he drove off Val hung up her shirt, leaned over, and suddenly started snogging him. The three of us creased up in the back of the taxi, trying not to laugh out loud. Of course the taxi driver thought it was Christmas. As we got out of his cab and walked into the Star-Club Val didn't mention it, which made it even funnier. I think she felt like doing something completely stupid to amuse us.

There was a little guy in the Star-Club who was plump and walked like a duck—everyone used to make fun of him because of the way he looked. One day, without any warning, Val grabbed his face and just started kissing him. Maybe she liked having control, thinking, *I'll get his hopes up and then I'll just let him drop.* Or Mike, the good-looking waiter in the Star-Club, with whom she had a two-day affair. He was mad about her but then she passed him up after just a few days.

She also had a fling with Mick Cummins, the guitarist from the All-Stars, who didn't have a decent tooth in his head. Lee would say to him, "Go to the bloody dentist!" One man who lasted longer than most was Shay McCarthy from the Crickets. Val dated him for about six months and used to say to me, "I can't believe the size of it." Shay was only small, a tiny fella. Val would add, "It's a wonder he can stand up." She had a very dry wit.

Even though she loved him, Val was sometimes noncommittal about Shay, always putting her music first, and the relationship didn't last. He was brokenhearted and never really got over it. Years later I met Billy Harrison, the guitarist from Van Morrison's band Them, who was a good friend of Shay's. He said to me, "Wasn't your guitarist the one who broke Shay's heart?"

"We lost contact with him but I can imagine."

"Well, it completely ruined him. He never got over it."

I'm not sure it's fair to blame Val for his reaction to their breakup but she did have a strange magnetism in relationships.

One night, long after the Star-Club days, Val told me about a traumatic incident that partly explained her eccentric behavior around men. It happened when she was fifteen, walking home after school along the alleyway near their house. The family lived opposite the docks, and sometimes unsavory characters would hover around the area. That day a drunken seaman lurched up, grabbed her and raped her. After the horrendous attack Val ran to her house, threw open the door and screamed, "That man just raped me!" She pointed at the assailant, who was still staggering down the lane.

Instead of helping her daughter, Mrs. Gell pulled Val into the kitchen, battered and slapped her, and then hissed, "Don't you *ever* tell anybody."

Val's father, Tom, tried to intervene.

"Leave her alone, she's had enough."

"You keep out of it!" yelled Mrs. Gell. "I don't want anyone to know what happened to her."

Mr. Gell was a kind man but not strong enough to stand up to his wife. It's hard to understand Mrs. Gell's violence, but maybe because she was strongly religious, and keeping up the appearance of the perfect family was more important than her daughter's well-being. And maybe she thought the rape would bring shame on the family. Whatever her mother's motivation, Val was forced to keep quiet about the rape, repressing the memory for years. That would explain Val's instinct for self-protection and her desire to sexually control men. No wonder music became her liberation, a space where she could find strength and the freedom to fully express herself.

Then, in the summer of 1965, Val met someone who would completely change her world. We were playing in a club on Leopoldstrasse in Munich called the Big Apple—a key venue for beat bands and the first place that Jimi Hendrix appeared when he came to Germany.

The stage was in the cellar and a lot smaller than the Star-Club, but it was the most famous club in Munich at the time. There was a good crowd, very stylish, and quite different from our rock-and-roll fans in Hamburg. They had a mod soul influence and people looked a lot richer, moving to the music with some fancy footwork. While we were onstage we noticed a beautiful boy dancing in front of us with black eyeliner and a red rose in his dark, shiny hair. We all were very impressed with him. "Have you seen that guy?" we said as we walked to the dressing room afterward.

When we came back out to the dancefloor he was waiting. We all started chatting and he said, "Would you like to come to my place tomorrow for a party?"

We glanced at each other.

"Well, why not? Yeah."

The boy introduced himself as Stephan and gave us his address. The next morning we took a taxi that drove us to an amazing house in Schoenwald, one of the wealthiest suburbs of Munich. Staff answered the door and took us through to a large garden where there was a lawn, shady trees, and a large swimming pool. It was like a mansion in a Hollywood film. And there was Stephan, lying in a hammock between two trees, swaying gently. It seemed almost staged.

It was a warm summer day so within a few minutes we had changed into our bikinis and were jumping into the pool. There was a table on the patio with a buffet and all kinds of drinks. We thought, *Well, this is Hollywood now.* The party was only us and two of his best friends. We were just settling in when Stephan's mother came out of the living room and clipped across the patio in kitten heels. Her hair was up in an impeccable chignon bun, like a glamorous movie actress. She wore expensive clothes and she spoke with a hint of arrogance. "Stephan, I've just had a phone call from one of our friends. They said the weather today in Rome is perfect for shopping. So, Daddy and I are off. We'll see you tomorrow."

And with that she disappeared off in a private jet from Munich airport.

We stayed at Stephan's house until midafternoon, swimming and lounging on hammocks while Val chatted to Stephan, looking animated. We knew she was the one he was going to pick. They ended up holding hands and walking round the garden with their arms around each other. Val liked doing that. She did that with David Davies the time we met the Kinks in London, and she used to do that with Shay from the Crickets. It made her feel safe and wanted.

We had another gig at the Big Apple that night, so we couldn't stay too late. Because we were feeling so positive and relaxed our set really rocked, with Stephan and his group of friends dancing near the stage all night. After the show he took our telephone number at the Hotel Pacific and he started coming to gigs, flying to wherever we were playing. He was seventeen years old, studying fashion in Vienna. He had his own elegant style, wearing tailored shirts and cool shoes, and he wanted to be a fashion designer. His parents had bought him a flat in Vienna so he had somewhere to stay while at college, and he would commute back to Munich at the weekends. But after he met us, and Val in particular, he followed us around. He could afford to do that because his father, Michael Hausner, co-owned Triumph International, the underwear company that had a 50 percent market share for corsetry in Germany, and branches throughout Europe, Hong Kong, and Japan. When we met Stephan, the company was generating sales of 620 million marks and employed nearly 23,000 people. The Hausners were super rich.

Once we got to know Stephan, our style began to change. He gave us advice about what to wear, and we had shirts made by his tailor. Astrid liked the frills and ruffles, but Stephan had more of a mod influence with ties and straight lines and skinny-legged trousers that flowed at the bottom with pleats up the side. Though he joined us on tour his mother, Frau Hausner, didn't seem to mind—she probably thought his relationship with Val wasn't anything serious. Also, at that point I don't think for one minute that Stephan was ready to settle down. He had his whole future ahead of him.

Stephan also came along if we were doing a TV appearance. Bands from the Star-Club would frequently appear on German TV, along with star guests. It was two decades before MTV and there weren't many pop shows on television, so bands could have huge hits in Europe without people knowing what they looked like. Lee Curtis told us about one afternoon going to TV studios in Bremen to perform on *Beat Club*, the German version of the British pop program *Thank Your Lucky Stars*. The star band that night were the Who, and he was sitting in the dressing room with their bassist John Entwhistle. The German TV producer came in looking worried.

"We need to rehearse with the Who and we're running out of time. I'll be very happy when they get here."

After he left the room, Lee said to Entwhistle, "They're looking for your band."

"Yes, I know. I understand," he said, smiling. "Let them look."

He enjoyed having his bit of fun.

By the mid-sixties many of the bands we toured with when we started out were playing at a whole different level. In 1963 a bunch of kids had thrown cream buns at the Rolling Stones in Nuneaton, but two years later in September 1965, when the band played the Waldbühne in Berlin—a 22,000-seater woodland theater at Olympia Park—their set was cut short after twenty minutes by a full-scale riot. Frenzied fans stormed the stage, and police caused a rampage trying to control them with rubber truncheons and fire hoses. The crowd destroyed seating and fire hydrants and caused over 270,000 marks of damage. *Bild* newspaper headlines screamed, "We knew hell!"

The following year forty-four fans were arrested for rioting at the Beatles concert in the Ernst-Merck-Halle arena. The scenes weren't just about rock-and-roll abandon—these fans were part of a widespread rebellion in Germany against an older generation who would not take responsibility for what they had done in the war. Trouble was brewing, along with the music and politics of a new youth culture, in what would become known as the '68 generation.

16. SYLVIA

To My Little Sweetheart

As our lives became more settled I was looking for a relationship and for a while I went out with Joe Walsh, the drummer with Lee Curtis and the All-Stars. Joe used to come over and we'd snuggle on my bed. He was engaged to a girl in Liverpool. He wanted to be true to her, but fancied me as well…and I fancied him. So we tried sex, a few times, but we were both so inexperienced that we couldn't do it. One day he just went home to his fiancée and never came back.

I also got together with Bob Garner, the former bass player from Tony Sheridan's band. He joined psychedelic group the Creation and had a hit with the single "Painter Man." When they performed the song live, the vocalist, Kenny Pickett, spray-painted a canvas, which one of the roadies set on fire afterward. All in the name of art. Bob and I did like each other, he was a nice fella, but we were both so busy touring it didn't last.

But then I had my eye on someone closer to home, a regular musician at the Star-Club. I'd always noticed John Wiggins because he played keyboard for Bobby Patrick's Big Six, one of the best-known

Star-Club bands. Originally from Glasgow, they first arrived in Hamburg in 1962 to play at the Top Ten Club on the Reeperbahn, and became friends with the Beatles. The band played slick, tight American-style R&B, and were such strong musicians that the Beatles checked them out every night to pick up tips and techniques. The Big Six had released two singles on the German label Ariola and were backing Tony Sheridan on top Star-Club dates around Germany.

John had dark brown curly hair, a cheeky smile, and his own style, wearing cool corduroy jackets and grandad shirts. The night we met the Liverbirds were coming off stage and the Big Six were about to go on. In the darkness backstage, John's hand accidentally brushed on my bust and I jumped.

"Oh!"

"Oh, sorry."

Afterward he said to me, "I thought, *that's not a fella.*"

A dynamic keyboardist with a catchy R&B style, John joined Bobby Patrick's Big Six because he was a good friend of tenor sax player Alex Young. In the early sixties Alex's family immigrated to Australia, but his career was taking off so he stayed in Glasgow. (His younger brothers Angus and Malcolm went on to become 1970s guitar legends in hard rock band AC/DC.) Bobby Patrick's Big Six used to back artists from America who couldn't get permission for a green card for U.S. musicians. They backed American stars like rockabilly firebrand Brenda Lee, and Smokey Robinson and the Miracles. They also played with Jerry Lee Lewis at the BBC Studios in London. "He got a bottle of bourbon out and insisted we all drank it before playing a note," John said. By 1965 Bobby Patrick left and the band became the Big Six, moving into a jazz direction on their single "Comin' Home Baby," but they didn't have much chart success. John always said that apart from their first lead singer, Barry St. John, the band lacked a strong front person, and that's why, despite being hugely admired in the industry, they didn't have big hits.

John often had to improvise and think on his feet. When Smokey Robinson came over to the UK in 1964 to play the Royal Albert Hall, for instance, the Motown star lost all his music. Five minutes before they were due to go onstage Robinson's people gave John some music to sight-read. He said it was stressful and terrifying, but because he's such a talented player, he could do it.

I used to see John in the Star-Club and think, *Ooh, I fancy him.* I began thinking about him a lot and would always go to the Beer Shop after our set to see if he was there. But he was engaged to a German girl called Randy, a very serious relationship, and he had a ring on his finger. In Germany men have engagement rings as well, and the practice is to wear it on the left hand and once you're married, you move it to the right. John's ring was on his left hand.

I kept my distance because he was engaged, but then one day after he'd come back from a British tour I saw him in the Beer Shop and he no longer had the ring on his finger.

"Hi, John, are you all right?" We sat nursing a couple of beers and talked. "Are you all right? Where's your ring?"

"Oh. We're finished."

"Oh gosh," I said, pretending to be concerned but in my mind thinking, *Ooh, great!*

"Can I ask you why? Is there anything wrong?"

"Well, I shouldn't say this." John was a very quiet person, but gradually he opened up. "When I was back home she went off with another musician."

He was still hurt about Randy, so nothing happened that night and it was a while before we got together. She tried to rekindle their relationship, crying and pleading with him, and some nights he would see her and come back later saying she was in a terrible state. But she had hurt him so much he was reluctant to go back. I walked away from it, saying I didn't want to be involved. Her parents lived in an apartment not far from the Star-Club and loved John as well. I just had to wait, I felt that if John wanted Randy there was nothing I could do.

A few months later the Liverbirds played a gig in Frankfurt and went dancing afterward. We had only been in the club five minutes when all the musicians from the Big Six walked in.

"God, John's here in Frankfurt!" I said to Mary. He walked over to me.

"D'you want a dance?"

"Oh yeah!"

He couldn't dance but he kept me on the floor all night, laughing and exchanging kisses. It turned out that Randy was history, and he loved me more. Much later on, after we were married, I asked him to get on the dancefloor with me and he refused.

"But you had a dance that first night."

"That was because I couldn't afford to buy you a drink."

In those days even a Coca-Cola in Frankfurt cost about five pounds. But the dancing worked, because that night in Frankfurt we got together, and from then on we were inseparable. We would hang out in bars or in the Star-Club with the musicians, or go to Granny's for sausages and *schnitzel*. Once we had steak and chips at a place called Manga Shanga, with a *spiegelei* (fried egg) on top. As we were leaving we found out that the steak was horsemeat, but it tasted beautiful! We didn't go out on many dates, but we did go to the cinema to see *Doctor Zhivago*, the epic historical romance starring Omar Sharif and Julie Christie. It was the first film I saw dubbed in German. I knew a few phrases but I wasn't fluent like John, so he translated it for me and everyone kept telling us to be quiet. We couldn't help giggling; it was like we were in our own little world.

John's family was from Glasgow. His father, Bobby Wiggins, worked in a Hoover factory assembling vacuum cleaners, and also had the first mobile grocery van in the city, selling bread and eggs around the estates. He was married young to John's mother, Peggy, who cleaned houses in the west end of Glasgow. She also taught ballroom dancing and played the piano, a shiny C. F. Glass & Co upright with candlesticks on either side that had been in the family for years. When she moved out of the tenement flat where John grew up, the piano was so heavy it took six people to carry it down four flights of stairs.

John inherited her talent, learning piano from the age of five and when he was older accompanying his parents to their ballroom-dancing classes. Bobby played Hawaiian guitar and was a right character. He used to go to the joke shop and buy fart cushions or sugar lumps that dissolved into flies when you put them in your tea.

John was close to his maternal grandmother, Nanny Quigley, an energetic lady who worked on the ships doing laundry and cleaning. She traveled all over the world and would bring back exotic gifts for John. They were very close. She died just before his twenty-sixth birthday, and he received a card after she passed away. He had been on tour and found it lying on the doormat in his Hamburg flat. "To my little sweetheart," she had written, "Happy birthday." He thought an awful lot of his granny.

The first time I flew to Scotland to meet John's family I was wearing a bright green-and-white-striped jumper. Bobby collected us from the airport in an old Jaguar, and the first thing he said to me was, "Great, hen, I'm glad you stick up for the right team—Celtic!" I supported Liverpool but I didn't know anything about Scottish football, so my jumper was a happy accident, ensuring that Bobby loved me from the start.

John told me so many stories, how he used to write out lyrics for the Beatles, because he had more records than anyone else. He was friends with Stu Sutcliffe and Pete Best, and he used to get Ringo drunk on all-night benders. Big Six's drummer Freddie Smith fancied a Star-Club barmaid called Goldie, and so did Ringo. John would encourage Ringo to get sozzled and carry him home, so Freddie could get together with Goldie.

He didn't like John Lennon because he used to talk about people and cause trouble. That reminded me of how Lennon had provoked us during that first encounter backstage at the Cavern, saying that girls couldn't play guitars. My John wasn't a violent man, but he had Lennon up against a wall one time over something the Beatle had said. John told me Lennon was quite cynical and sarcastic and a winder-upper. Often he would start an argument between musicians and then walk away when it got a bit heated. On that occasion Lennon started a fight between the Big Six and their mates, the Big Three, over something silly. "I went to grab him but he bolted and the last time I saw Lennon I was chasing him up a back alley in St. Pauli. He could certainly run!"

My John had been in Hamburg with the Beatles since 1962, all sharing bunk beds in a room above the Top Ten club. The club owner, Peter Eckhorn, was usually out of his head on the amphetamine Preludin and sometimes cocaine. They used to feed the dog with Preludin until it ran around in circles barking manically. One night Eckhorn came in with a gun and started shooting everywhere, so they had to dive out of the way.

John was a quiet man—you had to pry things out of him, he wasn't one to brag, and he would never talk about himself until he was close to someone. I found that really appealing. He was six years older than me, but there was a spark between us. I thought he was so different from all my other boyfriends—calm and considerate with huge dark puppy eyes. I knew he was The One.

In 1966 we recorded our second album, *More of the Liverbirds*, in the Friedrich Ebert Halle, a school and concert hall in Harburg, a western suburb of Hamburg. There was a studio in the basement, where five years earlier the Beatles had backed Tony Sheridan on his album *My Bonnie*. After the school classes were over at four o'clock, a car would come for us at the Hotel Pacific and we recorded the album in four long sessions, with the mixing done afterward. In the two years between our debut album and the follow-up, the process had become slicker and more sophisticated.

We had been playing a lot that year and our whole technique in the studio was more confident. The studio technology had also improved with eight-track tape, so if one of us made a mistake, it could be edited out and replaced. We could dub and layer sounds as well. For instance, on the song "Why Do You Hang Around Me," Val doubled the guitar solo, and was excited to have two solos on one track. Siggi Loch, a key producer on many Star-Club recordings, produced the album, experimenting with a different sound that was less raw R&B and more influenced by the sheen of Motown. By then artists like the Supremes, the Temptations, and the Marvelettes were dominating the charts with high, crystal-clear vocals and thumping chart pop.

We included the song "Heatwave," which had been a number-one hit for Motown girl group Martha & the Vandellas. Pam was the driving force behind that decision, persuading us to do something we weren't sure about. I like the way my drumming stands out and the definition in Val's guitar, but the song isn't at Pam's natural pitch, so her voice comes across as high and a little screechy. At that point her sister Dyan had started performing with the band Arrival, creating a soulful rock sound that was to hit the UK charts in 1969 with the song "Friends." Pam admired her sister's musical talent and wanted Dyan's approval, for her to say, "Wow, I love the way you sing that song." When it came to choosing "Heatwave" we weren't sure if it was our song or there to impress Dyan. Once Pam made up her mind, however, it was hard to shift her off course.

Having said that, our favorite track on the album was one written by Pam. "Why Do You Hang Around Me" is another song about her thwarted romance with Lee Curtis, built around the central question, why do you hang around me when you've still got your wife? Val and Pam's punchy harmonies blend well together, and Frank joined this session to play a mean tambourine. By then Frank was doing really well in the Rattles, helping to develop their style with more of a gritty Wilson Pickett influence.

Earlier that year when Mary was at home in Liverpool for a visit he sent her a telegram saying, "Would you mind if I joined the Rattles?" That was a nice surprise. She sent a jokey telegram back: "Be great if you joined them, but leave the groupies alone!" Their vocalist Achim had to go into the army for eighteen months to do his National Service. Because Frank's group, the Faces, won the Star-Club beat competition, the Rattles asked him to join them and take Achim's place as lead singer. Frank said he would only do it if they took the Faces piano player as well, so he and Bernd Schulz joined and changed the Rattles' music. Frank had a deep voice, singing and dancing in an Otis Redding soul style that went down very well. When he was on tour with the band in Dortmund, for instance, a female reviewer for the local paper wrote "Frank Dostal moves onstage like a tiger."

We were all trying out new sounds and technology. When we were touring that year Pam played a funny thing called a Tubon, a battery-powered tubular keytar designed in Sweden that looked like an inflatable microphone and made deep woodwind sounds. Paul McCartney used a Tubon on the original demo of "Strawberry Fields Forever," and later Ralf Hütter used it in 1970s Kraftwerk. It gave our shows another musical dimension. We also experimented with our image, wearing vivid makeup and false eyelashes, and doing photo shoots with colorful props and designer clothes.

By then I was writing longer postcards home. I sent one via the

Liverbirds European Fan Club, run by Frank's brother Fred. "Dear Mum and Dad. Here is a picture of the hotel that we are staying in, in Göttingen. The tour is still going good. We are also working with Henry Henroid, we all have a great laugh. See you soon, love Sylvie."

And in August 1966 I sent a postcard home about our new album: "Dear Mum and Dad. Still going down great. The next record I think might get somewhere. Every time we play it, the crowds go mad. Recording it when we're back in Hamburg. Love Sylvia, xxxxxxx." I followed this up with another postcard at the end of the studio session that read: "Dear Mum and Dad. Just a line to say our recording was fab. The men in the studio were very pleased, I can't explain how great they thought we were. We recorded for two days from nine until seven at night. We were all very tired, but it was worth it. Our LP and single will be released in Nov. Love Sylvia xxx"

My mum kept everything, in boxes and boxes, and now many years later it has come back to me.

17. MARY

Tomorrow Is Not Your Birthday

Although we were very different personalities something gelled, and we always worked well as a band. At the time I thought I wasn't musically important. I kept thinking, *I'm the lucky one.* Now when I listen to the records I know my bass-playing was good, but I thought any other girl could have done it as well. My scary old teacher Miss Callaghan could never believe that I went onstage in front of thousands of people. But the girls believed in me. Val always encouraged me, saying things like, "You're fantastic. You are my little bass player. Go on!"

By 1966 we were still just twenty years old and attracting large crowds, with a throng of people hanging around after gigs, clamoring for autographs. Our genial road manager, Oskar, said recently, "You were big stars then and you still are." We were touring all over Germany, Switzerland, Austria, Holland, Norway, and Denmark, and had a Top Five hit in Germany with our second single, "Diddley Daddy." People also loved "Peanut Butter," which had been a hit for

Chubby Checker and then became our signature song. Pam sang it live with a real deadpan humor and the crowd always joined in the chorus, doing formation dancing to the chugging rhythm.

When we first moved to Hamburg we had spontaneously seized opportunities and ended up staying in Germany longer than we expected. By now it had come to feel like home. We were happy, making money, doing well, and thrilled to tour round Europe, visiting countries we'd never been to before. We never regretted not going back to England, but we were ambitious to tour further and maybe even make it in the U.S. We did regret not going to America with Chuck Berry's manager, because we had a different sound from Goldie & the Gingerbreads and it would have been great to try our luck as an all-girl band over there. We were open to new possibilities.

We gave a sassy performance of that song in our first movie appearance—the Rattles' film *Hurra! Die Rattles Kommen*. The Rattles were always heralded as the German Beatles, so the film revolved around a plot that was very similar to *A Hard Day's Night*, with shots of the band being mobbed on the streets of Hamburg and Berlin and running away from chasing girls. Our scenes were filmed onstage in the Star-Club, and while we're playing the Rattles look up at us and say, "Oh, they're not bad."

As our life revolved around tour dates and sell-out shows, Oskar kept us organized, a strong, capable presence over four years. He could cook, he'd worked in a bar, and wherever we played he would bring the equipment in and set up onstage every day at six o'clock, before coming to find us girls. We were often late. Sylvia would bring her snare drum, cymbals, and high hat, and at the last minute Oskar would always have to look for her bass pedal. Pam took a long time getting her hair ready and was very particular about her clothes— she always had them on a hanger, carrying them around like a lady. Years later when Pam was working in a Hamburg bar and Oskar had a restaurant next door, she would introduce him to people as her roadie.

One night we were playing down south in Bavaria and before the gig went to a nearby restaurant for a bite to eat. As we walked in there were two young couples eating and the girls started laughing at us, making fun of our clothes. At that time not many girls wore trousers, and we had a boyish beat style with jeans and fitted waistcoats. I was feeling strong that day so I said, "What d'you think you're laughing at?"

With that, one of the men stood up and hit me so hard in the face I went flying into the corner of the room. Oskar immediately went to the manager and he threw the people out. They looked like Nazis: the men had slick side partings and mustaches, and the girls were very blond. But it wasn't just the right-wing youth who were reactionary—sometimes, when we walked round the streets, older people would laugh at us. We stood out because we looked different. Although we were popular, there were some people who hated us, viewing an all-female group as some sort of threat.

Sometimes the job could be hazardous in other ways. One day at the Star-Club in Kiel when I went up to the mike to sing, it stuck to my lips and I was electrocuted. I felt a terrible pain, jumped into the air and fell down in a complete shock. I was so dizzy I had to be taken to the hospital for an overnight stay. Caused by a loose wire, this accident happened well before the health and safety legislation of the 1970s. I was lucky to get away with just feeling shocked and bruised—it could have been so much worse.

We got to know about other crews and share their stories. Remo Four's roadie, for instance, was a guy called Peter Brandt who had blond hair and looked like Brian Jones. He learned his English from the band so he spoke with a Liverpool dialect. Some of the groups swore a lot, but the Remos weren't swearers, they were gentlemen. If pushed, though, they liked a practical joke and could be mischievous.

Oskar told us that Brandt was full of himself; he thought he was something special. Once when the Remos were touring Scotland they decided to cut him down to size. They were driving from England and just before they got to the border they said, "Have you got your Scottish passport?"

He started sweating. "I don't have any papers." He didn't know that a passport wasn't necessary.

"We've got to hide you on the bus."

Brandt squeezed himself under seats at the back of the bus, and as they neared the border the musicians spotted an AA man on his motorcycle. They pulled over and got out to talk, letting him in on the joke. They got the AA man to stride on the bus, barking, "Passports…give me your passports!" while Brandt cowered at the back. Once they passed through the border the Remos burst out laughing and told him it was just a practical joke. He didn't speak to them for days.

~

By mid-1966 Frank and I were in a settled relationship. We went to the cinema to see *Doctor Zhivago*, a film that most couples saw that year! On our way home he looked thoughtful, and then said to me, "Do you know what? I think we should get married, but in seven years." And that's what we did—we got married seven years later. Frank had probably worked out that we'd be twenty-seven, and that would be a good age.

All of us were enjoying our relationships—even Pam and Lee were having a harmonious phase. Stephan was a frequent visitor to the Hotel Pacific, staying there with Val as often as he could. On the morning of his eighteenth birthday in July he flew back to Munich to do his driving test, because his parents were giving him a car. Late morning he phoned Val.

"I've passed my test, I've got my car. I'll see you tomorrow!"

"But tomorrow is not your birthday." She wanted to see him that day, to celebrate.

Anxious not to disappoint her, Stephan got into his new car, having just passed his test, and drove the eight-hour journey to Hamburg. Twenty kilometers before reaching the city he fell asleep at the wheel, and the car crashed through a barrier onto the autobahn below.

We were practicing at the Star-Club that evening when there was a call for Val. The stage manager came and told her that Stephan had been in an accident and that she had to go to Bamberg Hospital. So of course we stopped playing right away and she raced off to the emergency room to find him lying unconscious, swathed in bandages and connected up to a drip. Val was shocked at his condition. When Stephan regained consciousness he was woozy, but determined to talk.

"Did they find the rings?" he asked.

"What rings?"

"The rings in the car. I was bringing them to get engaged. I'd come to ask you to marry me."

The car was all smashed up, and the rings were never found. We don't know if he really had brought one, but that's what he told Val, and she agreed to marry him. She did love him; they'd been going out for eight months and spent a lot of time together. In a way it helped her, but it also reinforced the feeling that she had to take care of Stephan. She found out right away how bad it was, that he was paralyzed and probably would never be able to walk again. Val wasn't very good at showing her feelings and over those few days she was like a zombie. She would be talking but it was obvious her thoughts were somewhere else. I could tell right away she was hoping that whatever happened she could still stay in the group. She couldn't know how tough it was going to be in the years ahead, but she knew that she still needed the Liverbirds to keep her going.

Val always felt terrible guilt. She must have regretted saying "tomorrow is not your birthday" for the rest of her life. We're sure Stephan reminded her of that later on, if ever she was fed up or they had an argument, because from that year onward, he refused to celebrate his birthday.

18. SYLVIA

The Most Beautiful
Man in Munich

Stephan was in the hospital for a long time, nearly two months. The doctors tried to get him doing rehabilitation exercises to move his muscles, but it was clear early on that he was paralyzed. His spine was so damaged that he wouldn't be able to walk. He had been so badly injured that he could hardly move his hands or grasp objects. He could pick up a glass but he couldn't clean his own teeth or wash himself; he could barely do anything.

A few weeks after the accident, Val went home to Liverpool for her twenty-first birthday. She felt torn leaving Stephan in Hamburg, but her parents had hired a hall and made arrangements for drinks to be brought in, and my brother-in-law Bob, who was then a chef in the children's hospital, had baked a cake in the shape of a guitar. The party on August 14 was fun but Val went back to Hamburg and Stephan as soon as she could.

The question was, could she keep on playing in the band? We had a break for six weeks until his parents decided whether he would go back to the family home in Munich or stay in Hamburg. When

Stephan was discharged from hospital his mind and his speech were OK, so he and Val decided to stay in Hamburg, and she came to an agreement with Stephan's family to live with him and to become his carer. Herr and Frau Hausner bought a Mercedes for Val to drive him around in, and a split-level, ground-floor flat so there was wheelchair access and a drive big enough to strap Stephan into the car. Val got her driver's license right away and soon became a very competent driver. Stephan could sit up if he was strapped in, so Val would lift him in and out of the car or wheelchair, tightening straps around him for support. Over time she completely ruined her back, but they just got on with it, didn't they?

The arrangement was that if she took care of Stephan she could carry on playing in the band. Val used to drive to wherever we were performing with Stephan in the Mercedes next to her, then leave him in the car while she dashed out to play a gig with us. She was always the last one to get to the venue. It was obvious that Val was absolutely shattered, especially when we did out-of-town gigs in quick succession. After the concert, even if we had played a venue miles away, she would drive Stephan home because he felt more comfortable in his own house—he had everything that he needed there. He could have stayed in the flat and have somebody to look after him but that was out of the question; she was the only one allowed to touch him. There was an element of control that he clearly wanted to have over the situation. He wanted to know that Val wouldn't leave him. It was exhausting for them both, but she never moaned, even though all their hopes of a bright future had been destroyed.

Before the accident Stephan was so young and so very, very popular. Years later, when Mary went with Frank to Munich for meetings with GEMA, the musical rights organization, she met the wife of a famous German composer. This woman was well connected. "Oh, Stephan, you know Stephan," she said. "Did you know that Stephan was called the most beautiful man in Munich at the time?" Stephan knew he had been the most beautiful man in Munich, and could never get used to his terrible, life-changing injuries.

Soon after the accident, Val and Stephan got married. I was her maid of honor and her only friend at the ceremony. She didn't want a big wedding, so very few people were there, but her mother, Mrs. Gell, thought a lot of me and wanted me to be there as one of Val's oldest friends. I got the feeling Stephan's parents didn't want people to know about the wedding because the ceremony was in Liverpool and there was no celebration in Munich. Herr and Frau Hausner flew over and stayed just one night with Stephan in the Adelphi Hotel. Val was at her mum and dad's house, so we went from their house to the registry office. They said their vows, exchanged rings, we had a big meal in the Adelphi, and that was it. I flew back to Hamburg, and his mother and father returned to Munich. I thought they were very cold. Somebody signed the register for him, but nobody else—none of his friends or wider family—were there to witness the wedding. It was like, "Let's just get them married."

Val and Stephan flew back to the apartment that his parents had bought, and we carried on playing in the band. Stephan's parents didn't want to be responsible for him, so that must have seemed like the ideal solution. They gave Stephan and Val material things, whatever they wanted. Herr Hausner seemed to like Val, and he must have been pleased afterward at the way she looked after Stephan. But years later Stephan's mother said to her, "I don't know who you think you are, you're only out of the gutter in Liverpool."

When Val moved in with Stephan, that signaled the end of our time at the Hotel Pacific. Pam and Lee found a small apartment on the ground floor of a brothel in the Reeperbahn, one room with a kitchenette and a shower. This domestic nest was the ideal place for Pam, because she wanted to stay where she felt comfortable, in our district near the Star-Club. Lee was still married to his wife, Beryl, but she was at home in Liverpool with the children and turned a blind eye to his affairs. He probably told her, "You're the one I come back to, you're the one with my children and my name." That was the excuse some of the married musicians used. At this point, whenever he was in Germany Lee spent most of his time with Pam, but he also saw other women and even started a liaison with the beautiful sex worker Karin. Pam knew about the other women and wasn't only true to Lee, and maybe this was the way she coped with it.

As for Mary and me, we rented a flat in a leafy part of Hamburg called Wandsbek so we could have a bedroom each and some privacy. We missed the Hotel Pacific, but by then things were already beginning to change and it didn't feel like home anymore. Many bands local to the Star-Club had gone back to England, and the musicians who stayed were moving into their own places.

Throughout 1966 and '67 we were touring big arenas as well as regular slots in Hamburg. We played the Wiener Stadthalle, the biggest hall in Vienna, and we performed in front of 22,000 people at the Waldbühne in Berlin, the same venue where a year earlier Rolling Stones fans had caused a riot. We also played in Tivoli Gardens in Copenhagen, and went back to the Big Apple in Munich, or other Star-Clubs dotted around Germany. But because of Val and Stephan most gigs had to be within driving distance of Hamburg, and it meant restricting our touring schedule. "We've played, we've got our money, let's go back to Hamburg," we would say.

In those days cars would break down more often and there was no legal drink-driving limit until 1967, so for musicians who spent a lot of time driving from place to place car accidents were unnervingly frequent, sometimes with tragic consequences. One musician we really liked from the early days, who was killed in a car crash, was Johnny Kidd. He was so nice and down to earth. Johnny liked to drink in a rough bar along the road from the hotel, and sometimes we'd sit with him there and chat. He signed a publicity photo for me with the line: "To my favorite drummer—girl drummer."

Johnny was a real innovator, fusing blues and R&B before many of the other British rock-and-rollers. He came from Willesden in north London and in the late 1950s had a skiffle band called the Nutters. After the group became Johnny Kidd and the Pirates he had a number-one hit in 1960 with his self-penned song "Shakin' All Over." He wrote dozens of songs and had such a distinctive stage show—he would wear an eyepatch, swing a cutlass and do high kicks to the beat. When we first came to Hamburg he was one of the biggest acts at the Star-Club, but now his career was slowing down and he was looking for new material to revive it.

Pam was thinking about her love affair with Lee and had just written the song "It's Gotta Be You." We played it one night during our set, and afterward Johnny came into the dressing room. "I want to record that, I think it's a lovely song." He went off and recorded it with stabs of brass and soulful harmonies, giving the words his flamboyant rock-and-roll spin. A few weeks later he came into the bar and told us, "If I don't make it with this song I'm not going to record another." Johnny's version of "It's Gotta Be You" was released in 1966, the first single to kick off shows with his new Pirates backing band. Johnny went back to England in October and was working toward a big comeback album when he was killed in a head-on collision on the road to Bolton, Lancashire. His version of "It's Gotta Be You" was the last song he recorded before he died. When he was killed we just couldn't believe it—he was one of the good ones. It was so very sad.

The following year Lee and his guitarist Dave were driving back to Hamburg after a performance. Both of them had been drinking. The car left the road and smashed into a tree. They survived, but Lee was badly injured with a semicircular scar on his cheek. After the accident he lost his confidence—he had always been such a good-looking man, and he was reluctant to perform with the facial scars, so that affected his work. It also affected his relationship with Pam, because that's when he started thinking about going back to Liverpool, where his wife lived, for good, and leaving Germany behind.

19. MARY

The Best Joints in Hamburg

1967 was a big year for Sylvia and me because we both turned twenty-one. My family had organized a party for me at home in Liverpool, and the night before we went Frank and I saw Motown vocal group the Four Tops at the Star-Club. They were such a cool group, fantastically slick dancers and singers, and their hit "Reach Out (I'll Be There)" was being played on the radio everywhere. Backstage after the show we made a cheeky request.

"Why don't you call in and play Mary's party?"

"We'll have a look at the plan."

They happened to play Sheffield City Hall on February 2, the day I turned twenty-one, so we all went to the concert. While the Four Tops were on stage their lead singer, Levi Stubbs, declared: "It's Mary's twenty-first birthday today. Happy birthday! Let's sing a song for her."

The next high point was seeing Jimi Hendrix, who played the Star-Club for three nights in March. With his arrival we sensed that music was changing, moving from beat pop to psychedelic sounds and longer, more complicated guitar solos. There was huge anticipation when his set began with feedback, which gradually grew louder until the curtains opened and Jimi lunged into the opening chord of "Foxy Lady." As he stood there with his Afro hair, silk shirt, and red velvet trousers, he had a magnetic, elemental presence. His set included "Purple Haze," "Hey Joe," a version of the Howlin' Wolf song "Killing Floor," and Chip Taylor's "Wild Thing," which the Troggs had taken to number one in Britain the previous year. Jimi's version, however, was deeper, darker, and much more sensual. He had the audience absolutely mesmerized.

After the show we walked into the dressing room and Jimi was sitting there, surrounded by musicians and fans. He looked up and announced: "Which one's Mary?"

"Me."

"I've been waiting for you."

"Why?"

"I've been told you make the best joints in Hamburg."

I had walked in with my little doctor's bag, which held all my equipment for rolling joints. I once smoked marijuana but it wasn't really my thing. I didn't like drugs because I didn't like being out of control, but I was very good at rolling joints for other people. Frank taught me how to make them, and I always had my little bag with the roller and the weed. I made Jimi one and he really liked it—a welcome gift from the Liverbirds!

Drugs were all around us in Hamburg. Half the reason for the energy of the bands was what they ingested backstage along with the beer. Amphetamines were so cheap and came in the form of Preludin and Captagon, which decades later became known as the jihadists' drug, used by militants in Syria. Mixed with other stimulants, it was highly addictive. Preludin was originally a treatment for narcolepsy and depression, introduced by a German chemical company in 1962, but the pills came to be to be taken recreationally and known as "Prellies."

You could buy forty pills for five marks in the chemist. Gibson Kemp told us that for his eighteenth birthday all the doormen on the strip clubs gave him industrial bottles of Prellies, 250 in a bottle from five doormen. "There I was with 2,500 pills. I was the most popular guy in the dressing room!" he recalls. If you wanted to buy a tube the musicians had their contacts, and the audience in the Star-Club would go to a woman in the toilets, a little old lady who looked like butter wouldn't melt in her mouth. You could buy one or two Prellies from her and she would pocket the money.

"It was rife, it's what everybody did," Gibson says. "Cannabis never really took off because it made us lethargic. If you got up early and had to work until six in the morning you needed Prellies, what the Rolling Stones called 'Mother's Little Helper.'"

There were some hair-raising moments. Once Ian Edwards and his wife, Betty, were asleep in the Hotel Pacific annex and their little boy Steven got up in the middle of the night and found a Prellie on the floor and sucked it. When they opened their eyes in the morning he was running around in circles, waving his arms. It could have been terrible but luckily he eventually calmed down.

Our friend Tony Coates remembers doing a gig with the Hi-Fis and in the audience was Don Black, a lyricist who worked with Bond film composer John Barry:

He asked me to do a session the next day. We were playing until seven in the morning and they said a car would pick me up and take me to the studio to do vocals with a female singer. I agreed to do it and got chatting with the singer, Les Humphries. He said, "You're gonna need these," and gave me Prellies. I took them and stayed awake for twenty-four hours, playing all night and doing the session all the next day. Then I crashed out.

Everybody was walking around with tubes full of pills. One night not long after Tony arrived in Hamburg, Bettina Derlein, a blond, curvy barmaid at the Star-Club, came over to the Hi-Fis and opened her handbag. It was full of Prellies. "Here you are, lads." Bettina was a character. Serving customers from a small bar on her own inside the Star-Club, she was very popular with the bands—Pete Best remembered her nestling his head between her breasts. "It was a nice way to go deaf for a few seconds," he said. John Lennon, however, was her special friend, and she would buy him clothes, shoes, and Prellies. There is a Star-Club recording from December 1962 where, after the song "Glad All Over," George Harrison refers to Bettina as Lennon's *mutti* (mother), and Lennon replies, "No, she's my liebling [darling]."

Everybody asked us if we'd like to take Prellies but we said, "No, we're good girls, we're not taking drugs." Then one evening after she had styled us and we were sitting with rollers in our hair, Astrid offered us a Prellie each. I looked at Sylvia.

"Go on, shall we try it? We can just have half each."

We broke one in half, swallowed it and sat there for a while.

"Anything happening for you?" I asked Sylvia.

"No...no, nothing's happening to me neither. Shall we take the other half?"

We each had another half, and then we couldn't stop talking all night. We danced, we hardly ate, and we didn't sleep for four days. We found we could just go and go. Though we enjoyed the experience once was enough for me, and in the end, too much.

Sylvia, though, liked the adrenaline rush. She had a very energetic way of playing drums, shaking her head and going wild, and when we were playing night after night the pills often gave her a boost. She admits that it could have got out of control, and she was getting careless. After a night at the Star-Club she would always take her cymbals home in case they were pinched from the venue, and more than once when putting the key in the lock to her room she'd drop the cymbals and nearly cut her toes off.

One night things came to a head, not long after Sylvia had started courting John. Pills and drink made her irritable and bad-tempered when she was coming down, and one night they were arguing over something silly when she began shouting and throwing things at him, so he held the bedroom quilt up to protect himself.

"Look, Syl, you're gonna have to stop this!" he said. From that night she began to cut down, and when she knew that she and John were serious, she stopped completely.

For Pam it was different—she started taking pills to keep herself awake and she grew to like their speedy effect. Drugs had become an integral part of the scene. One day in March when Frank was away and Lee was touring, Pam and I decided to go on a spontaneous trip to Dortmund to see the Rolling Stones on their *Between the Buttons* tour. Once we got there we took a taxi to their hotel, which was right next to the Westfalenhalle arena. As we threaded through fans and paparazzi, the policeman by reception made room for us. Pam, of course, was tall, elegant and blond, and we overheard people saying, "I think that's Marianne Faithfull."

In the hotel the Stones were all sitting in the bar. "Ah, it's the Liverbirds," they said, greeting us warmly. Brian Jones then edged up to Pam.

"Have you got any coke?"

I thought he meant Coca-Cola, that's how innocent I was then. And even with Pam he was a few years too early—she hadn't yet graduated to cocaine.

"No, sorry, Brian."

He was still good-looking, with his long blond hair and expressive doe eyes, and he seemed happy, looking forward to going onstage.

That night the Stones were a phenomenal force, playing all the hits—from "The Last Time" to "Ruby Tuesday" and a fiery version of "(I Can't Get No) Satisfaction." Feeling like naughty schoolgirls bunking off, Pam and I vowed not to tell Frank or Lee that we had been with the band in the hotel bar. Then, plastered on the front of the newspaper next day, there was a photo of me and Pam with the headline "Look Who Came to See the Rolling Stones Play!"

My memory of that day is poignant, because it was the last time we saw Brian Jones alive. A few months later he was arrested for drug possession, his girlfriend Anita Pallenburg left him for Keith Richards, and he became increasingly alienated from the band. He went into a downward spiral, with further drug convictions, until he was found dead in July 1969, at the bottom of his swimming pool. The coroner's report stated that it was a drowning—"death by misadventure." It's so sad, when I think of the beautiful blond boy we knew from those early UK tours up and down the M1. Mick Jagger said later to Jann Wenner from *Rolling Stone* magazine: "No one seemed to know much about drug addiction. Things like LSD were all new. No one knew the harm. People thought cocaine was good for you."

In the 1960s drugs were seen as the portal to a new world. The Beatles were famously experimenting with LSD and expanding their consciousness with transcendental meditation and a trip to India to receive wisdom from their guru, the Maharishi. In May they released their psychedelic concept album *Sergeant Pepper's Lonely Hearts Club Band*, and newspaper headlines announced the dawning of a hippie era of peace and love. Pam brought the record into rehearsals saying, "Come on, girls, we've got to listen to this now." We were blown away by the music and how the Beatles had developed. *Sergeant Pepper* was a different world. There was a feeling of excitement, that something was changing and getting even better, not just with the Beatles but also with bands like the Stones and the Kinks. The invention of eight-track tape created so many possibilities in the studio, and the sounds were further influenced by cannabis and acid. Frank was smoking a lot at the time, and you could hear that in the music for his new group, Wonderland. He would take acid with other band members, sit by the riverside in the sun, and then come back and write lyrics populated with fantastic imaginary characters. You could tell they were on a different planet.

We enjoyed listening to psychedelic music, but in the Liverbirds we stayed with the music we knew and loved, the Bo Diddley–inspired rock 'n' roll with the driving beat. There were always new songs in this genre, and Pam in particular kept finding ones for us to play. Even though we didn't experiment like other bands, we were getting more experienced and more advanced on our instruments. There is a German term, *musikalisch*, which means more than being able to play well—it translates as "belonging to the music," and we definitely had that instinctive feel for rock 'n' roll.

Frank asked me to move into the apartment he shared with his mum and younger brother, Fred. They lived in Harvestehude, a part of Hamburg close to the River Alster, with its own scene of restaurants and bars. The flat was in a prewar apartment block, with high ceilings and spacious rooms, which in the early 1900s included servants' quarters. Frank had his own en-suite bathroom, so we turned his room into a bedsit. We would eat meals together with his mum and Fred, but were very independent and both of us spent a lot of time away touring. When Frank was away I used to dress Fred up in his best clothes and take him to the Star-Club. Even though he was only thirteen at the time, and a typical teenager, he liked being part of the scene.

Frank was still going to school the first year after we met. His mum was reserved with me, adamant that we were too young to settle down, and that his leaving school was my fault—it wasn't, but it turned out to be the best thing he could have done, because he ended up having a brilliant career as a singer and songwriter. There was no way he could have toured with the Rattles and completed his *abitur*. By then the Rattles were incredibly successful in Germany. They developed their musical style, and after Frank left the band in 1967 to start his group Wonderland with Achim, they went on to have a global hit in 1970 with acid rock single "The Witch," sung by the Israeli-German singer Edna Béjarano.

By now our friend Karin, the star sex worker from St. Pauli, had settled down with a famous rock musician. She was still working, so they had a fantastic apartment with expensive antique furniture, and she also bought a giant detached house near the Alster lakes and turned it into a private brothel. Frank and I were invited to parties there—Karin's specialty was as a dominatrix, and she would take us through the house, showing us a room full of whips, or a kinky dungeon in another. She had everything in that house, including full-time maids, a gleaming kitchen, and an opulent dining room.

After her relationship with the musician finished, she started getting more serious with Lee. He was another big love of hers, even though he was living with Pam. Later on, after he and Pam had broken up, he would come to Hamburg and see her, and the relationship carried on for about thirty years. I always remember one night when Karin showed us round, she left something on the bed. Pam had bought a toy rabbit for Lee and written on it "To the love of my life." For some reason, Karin had the rabbit. She laid it on the bed specially so I could see it.

There was only one sex worker I met who felt exploited and didn't enjoy the job. She became a good friend, confiding in me that she did it not out of choice but to support her boyfriend, who needed financial help. The other sex workers I met seemed to enjoy the job—they felt emancipated, they were doing their own thing, deciding to accept or reject punters on their own terms. The girls all looked good, wearing clothes that women with office jobs couldn't afford, and most of them employed bodyguards. The scene back then was different and on a much smaller scale. It changed very quickly at the beginning of the 1970s when mafia gangs took over the red-light district, leading to the huge problems with crime and sex trafficking we see today in places like Berlin and Amsterdam. Through the seventies more and more girls became controlled by their pimps, but for a while in the 1960s there was a window of emancipation, a genuinely liberating time when young women were trying new things. The same was happening in London when working-class musicians mixed with aristocrats, artists, and celebrated sex workers like Christine Keeler. The culture felt egalitarian; there was nothing to hold women back.

20. SYLVIA

You'd Better Treat Her Right

By the summer of 1967 John and I had found a little house on a *klein-garten* (allotment) in Barmbek, and moved in together. The woman who rented it to us said, "You can have it for next to nothing as long as you mow the lawn and look after the apples." There were apple trees and pear trees and strawberry beds, and an old lawnmower with no petrol. The actual plot was so extensive it took John three days to mow the lawn, but it was idyllic. We lived there while we were courting and were very happy, with him playing in the Big Six and me touring with the Liverbirds, tending to the *kleingarten* whenever we were home. It felt like a haven, so peaceful under the fruit trees.

While John was away for a few days backing Tony Sheridan on tour I realized I had missed a period. I'd been on the pill for a while before I met John. The pill was meant to be a liberating force for women but it was a lot more potent in those days and I had severe side effects, so I went to the doctor and he advised me to stop taking it. I spoke to John.

"I've come off the pill. You know what that will mean, unless we take precautions. Is that all right?"

"Yes, that's fine."

"...if a baby comes along?"

"Yes, if it happens we'll deal with it."

And of course it did, quite quickly. I didn't consider other kinds of birth control because John and I had been together eighteen months and the relationship was solid. I went to the doctor, took a test, and got the results the next day. The moment I found out I was pregnant I was surprised but very happy.

"What are we gonna do?" I asked John.

"We love each other, we'll get married."

I was made up about that, but then worried about what my mum would think. "Ooh, we've got to tell my mother. You'll have to speak to her."

I made my usual Friday phone call at eight o'clock from the Star-Club, babbling nervously without taking a breath: "Mum, John wants to ask you something. Also, I'm pregnant. Here's John."

I handed over the receiver.

"Hello Mrs. Saunders. I'd like to marry your daughter. I'd like your permission."

There was silence at the other end. Then: "It's a bit late now for that, isn't it?"

"Could I speak to Mr. Saunders please?"

My dad came on the phone.

"Your daughter is pregnant and we want to get married, if that's all right."

"Yes. But you'd better treat her right."

By sheer coincidence, my brother Chris had come to Cumpsty Road that night to tell my mum that his wife Val was having a baby too. It was a lot of news for Mum to digest.

"The family are going to get me down the sticks now," she said.

Chris tried to reassure her. "What are you worried for? Look, she phoned you up to tell you she's pregnant. Would you rather she ring up and say, 'Mum, in nine months I'm going to die of cancer'?"

Mum fretted and worried about what the neighbors and relations might think, but she gradually came around. Once the initial shock was over my parents were supportive and Mum was ready to come to Germany and get us married as quickly as possible. "Just say we're going over for a holiday, not a wedding," she instructed. "And don't forget to tell them you were married three months before you told me."

Being pregnant out of wedlock mattered in those days. Young unmarried mothers were shipped off and sent away to Catholic orphanages, forced to give away their babies for adoption and, in so doing, lose a part of themselves. Every year on the baby's birthday the thought must come like a thunder-hammer, *What's he or she doing now?* It was an inhumane practice.

I first shared news of my pregnancy with Mary and then told the other girls. They were all excited for me. It didn't occur to me at that point what having a baby might do to the group, and I don't think any of them thought it would be a problem. They were a little surprised but they knew John and I were happy and building a life together.

Our Star-Club community of musicians was very in tune with ideals of sexual liberation but our parents saw the world differently. Social attitudes toward sex in the sixties were so mixed, with old-fashioned morality on one side and heady freedom on the other. Hamburg as a city was very forward-thinking about sex, in a way that could be challenging for the older generation. Once our engagement was announced, John's mum and dad came over from Glasgow, and one night we took them to a club behind the Star-Club, which featured very high-class transvestites, as we called them then. A lot of

The Liverbirds: Mary (above), Val and Sylvia (below left), and Pam (below right). We were four teenage girls from Liverpool with dreams of making it big as a rock 'n' roll band.

LEFT When we moved to Hamburg in 1963, the Hotel Pacific was our home for three years.

RIGHT Having a laugh in the dressing room before a gig at the Star-Club. We were all such close friends.

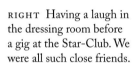

LEFT We couldn't believe our luck performing alongside the likes of Chuck Berry.

ABOVE Mary on the bass.

ABOVE LEFT AND BELOW Sylvia in action on the drums.

ABOVE, FROM LEFT Pam, Mary, Sylvia, and Val at Club Big Apple in Munich.

LEFT A promo shot in 1965 once we'd found a new style with matching shirts and ties!

RIGHT Arriving
at Schiphol
Airport in 1965.

BELOW "Listen, watch!" TV series in Germany, 1966.

LEFT Val's husband, Stephan, who was known as the most beautiful man in all of Munich.

RIGHT Stephan with Val after his accident.

ABOVE Pam and Val with our friends the Crickets, Lee Curtis and the All-Stars, and Freddie Starr.

Pam in happier times with Lee Curtis.

Mary, her husband, Frank, and their daughter.

Sylvia and her husband, John, in Germany.

Sylvia and John outside their pub in Benidorm.

Pam, Mary, and Val during a reunion gig in 1998.

In 2023 we returned to the studio to record a new Liverbirds album. Musicians Molly Grace Cutler (left) and Liza Wright (right) stood in for Pam and Val.

them had the complete operation, had completely transitioned, and were sitting there looking beautiful. John spoke perfect German. The club owner said to him, "I've got a letter here from an English person and I can't understand it. Can you translate it for me?" They'd sent a picture of themselves dressed up. They were going for an operation and wanted to know if there would be a job afterward working in the club revue. John's mum and dad watched him translate the letter.

"Why would she/he want to come and work here?" Bobby asked.

"Dad, look around, everybody in this club is a man."

Bobby's jaw dropped. "You're kidding." Trans artists of all different nationalities were sitting drinking around us. That was quite a lesson for his parents.

Within two weeks of our engagement Mum and Dad came over to Hamburg for the wedding, traveling with Val's mother and father by car and boat. Mr. and Mrs. Gell stayed in a hotel, and Mum and Dad slept over at ours. Before they appeared I said to John, "You're going to have to move all your things. Get your socks out of that drawer, get your underpants, they mustn't know we're sleeping together."

In the back room we had bunk beds, like Huckleberry Finn's cot, though we normally slept on a sofa bed in the living room. While moving the furniture around I remember saying to John, "We'll go in the bunks and my parents can sleep on the sofa bed. And we'll move your socks to the drawers in the back room."

The next morning Mum and Dad put the sofa bed back and were sitting there, when John wailed, "Where're my socks? Where're my underpants?"

"Where they always are, John," I said, grimacing at him. "In that drawer in the bedroom." It's strange—even though I was pregnant I felt embarrassed about letting my parents know we slept together.

We were married on August 18 in the British consulate, a grand old building by the River Alster. John and I were elated, and looking forward to having the baby. Deep down I'd always known that we were going to get married, and moving into our little cabin in the *kleingarten* had brought us even closer together.

The wedding was sooner than expected, though, so in some ways I was a little unprepared. I didn't think about flowers until my maid of honor and Star-Club friend, Monika Pricken, brought a bunch of gladioli and plonked them in my arms when we were doing the wedding photos. Mary was there, and Val arrived in her Mercedes looking very rock 'n' roll in her velvet bell-bottomed trousers and jacket. Pam couldn't make it because the wedding was last minute and she was away on holiday with Lee somewhere. Years later, Mary asked me why I didn't ask any of the Liverbirds to be my maid of honor, but I didn't want to pick one. Val was my friend to start with, and Mary was mine in the Hotel Pacific. I didn't realize at the time that I might have hurt them—in the run-up to the wedding John said, "We met in Germany, we're getting married in Germany, so let's have German witnesses." So Monika, and Horst who ran the Beer Shop, did the honors.

The Consul General officiated the actual ceremony, rushing through the proceedings and forgetting important rituals. After we exchanged vows he said, "Right, now you're married."

"What about the rings?" I said.

"Oh…yes, yes. Put the rings on."

I think he'd had a few drinks and was after the big bottle of champagne standing on the table for the reception.

Many musicians were there including the Hi-Fis, who turned up with their guitars, holding them high for the wedding picture. That was a fantastic surprise. We had a British flag draped over the table, which was piled high with sandwiches and a tiered wedding cake, and everyone toasted us with the champagne.

After the wedding we went back to the *kleingarten*. Our parents and Mr. and Mrs. Gell had to get the boat to England, so they didn't stay. Thank goodness they didn't, because the party continued uproariously in our massive garden. It was August and beautiful weather, and all the musicians brought their own drinks, ensuring that everybody got sozzled. Over the course of the day people would peel off to play their slot at the Star-Club, then come back, and another band would go and take their place. We were married at midday so the party continued from midafternoon to the early hours of the morning. At the back of the allotment was a hut, which housed a very basic toilet—a wooden plank with a hole over a big bucket. By the evening I was aware that everybody had been drinking all day and we might have a crisis.

"John, it's getting full. We're going to have to do something about it."

"OK, leave it to me."

"Whatever, just do it, John, because nobody else can go in there. It's nearly overflowing."

He must have told the lads, because the next thing I see is Ian and the Zodiacs striding down the garden carrying the bucket aloft. One of them brandished a book as if it were a Bible and they chanted mock prayers, ceremoniously digging a hole and pouring in the contents of the bucket. That's how you had to get rid of it.

The Zodiacs had to really dig deep, but that was what we had to do every day, turning the soil in different parts of the garden, emptying the toilet bucket, and stuffing bleach and disinfectant down the hole. Back to nature indeed. Yet in our garden the flowers were lovely and the pear trees were fantastic, they grew so tall.

The Summer of Love was a hopeful time, and the music matched the mood. Six months after *Sergeant Pepper*, the Rolling Stones released *Their Satanic Majesties Request*, a sprawling psychedelic album that included Moroccan rhythms and the swirling, pretty song "She's a Rainbow." The Stones were in trouble because in February there had been a drug bust at Keith Richards's home in Redlands, Sussex, and both he and Mick Jagger were convicted in June of cannabis possession, spending a night in prison before being released on bail. Many of us felt they had been unjustly targeted. The connection between drugs and music was no surprise to us or other musicians, it was only news to the public, a story the tabloid papers sensationalized because the Stones were so popular. The *Times* editor William Rees-Mogg wrote an article critical of the sentences, and in August his paper carried a full-page advert calling for the legalization of marijuana, signed by sixty-four celebrities including the Beatles, the artist David Hockney, and the writer Graham Greene. This helped the Stones' appeal, leading to Mick Jagger's conditional discharge and Keith Richards's sentence being overturned.

Jagger wrote the lyrics to "2000 Light Years from Home" the night he was in Brixton Prison, and the song became a big hit in Germany. Even though some fans didn't like the Stones' move toward a more trippy flower-power style, everyone was trying out new sounds and arrangements. In the Liverbirds we weren't experimenting with hippie styles, but Pam was writing more songs and we were maturing as a band, getting deeper into the bluesy rock 'n' roll we loved. At that point we received some exciting news.

Yamaha in Japan got in touch with us via Frank because they were interested in the Liverbirds being the "face" of their new campaign. The company was founded in 1900 as a piano manufacturer and specialized in acoustic instruments—this is reflected in the company logo, which is a trio of interlocking tuning forks. In the late sixties they were branching out into electrical instruments, making amplifiers and guitars, and they wanted musicians to come over and promote their new product. By then we had a striking image with our bright tailored trousers and custom-made shirts, a girl band who stood out from all the other male beat groups. Someone from Yamaha saw us at the Star-Club and chose us for the campaign, which was organized with a music shop in Hamburg and involved a Japanese tour the following spring.

We were feverishly making plans for the trip to Japan when I had problems with bleeding. I was worried because I was only four months pregnant, so I went to the doctor to be examined. In those days they didn't have scans, and to determine if a woman was pregnant they just used to *feel*. After prodding around the doctor said, with a serious look on his face, "You have to make up your mind. Either you play the drums or you don't have a baby. Because of the exertion when you play, you're going to lose it."

When I was drumming, my whole body moved and I expressed my personality. My style wasn't just doing a little tinkle here or a roll there, I wanted to hit the drums with power. I loved it when the girls shouted, "Shake your head, Sylvia!" When I was younger, girls were told that it wasn't ladylike to be loud or noisy, and drumming is the opposite of that, it's so emphatic. When were at the Star-Club we played like the lads, there was no holding back, and I loved my role. My heart sank, knowing it would be horrible to give up the drums.

I went home to John and told him what the doctor said.

"It's up to you, but to me there's only one choice," he said. "You've got to pack in the drums. We have to start now, we have to start our married life thinking together."

I knew he was right, but it was very upsetting because I loved the band so much. How on earth was I going to tell the girls?

21. MARY

Liverbirdmania in Japan

It was November 1967 and we were practicing at the Star-Club, all enthused about the Japanese trip. We had rehearsed a few songs when suddenly, Sylvia laid down her drumsticks. It was clear she was nervous and had something on her mind she couldn't face telling us. Then she told us that she had been having trouble with bleeding, that she had been to the doctor and he advised that she give up drumming straight away.

"I can't go on any longer. I have to make the decision now and there is no time to wait," she said. "If I carry on playing it could cause a miscarriage."

We were stunned. It took a moment for the news to sink in, and then it was obvious to us there was no way out. We just looked at each other, feeling sick and helpless. There was no need to carry on practicing—it would have been a waste of time because she was going to leave anyway. We knew the band wasn't going to last forever; that wasn't our plan: Val was a full-time carer to Stephan, so it was obvious that she was with us on borrowed time. But we did envisage it continuing for another two or three years before everyone went our separate ways. We assumed that because of the way we started—confidently choosing our direction—we would decide ourselves the way we finished. We thought that one day we'd look at each other and say, "That's been great and that's it now."

We didn't have a big five-year career plan like bands do now; we were happy the way it was. We were earning good money and touring a lot and could have been very content. Because we were so young when we started, there had been times when we wondered if we were getting to an age where we should stop—even though we were only in our early twenties! At that point we tried to hide the fact that we were over twenty-one because no one could imagine rock-and-roll musicians getting old. Who would have thought that the Beatles and the Stones—especially the Stones—would have carried on the way they did for so long? If anyone had said at the time that the Stones would be playing when they're eighty years old, we'd have laughed: "You're nuts!"

I knew we wanted to have babies. I saw a possible future in Hamburg with Frank, and Pam thought that maybe in a few years she would have a baby, but not then. We didn't think of stopping. But that was all turned on its head when Sylvia had to leave us.

We'd already been to the music shop to sign contracts for our new Yamaha guitars. Sylvia had signed for the drum kit, thinking at that point that she'd stay in the band. It took a few days to decide whether to stop there and then or carry on, and much depended on whether we could find a replacement. We confided in our good friends the Hi-Fis, and Tony Coates said they had just been performing near Dortmund with a German band who had a girl drummer called Dixie Wassermeyer. We got in touch with her and arranged an audition. She didn't have Sylvia's personality or drumming power, but she was a kind person and had decent technique, so it felt like a workable compromise. In the meantime, there was more bad news.

Val turned up at the next rehearsal looking downcast. "I can't come to Japan," she said.

Stephan wouldn't let her. The Hausners could have easily paid for a nurse, but Stephan would only let Val touch him, and when the opportunity came up for the Liverbirds to play Japan he said, "No way." She was shattered.

"Maybe it's best if you look for a drummer and a guitarist at the same time," she said. Val didn't want to give up the band; it was still her main enjoyment in life, as hard as it was. She told me years later that when she couldn't come to Japan she pulled her beloved Fender guitar out of its case and scratched it to pieces.

Val's departure was the second shock for us. We knew a girl drummer at least existed, but it was going to be hard to find a girl who could play guitar the way Val did. We couldn't find anyone to take her place. Frank's band Wonderland had a record in the charts so they were touring a lot. Their road manager, Juergen, knew of a female guitarist in Sweden and offered to take us there, so we drove to Denmark, took a boat to Stockholm, and met a very professional all-girl lesbian band. The only problem was the guitarist lived with the drummer and would only join the Liverbirds if we took her girlfriend too. We had already said yes to Dixie because she was based in Germany, so nothing came of that.

It was just impossible to replace Val. We had to keep looking for a girl guitarist, and the more we looked the more we realized how rare it was to find someone with the same level of skill and creativity. Dixie told us about Chris Schulz, a guitarist from Berlin who played rhythm in a male band, so we thought that if she played rhythm then maybe she could play lead as well. When Chris came to Hamburg we filmed her audition. We had already started practicing in a cellar with Dixie, and when Chris arrived and started playing guitar riffs

Pam and I looked at each other as if to say, *At least she can play a few chords.*

We had six weeks to practice hard, helping Chris improve the solo work. She couldn't sing, so that meant that Pam did all the singing. We practiced and practiced and practiced, and she did improve, marginally. It was frustrating, however. Pam helped Chris a lot and attempted a few simple solos herself, but when Chris botched a solo Pam would say, "What was that? What was *that*?" She had trouble trying to play the same guitar riffs as Val, and on "Why Do You Hang Around Me" she just couldn't get it right. Val had such a unique sound—the "fiddly bits" she had created were so complex she was hard to imitate.

In the spring of 1968 we flew to Japan from Hamburg. I've always been frightened of flying, and I couldn't imagine cruising from Hamburg to Tokyo without the plane crashing. That fear was slightly alleviated by a two-hour stop-off in Alaska on the way, but I was glad when we touched down in Tokyo. And it was quite a reception. You'd have thought the Beatles were arriving. As soon as the plane landed on the tarmac and we walked down the steps we were met by a barrage of photographers and a hysterical crowd of screaming boys and girls. People were on all sides, offering us flowers. We had experienced Liverbirdmania in Germany and Denmark, where we had worked our way up and people had seen us on television, but we weren't expecting that explosive reception in Japan. We soon realized that people liked our song "Diddley Daddy." A few months earlier we had recorded a new version for Japan, and the song had been played there many times on the radio, along with "Peanut Butter." A hit single travels everywhere, and Japan is a big market.

We toured the country for six weeks, accompanied by chaperones and translators, playing all the major towns and doing countless TV shows. We were showered with expensive gifts like silk kimonos, tea sets, pearl bracelets, and gold necklaces. In the middle of the tour we stayed for a five-day rest on a little island owned by Yamaha. Japan was futuristic with advanced high tech, like the exhibition room in the company building where we could phone someone in another room and see them on a screen. Now we think nothing of doing Face-Time on a mobile phone, but back then video calls were like science fiction. Everything seemed so advanced, even compared to Germany. They had superfast bullet trains and modern shopping arcades with cool fashion. The only thing I didn't like was the Japanese food— sushi was too raw for me and the little yakitori stands down side streets smelled strange, so our gracious chaperones took us to American hamburger joints.

We were made to feel so welcome, especially by the young people who loved American rock 'n' roll and English beat music. Keen to learn English, they would try and talk to us whenever possible. Pam stood out in Japan, like she was from a different world, because she was tall and blond. She'd grown her fringe down to her eyes and wore a black cape and trilby hats, so they called her Mount Fujiama, after the sacred mountain that dominates the landscape south of Tokyo, sheer and dark with a snow-capped top.

One of the few affairs in my life was with a musician called Pea (aka Minoru Hitomi), drummer of a Japanese band called the Tigers. It was out of character for me. I loved Frank but at that point I wasn't getting on with his mum and I didn't know how things were going to work out with the band when I got back. If the Liverbirds split, would she put pressure on me to go back to England? I even wondered if I might have to return to Liverpool and work at James Brown & Company! Pea's attention took my mind off those problems back home.

In Japan, the Tigers were as big as the Beatles, and whenever Pea came to the hotel screaming fans would gather outside. The five-piece band formed in Kyoto in 1965, and within two years they had moved to Tokyo, signing with a top management company called Watanabe Production. Leading figures in the Group Sounds boom—a musical craze that fused *kayokyoku* (melodic Japanese pop) with Western beat rock—they looked beautiful in that groomed pop idol way. They were one of the first Japanese male bands to get their hair permed, styled, and set in the beauty parlors.

Pea was a real extrovert, a driving force in the band, and from the moment we met backstage at a TV show he pursued me. I was fascinated by him because he was handsome, and his band was massive. We were going down well and had a lot of fans, but the Tigers played stadiums and were at number one in the Japanese pop charts with a frenetic song called "Cee Cee Cee." His birth-control method was to run me a bath before we went to bed and put minerals in the water that apparently prevented pregnancy. Or maybe he was just very hygienic. Either way, it worked.

In the hotels the baths were luxurious, edged by gleaming marble steps. Submerged in the tub I could deeply relax, feeling like a liberated lady, leading my own life. There weren't many women there traveling independently like us, and we attracted attention. One night Pam and I had a small party in the hotel room with Pea and a guitarist from the Tigers. As we played music and danced she began smooching with the guitarist, who was decidedly shorter than her. Afterward she said to me, "He was wiping his nose on my shoulder."

Dixie and Chris had separate bedrooms from us and didn't flirt with the musicians. We did go out with them sometimes, we didn't ignore them, but the energy wasn't the same. The Japanese were delighted with this incarnation of the Liverbirds and wanted us to return a year later, but Pam and I didn't enjoy it because Val and Sylvia weren't there to share it with us. Yamaha treated us like queens and we earned lot of money. They put us in limousines, we stayed in fantastic hotels, and every time we did a Japanese TV show they'd give us more money and presents. Each one of us received a photo album with pictures from the tour. Some of the shots show Pam grimacing while Chris plays solo. It wasn't just the way she played, she had a completely different feel, and to be fair to her the original Liverbirds had grown together and each one knew exactly what the other was thinking. We realized it was never going to be like that again.

When it was time to leave, a stewardess at the Tokyo Airlines desk said to me, "There's someone waiting to say goodbye to you." She took me to the VIP lounge, where Pea was waiting with a bouquet of flowers in one hand and a large signed photograph of himself in the other. I smiled and thanked him, thinking, *How am I going to get rid of this? How will I get this home and explain myself to Frank?*

After I got off the plane in Hamburg Frank was there to meet me. I told him that the picture was from an admirer. I had no choice really. The Tigers flew to the U.S. a few days after we left, and Pea kept writing to me. At the time Frank and I were living in the family apartment with his mother. Pea wasn't just writing letters, he also sent postcards with passionate messages that Frank could see, like "Dear Mary, I enjoyed our time together…and I miss you…can't wait to see you again. I'll come and pay you a visit soon and get the bath ready."

Frank had remarkable patience—he wasn't jealous and he knew our liaison had been harmless. Pea was smitten, inviting me to come back and stay in Tokyo, but that was out of the question. Finally, after more and more letters arrived, Frank said, "I think you should tell him now, Mary, don't you?" I did tell Pea that I had a boyfriend and there was no way I was interested in him, but for a long time he didn't give up.

The following year Pea went to England with the Tigers to shoot a mod musical film called *Hi! London*. Featuring a cameo appearance with Barry Gibb from the Bee Gees, it has since become a cult rock-and-roll movie classic. Gibb also penned the only single release they had in the UK, a baroque pop song called "Smile for Me," which led to them being cover stars of *Rolling Stone* magazine, the face of Japanese new rock. Despite his fame and his amorous attention, Pea was never more than an attractive diversion. Frank knew that he was no threat, that I'd had an affair with Pea to take my mind off what was happening with the Liverbirds.

Pam and I had realized when we were in Japan that it was time to finish the band. Back in Germany, Pam, Chris, Dixie, and I honored the last few Liverbirds bookings. The final date, in August 1968, was sad, but we knew it was the right decision—without Sylvia and Val we no longer felt like the Liverbirds anymore. That rehearsal when Sylvia had put down her drumsticks and said she couldn't carry on had been the last time that the four of us had played together, and it would remain the last time for many years to come.

We had planned to go home for a holiday and then come back to the Star-Club, but we never played there again. Just before I went back to England, Chris asked me, "Can I pay you a visit in Liverpool?" I said yes, and she came to Liverpool for a week, staying at our house in Ternhall Road. I took her around and showed her the sights of the city. All the time I think she was hoping I'd say, "Come on, let's have another go. Get together and practice a bit more." But we didn't. Pam and I knew it was time to call it a day and now we wanted to move on.

As for Dixie, our drummer from Dortmund—her story is a tragic one. When the band split up she went back to her job as a plain-clothes policewoman and fell in love with one of her married colleagues. A year later she became pregnant and had a baby, thinking he was going to leave his wife, but he didn't. When her baby was about nine months old, Dixie took the little girl to her mother. She then went home, sat in the bath with a bottle of gin, and shot herself.

Her parents brought up the baby girl. She was born the same time as my daughter Melanie and now they are both in their fifties. I like to think that Dixie's daughter had a good life with her grandparents, that something good came out of that terrible event. Life can sometimes be so cruel.

22. SYLVIA

Big Blue Eyes and Jet-Black Hair

I would have loved to go to Japan, but I was taken up with the fact that I was pregnant, that John and I were starting a new life. Then, when Mary and Pam returned and told me about the tour, I realized what I had missed and I was gutted.

John was getting a lot of session work in Germany. He played keyboards with Tony Jackson, former lead singer and bassist of the Searchers, who by then had his own backing band called the Vibrations. Then Tony Sheridan offered him a tour, saying, "Come with me, we've got a gig in Vietnam entertaining American troops." Because of my pregnancy John felt it was too risky to make the trip, but that ruined his working relationship with Sheridan, who never spoke to him again.

John could have stayed working in Hamburg, but I felt vulnerable with my pregnancy and wanted to be nearer my parents, so he decided to come back to England for me. I kept my snare drum and to raise money for the trip I sold the rest of my kit to a German band. We were planning on going to London, but didn't have anywhere to stay. The Londoners' singer, Brian Morris, had already taken a German girl back home with him, and was going to get married. He wrote, saying, "Come to London. You can stay with us, we've got a big house. And then you can decide what you want to do."

So in November 1967 on the day it came to leave Hamburg, the Hi-Fis' keyboard player, Brian Bennett, helped us secure our cases to the roof of his Mini. I'd already said goodbye to Val and Pam the day before, and Mary was there to see me off. She told me later that she looked at the little Mini full of cases and thought, *That's Sylvia's life in there and now she's going.* The girls in the group were the most important thing to me, and it was horrible saying goodbye to them. Leaving them was so sad.

As we drove farther and farther through Germany and Holland, though, I realized I could focus more now on the joy of having a baby and our new life. After we crossed the North Sea in the car ferry to Harwich, Brian drove us to London, dropped us off in the middle of the city, and headed off. There were no wheelie suitcases in those days—Bernard D. Sadow's "rolling luggage" had yet to be invented—so we hauled our suitcases along the street, stopping people to ask the way. They were very aloof and wouldn't speak to us, probably put off by John's long hair, the cases, and my pregnant tummy—it must have looked like we were doing a daylight flit from somewhere. Eventually we found Brian Morris's address, knocked on the door, and he opened it. "Oh, hi."

His mother bustled down the hall. "Who is it, what is it?"

"Oh, hello. How are you?" I asked politely.

She saw our cases. "What's going on?"

Brian looked away, embarrassed.

"Sorry," she said. "You can't stay here."

We thought, *Oh God. What are we going to do?* But said to her, "Oh, it's all right," because we didn't want to cause any trouble.

After that we tramped the streets until we found a cheap B & B hotel. "We don't want to stay long, but we're looking for a flat," I said to the landlady on reception. I tried to cover my tummy with the suitcase because they didn't want babies in their rented accommodation.

"Oh yes, come in."

It was hard being in my condition. We rented a room with a bath, but the toilet was upstairs and I always wanted the toilet. I had to wee in the sink so the landlady wouldn't see me and my pregnant tummy going up the stairs.

Every day for a week we bought the London *Evening Standard* paper, scouring the vacancies to see what flats were available. We found a place that was just one big room next to a shared kitchen. Our room had an old-fashioned fireplace with a chimney, and the only furniture were a mattress, a settee, a nightstand, and that was it. What kept us going was my parents' generosity—when we got married Mum gave us a Post Office account in my name, which contained five hundred pounds, all the money I'd send home to them from the Star-Club. That really helped us during those early weeks in London, plus John started doing session work in a recording studio.

Then, not long after we moved in, I awoke to find blood on the mattress. I had started bleeding again, so I had to go to hospital and rest there for a week. They checked the heartbeat every day to check that the baby was OK, and even did that examination again—the one that could cause miscarriage. It was stressful being in London so I said it was time to leave.

"Where should we go?" I asked John.

"Well, because I'm Scottish I'd like the baby to be born in Scotland," John admitted.

So we went to Glasgow and stayed with his mum and dad. My parents didn't mind, as long as I was being looked after and close to family.

John always said he wanted to be there when I gave birth, but was offered a gig in January touring around Italy and France with the Krew, a band formed by tenor sax player Howie Casey. His wife,

Barry St. John, was on lead vocals, and another Big Six member, Archie Legget, played bass.

"What do you think?" he said.

"Well, we need money."

"I promise, when the baby arrives I'll come home." But he never made it; the tour was going so well that he had to stay out there.

John's father, Bobby, was the one who let him know when the baby was on the way. John rang from a club in France while I was still in labor, but he thought the baby had already been born so all the waiters and musicians started celebrating. The band had said, "When the baby comes, we'll all take our trousers down," and that's what they did. Even the waiters stripped down to their underpants. Meanwhile, the labor dragged on and I was in terrible pain.

On February 13, 1968, I gave birth to little John Wiggins at the family house in Glasgow. My first thought when he arrived was, *Thank God it's all over.* I was nearly twenty hours in labor. Looking down at his big blue eyes and mop of jet-black hair I realized that it had all been worth it. I had been forced to give up the drums and leave the band, I had been bleeding and scared of miscarriage, I even had to leave Hamburg. But now, after all those months of uncertainty I was holding a tiny, healthy baby boy.

I'd never thought of my husband as particularly romantic, but he was always caring. Just after the baby was born he sent me a letter from the tour saying how much he missed and loved us. When little John was six weeks old I took him to Paris to meet his dad, and the moment he met us at Orly airport big John was overwhelmed. We stayed for a while in a flat in the center of the city, and I realized how child-friendly France could be. One day, for instance, we went into a shop with the carry cot. I was looking at clothes, and turned round to see the baby had gone. I was just about to panic when I noticed the shop assistant holding him and cooing, "Oh, he's so beautiful. You do your shopping and we'll look after him!"

That was very welcoming, but then we ended up in the middle of the May '68 riots. It was a period of civil unrest and demonstrations, with trade unions on general strike and students occupying universities, protesting against capitalism and American imperialism. Fearing revolution, the French president Charles de Gaulle secretly fled from France to West Germany on May 29. There were street battles with the police. I remember one morning walking with John and our son and suddenly we saw people running like mad down the street with the police chasing after them. "What's going on?" I cried. Paris police don't stand any messing, and the next minute they were firing smoke bombs at the protesters. We had to run into a nearby restaurant to get the baby out of the way. Those '68 riots were so frightening, a major turning point in the youth revolution that was shaking up old values and old certainties.

John's birth came at a time of change for all of us. Soon the Liverbirds were no more and we were separated. Having been a close unit for over five years we had formed a deep bond, but suddenly our lives were moving fast in different directions. It would be a long time before we found our way back together.

We had arrived in Hamburg in 1964, four excited young girls getting off the ferry and coming to the Star-Club for the first time. Our trip was originally meant to be six weeks and it ended up four years. So much happened during that time—playing with Chuck Berry, recording two albums, touring all over Europe to screaming fans, hanging out with Jimi Hendrix, drinking with Johnny Kidd and the Pirates, the Remo Four, the Big Six and all those fantastic musicians. We experimented with drugs and sex and fell in love. There was also Stephan's terrible accident, and the music changing, and everything changing. We were excited for the future, but we didn't know what the future held.

BOOK THREE: INDEPENDENCE

23. MARY

He's Somebody's Son

The Star-Club opened April 13, 1962, and closed its doors fourteen months after the Liverbirds ended—on New Year's Eve 1969, the very last day of the sixties. With that an era ended. It had been obvious that Manfred Weissleder was losing interest, so Frank and Achim ran the Star-Club for its last eighteen months because they wanted to rescue it and keep the venue on the right track. They sank into it all of their savings from Wonderland and the Rattles, hoping to make a million marks, but they lost out. They would go over to England to book groups, auditioning acts like Black Sabbath and Deep Purple, but nobody came to the gigs because the trend was now discotheques or sitting in the corner of a rock club smoking weed, not caring who was onstage. Frank was paying a venue hire of six thousand marks a month to Manfred, and even though he was our friend, when we had difficulty keeping up with the payments Manfred sent the bailiffs round to our apartment, putting stickers on the furniture. "That's business," he would say to Frank. Mrs. Dostal was appalled.

In 1970 the Star-Club was torn apart, refurbished and re-opened as a giant sex club featuring live intercourse onstage. It became a celebrity hangout: Liza Minnelli went there one night with her minders, finding the live sex hilarious. The times were definitely changing.

When the Liverbirds ended, I stayed in Germany. My life was there now—with Frank. Two years before that, when our friend Achim was nearing the end of National Service, he didn't want to go back to the Rattles, so he got in touch with Frank and suggested they start a band. They created Wonderland, a feast of adventurous psychedelic pop. They had a vivid light show and glittery jackets, and were produced by James Last (aka Hans Last), the German composer and big-band leader. Living in a palatial house on the outskirts of Hamburg, he was king of easy listening in the 1970s, selling millions of records worldwide. Songs of his like "Happy Heart" and "Games That Lovers Play" were covered by dozens of artists. With his goatee beard, wavy hair, and flamboyant suits, he would host extravagant all-night parties with an amazing buffet and endless champagne. He never stopped playing or making music—he would even record his own live albums at these parties.

Wonderland was only together for two years but they were very successful and toured constantly. Frank was the singer, business head, and main songwriter, and I would help him out with the fan club. They once did a six-week European tour with the Bee Gees, and Frank became good friends with Robin Gibb. When Frank met him forty years later in a studio, he was touched when Robin said that he enjoyed their time together and how much he liked his voice.

After the band split up, Frank and Achim produced other groups and worked together long term, promoting artists singing cool pop or rock with German lyrics. Until then German pop tended to be corny *schlager* music like the sentimental tunes performed by Sylvia's old flame Drafi Deutscher, so they changed that. It was a creative time— in those days, musicians used to spend weeks in the studios recording an album, and it was all paid for. Frank and Achim did really well out of these projects and the record company never said, "Do you think that two months in the studio is enough?" They worked like that for years.

Achim's wife, Erica, and I became good friends, and without her I think I might not have stayed in Germany. We socialized together when Wonderland was on tour, going for drinks or dancing at the Star-Club. I didn't speak much German at the time and Erica hardly spoke English, but we got on really well. She worked in a photo lab developing negatives, yet she was incredibly glamorous, looking like Brigitte Bardot. Frank's mother, Mrs. Dostal, knew how much I relied on my friendship with Erica, but she would say terrible things about me to other people, like she doesn't understand what Frank sees in me, that I'm not very pretty and a bit stupid. Even though her first name was Gertrude I always called her Mrs. Dostal. I saw her as being very German and strict. My mother or my parents would always say, "How are you?" but Mrs. Dostal would say, "How's business?" Strangely enough I found out a few years later that if any of her friends said nasty things about me she always defended me. I suppose she was just frightened of losing Frank.

My daughter Melanie was not planned—the contraceptive pill had just been invented, and like many women I was wary about taking it because there were rumors it would make you infertile. I was pleased when I became pregnant, however, because Frank wanted me to stay in Germany and was happy about having a baby, so even though we weren't married yet everything felt settled.

On June 4, 1969, I was nine months pregnant and Frank was going to the studio with James Last. I got up that morning to see a teeny-weeny bit of blood on my underpants. I alerted my gynecologist and he told Frank to take me to hospital. "This is just a little bit of blood," I told the nurse, expecting to go once they had checked me over.

"Oh no," said the doctor. "You're staying in here."

At that time men weren't allowed in the labor ward during birth, so Frank departed for the studio, leaving a phone number to call.

When my contractions started there was a girl in the next bed screaming her head off, and I thought, *Oh my God, I've got all that ahead of me.* Then all of a sudden I sat bolt upright, my body forcing me to push. As a strange noise came out of me the midwife looked and shouted, "Oh God, she's pressing!" She and the nurses dragged away the sheet and, a few minutes later, Melanie was born. A nurse phoned Frank in the studio for me, and they gave me the receiver.

"You won't believe this, Frank, but you got a baby daughter."

"What, already?"

He was shouting all over the studio. Frank had dropped me off at eleven o'clock that morning, and she was born at five. He was allowed to come in the maternity ward on his way home. I thought Melanie looked like a mini-Frank, and even now, you can tell she's his daughter. She wasn't very heavy, not quite seven pounds, and she was perfect.

We didn't get married until 1973 when Melanie was four because we were hippies, and hippies didn't get married. But shortly after Melanie's birth I told my parents that Frank and I were married—not because I was ashamed but I knew they would worry, thinking that he didn't really want me. "You don't know enough about each other," they would say. There was also a lurking fear about him being German, even though they knew he was partly Jewish. During the Second World War my father had to sit in a lifeboat watching his own brother go down with the ship that was torpedoed by Germans. Not only was it a German U-boat but the captain, Reinhard Suhren, was from Hamburg and lived there all his life. To my parents, the war was still raw.

When Frank first came over to Liverpool in 1967, for my twenty-first birthday, we didn't sleep together and he stayed in the spare room at my uncle's house. When he was walking down the road local kids would yell, "Heil, Hitler!" Though it took a while for Frank to be accepted in Liverpool, I knew my grandma loved Frank right away because when we visited her and Grandpa in their tiny, cramped apartment, she kept preparing food and putting it on the table.

"But, Mrs. Dunne, I've had enough, really," he said.

"Come on, put that down you. It'll do you good."

She thought he was too skinny. She would look at me and say, "He's somebody's son, isn't he?" Which meant, this German boy is still somebody's son, still worth loving.

My relationship with Mrs. Dostal changed after Melanie was born. I wasn't the favorite person in her life but I think the idea of having a grandchild helped, and she finally accepted me as the right partner for Frank. I saw her with different eyes after I watched the American TV series *Holocaust*, which was broadcast early in 1979 and drew an audience in West Germany of twenty million people, starting a huge cultural conversation about what happened during the war. I realized then that Mrs. Dostal had risked her life choosing to be with Frank's father. When she met Bedja Dostal in Berlin she was a Protestant, already married to somebody else, and had two children. Before the war Mrs. Dostal and her first husband ran a business together, selling jewelry. She had a flourishing jewelry stand in KaDeWe, the most famous department store in Berlin, when her husband joined the German army and was sent away to the Eastern front. After two years he went missing, and the authorities couldn't confirm if he was dead or alive.

Then she met Frank's father, Bedja, hiding out in Berlin. His parents were from Czechoslovakia and he told her right away that he was

Jewish, but she fell in love and stayed with him even though she knew she was risking her life. By 1944 the Nazis claimed that "Berlin was empty of the Jews," but it wasn't, of course. One of the few remaining Jews, Bedja assumed a false identity and came out of hiding. He and Mrs. Dostal knew they needed to escape from Berlin, so they packed everything together, sending her first two children, Barbara and Egon, to a relative somewhere in the country. By then Mrs. Dostal was pregnant with Frank, but that didn't stop her and Bedja from cycling 270 miles from Berlin to Flensburg near the Danish border. Once they were living there, Bedja helped many Jewish people escape over to Denmark.

In 1945, toward the end of the war, they moved to Hamburg and were beginning to feel safe and settled, with Bedja letting go of the false identity and reverting back to his original Dostal family name. Then all of a sudden, when she was heavily pregnant with Frank, Mrs. Dostal's first husband turned up. He took one look at her pregnant tummy and said: "You didn't know if I was alive. You thought I was dead, so I'm willing to carry on with our marriage and accept this child as my child."

"No, I don't love you anymore, I love him," Mrs. Dostal replied. But as a form of compensation she gave him the jewelry company and started another one.

Her first husband went on to become a multimillionaire but unfortunately Bedja, Frank's father, didn't live very long. The war ruined his heart. He was a gifted architect and had already bought some land in the center of Hamburg, with plans to build a multi-complex cinema. One morning in 1953, when Frank was eight and his younger brother Fred was two, Bedja stood up to go to the toilet and fell down dead. He left behind plans for many more buildings, none of which were realized. Mrs. Dostal completely fell apart and never got over it, which explained why she could be so tense and moody. In the meantime her first husband became very wealthy and helped financially with Frank and Fred, not just his own children.

The war had such a profound effect, creating long-lasting divisions not just between East and West Germany, but also between generations. In the late 1960s it seemed like the older generation wanted to forget about the war and move on, but young people needed to understand what happened.

The so-called '68 generation spawned the Red Army Faction, also known as the Baader-Meinhof Gang—a far-left urban guerrilla group led by Andreas Baader and Ulrike Meinhof that did terrible things like kidnapping politicians and even killing them. People who died included industrialist and former SS member Hanns Martin Schleyer, and the head of Dresdner Bank Jürgen Ponto. Starting with student riots in 1968, the movement grew stronger and stronger throughout the 1970s. Young people began to hate their parents for not taking responsibility for their actions during the Holocaust. One of the sayings that went around was, "According to what our parents say there was Hitler and just one other person in the Nazi party, because nobody else was there."

The Nazis got away with a lot, even after the war. Frank's grandmother and auntie were gassed to death in Sachsenhausen concentration camp. All the relatives on his father's side perished, so for Frank it was a very real thing having to deal with the past, and he felt it was important that it wasn't forgotten. One of the worst aspects of the Nuremberg war trials were Holocaust survivors on the witness stand recognizing judges as former Nazis. They'd say, "That judge, I saw him on the train platform saying 'you go right, you go left,'" ordering people to death. That is why the '68 generation emerged and why the Red Army Faction targeted campaigns against ex-Nazis who were still in power.

It is terrible that people were kidnapped and killed, but after this time of turmoil you could feel there was a strong pacifist movement and new hope for the future. Now that I'm older I can see what the country achieved. Although cities like Hamburg, Berlin, and Hanover were nearly flattened, Germany was very good at reconstruction. I'd see buildings that had gone up on massive bombsites and think, *How did they manage to do that? How did they rebuild so quickly?* The Germans are expert architects and engineers.

The '68 generation wanted to do everything in opposition to how their parents had done, bringing up children in a way that was free from strict rules. Our daughter Melanie was a very strong-willed child, but it was mainly our own fault because we wanted to encourage her to make her own decisions. The theory came from Summerhill School in the UK, where the founder, Alexander Sutherland Neill, believed that the school should be made to fit the child and not the other way around. That was different from the punitive world where children like me were caned for getting spellings wrong. This sort of education meant that children could have really good ideas and imaginative play. So rather than sending our kids to normal kindergarten, we joined an experimental group of parents who organized themselves, taking it in turns to look after eighteen wild little children who were allowed to do anything they wanted. Because he was more like a kid himself the children loved Frank, and his day became their favorite day.

Usually the children got on well together, and if one was getting picked on Melanie always protected them. I disagreed with the idea that if one child was a rowdy menace battering other children, you couldn't stop them because others had to learn to be strong. On the days we worked we wrote a report that would be discussed at a weekly parents' meeting. We had a girl called Christina who wouldn't have harmed a fly, but one little boy hated her so much he pulled her hair until her scalp was red raw. I told him off, saying, "Stop that now, that's enough, you shouldn't pull hair." At the parents' meeting I was asked, "Why did you do that, Mary? Why did you say that?" I replied, "You prefer to save it till he is grown up then?"

Our kids started going to normal school when they were six, and when they refused to do homework we realized that something had gone wrong. It must have been difficult for the children to adjust and follow rules when before there had been none. We completely changed our minds about the Summerhill-style education by the time our son Benny was born in 1974, because we saw that it just wasn't working. Friends would phone to invite us to a party and they'd say, "But can you do us a favor, can you leave Melanie at home?"

I can understand how the Nazi nightmare influenced the younger generation of German parents and how they turned away from authoritative, repressive education and felt the need to give their children more freedom and autonomy. But in many cases this lack of discipline went too much the other way. Many of our kids said school life was hard for them because they suddenly had to accept somebody being in charge. One of the mothers from the kindergarten became a successful TV producer, and when the children were eighteen she made a documentary about their experience. When they were interviewed, not one of those children said they would rear their kids the same way—even the ones that had been the rowdiest. They came to the conclusion that you need to draw boundaries somewhere.

Benny was the opposite in every way to Melanie, including his birth. I was twenty-seven and from day one had a terrible pregnancy, with dizziness and weight gain. I was massive, beyond massive, whereas when I was pregnant with Melanie I had a neat little bump. I assumed that with the second baby it was going to be an even easier birth than the first. Frank had started earning good money and we thought, "Well, let's have a private hospital this time." Melanie was born in a normal hospital, and that was perfect. The private one looked gorgeous—but they didn't have the expertise.

I was two weeks overdue and because we didn't have scans in those days the doctors thought it was a big baby. I was given too much anesthetic so it took a long time for me to wake up, and in the meantime Frank said there were bells going and people running everywhere. Benny was blue, weighing only five pounds; he looked like he was starving. I had an emergency Cesarean and we both nearly died. It was so frightening. The clinic photographed him few hours after he was born and I put the picture in our photo book. Years later Frank's mother found this photograph and said to me, "Look at this, Mary."

I couldn't see what she was looking at.

"This must be one of your relatives from Liverpool, but I wish you had thrown it away."

It was Benny. Because he didn't look good she reasoned that it couldn't have been one of her relatives; it had to be somebody from Liverpool. That was a stark reminder to me of the difference in the standard of living between Liverpool and Hamburg. My asthma, which had been so bad when I was a child, alleviated when I moved to Germany. And every time I went back when my children were young I'd get a bad cold on my chest.

Despite his traumatic birth, Benny was the most perfect baby. He slept well and, unlike Melanie, we had to wake him up. We'd give him something to drink and then he would go back to sleep again. Even when he was eighteen months old and just starting to talk, he would say, "I'm tired, can you take me to bed?" With Melanie, you'd have to beg her to go to bed.

But Melanie changed the day Benny was born: she became the perfect daughter and the perfect sister. She was just so happy to have a brother, sitting and playing with him for hours and hours.

24. MARY

Val Drives the Nürburgring

It's a strange irony that although it was a car accident that left Stephan paralyzed, he and Val had a garage full of cars. And one of their main hobbies was driving in the Nürburgring, on the German Grand Prix racing track. Val would strap Stephan into the front seat and drive at huge speeds—it was dangerous, but they entered rallies and she won prizes. They had dozens of expensive cars, and every time they went somewhere they liked to change the car. I remember one day they drove a bright yellow E-type Jaguar, and the next day she picked me up in a brand-new BMW, which had one of the first mobile phones. Stephan rang her on the phone and I heard her say, "You're crazy. Oh my God, Stephan, no!"

She replaced the handset and said, "He's just bought me a Ferrari."

In their own way, Val and Stephan had a good time because they had no financial troubles. Once he learned to accept the fact that she had to feed him in front of other people, they started going to lavish restaurants. They arranged their lives in a way that would give them something to look forward to. Munich in the 1970s was the disco center of Germany, and Stephan still wanted to be flamboyant and super sharp. Val would ring ahead, saying, "We're coming tonight and we want to book a table for four." She would push Stephan in the wheelchair to a VIP area of the club, where there would be a table with caviar and champagne. They went to the Blow Up Club, with go-go girls and psychedelic projections, and the P1 in the Englischer Garten, with acres of floor space and a 6,500-square-foot terrace. There was also the Yellow Submarine, a nightclub in a gigantic pool where you could look through portholes to see giant tortoises and thirty live sharks.

The city was a dynamic place—visitors came from all over the world for the 1972 Olympic Games. And at Musicland Studios near Arabellapark, the Rolling Stones recorded their album *Black and Blue*, and Giorgio Moroder created futurist electronic dance music with Donna Summer. Munich was also the center of the sexual revolution, with nudists and naked hippies cavorting in the Englischer Garten.

Everybody was happy to see Stephan because he and Val spent a fortune. His father, Herr Hausner, was such a successful man in Triumph he had both sons insured, and after the accident there was a large payout. Val and Stephan's flat was in Grünwald, near to his parents, in one of the wealthiest municipalities in Germany. It was split level over two floors, and the ground floor matched the basement, with identical windows and luxury furniture, right down to the white leather sofas, big TVs, and colorful paisley bedspreads. If it weren't for the stairs, you could mistakenly think you were in the same room.

They lived alone on the ground floor, and those were the days when Stephan wouldn't let anybody else but Val take care of him. Frank and I stayed for a week in the basement with Melanie when she was a baby, enjoying rooms with French windows that looked out onto a terrace and a lush, green garden. We went with them to his favorite restaurant in the Jahreszeiten (Four Seasons), the most expensive hotel in Munich. It had fantastic Chinese and Japanese food and luckily enough was on the ground floor, so Stephan had his own special table. He was made a fuss of whenever he went, probably because his family was so well known in the city. After the accident, Hausner family friends made clear how shocked they were that something like that could happen to someone like him.

At first Stephan had a lot of trouble accepting what had happened. He and Val met often with a close circle of friends and he was nice to them. But with strangers, he became very reserved. He developed a strange sense of humor, joking about himself in a self-deprecating way. He never talked about how much he missed dancing. He'd say, "I've just been for a dance" or "I think I'll just sit in this chair all day today." He and Val coped by finding ways to amuse themselves. One of her hobbies was to take photographs of me in strange positions or on the toilet—that was part of her dry sense of humor.

One night in particular stands out for me: it was the night of the moon landing in 1969. Melanie was about four weeks old, tucked up in the cot in the basement, and we were staying there overnight so that we could have a few drinks. Stephan said to Val, "Put four glasses out, let's have some Campari." As she went to the cupboard to get a bottle Frank said, "Stephan, I don't drink." Every now and then he might have had a cognac, but he was not a big drinker.

"Just one shot."

Out of politeness we drank the shots. Then Val and Stephan sat looking at us.

"How d'you feel?" he asked Frank.

"It's done nothing for me."

"It's supposed to make you randy!"

He and Val enjoyed doing tricks like that with people, and sometimes when we stayed the night they made sure we could hear them having sex. Val told me later that they found ways to satisfy each other, and for a while after the accident they did have the opportunity of having a baby, but ultimately decided against it. His manhood functioned for a few years, but not forever, and that's when he wanted to be the boss in other ways. Val confided in Stephan that she was interested in women as well, and later on when a nurse was employed to help out with his care he suggested that she could be sexual with her and he'd watch. Val told me they didn't do it, but I wouldn't be surprised if they did.

She and Stephan would come to Hamburg and stay in the most expensive hotels, places like the Atlantic on the shores of Lake Alster, not the grungy old Pacific. Because they were so thankful that Stephan was looked after by Val, his parents would treat them for dinner or take them on skiing holidays to St. Moritz, though of course he could do nothing there and Val didn't ski either.

Herr Hausner an exuberant person: he was warm toward Val and appreciated the help she gave Stephan. Although he was incredibly successful as a self-made millionaire, he was taking pills to keep him going and that ruined his heart, sadly leading to a fatal heart attack in the mid-1970s. According to Stephan, his father was taking twenty Captagon a day. Originally marketed for the diet market, it could easily be misused as an addictive amphetamine. Herr Hausner was under a lot of pressure at work, and trying to come to terms with the fact that his youngest son was permanently disabled with an uncertain future. After her husband died, we detected a hardening in Frau Hausner's attitude, and she became cold toward Val. Val worried that she was being seen as a gold digger. That couldn't have been further from the truth—if Val wanted an easy life she would not have chosen to be a full-time carer.

Stephan liked the special treatment, and he needed it because provisions for people with disabilities in the 1970s were pretty dire. Restaurants rarely had disabled toilets, so if they went somewhere new he'd make sure he didn't need to go or he would wear a nappy. Val had to do everything, which was very awkward for her because Stephan was so tall. He lost a lot of weight at first, but like a lot of wheelchair users he developed a big stomach and that was very heavy for her. He couldn't even clean his own teeth, so she had to wash him completely and feed him. I know how proud he was when after many years he learned how to hold a wineglass. But that was about it.

Although it's a waste of time, we try to imagine what might have become of them if the accident hadn't happened. We all said that Stephan wouldn't have stayed with Val. He had big plans. If things had been different he might have fulfilled his dream of being a fashion designer, achieving a vision like Karl Lagerfeld. He was the one who took us to the tailor in Munich where all the rich people went, and when we first went to his fantastic house in Munich he already had pinned to the wall all his fashion illustrations, executed with real flair. To be paralyzed would have been terrible for anyone, but for someone who imagined a future so bold, it must have been even harder.

25. SYLVIA

Which Side Do You Dress, Sir?

After those heady days at the Star-Club it was difficult settling down and making a living as a young family. John didn't last long with the Krew, the band he had been touring with when little John was born. They played a fiery multicultural festival at Santa Margherita Ligure near Genoa that summer. A drunk and obnoxious Iain Campbell joined the band and John left, considering the Krew finished. Late in 1968 he went on a tour of the Caribbean with Glasgow beat pop group O'Hara's Playboys, but then he wanted more freedom, and opted for freelance session work, so we could travel.

After a stint in Scotland with John's parents we made London our base so he could get easy session work, and we found a comfy maisonette in Seven Sisters, Tottenham. One day we were walking with the pram in the West End along Bond Street when we saw Georgie Fame, the chirpy R&B jazz musician who had a number-one hit in 1964 with the Latin soul classic "Yeh Yeh." A favorite at the Star-Club, he was always working with different musicians and had a good network of contacts. He jumped out of a van and shouted to John, "Hey, Wiggy Wiggy, what you doing here?"

"We've just come to London."

"Well, get in touch with Alan Price because he wants to go solo and needs someone to take his place."

The former keyboardist with the Animals had been gigging for a while with his band the Alan Price Set, but now that he was leaving the lead singer had taken over and rechristened it the Paul Williams Set. John was much in demand at that point. "If you play keyboards I'll give you a retainer for three months," said Price, who felt guilty about leaving and wanted to keep the band together.

Three months lengthened into a year while John was off touring with the Paul Williams Set. Most of the time I was on my own in Tottenham, isolated with the baby, because John was gigging so much. I found Londoners aloof and unfriendly and became so lonely, so I just blurted out to him one night, "It's horrible here for me."

We left for the north, renting a little two-up two-down in Kirk Road, Liverpool, and John found a job at the Landfall, a glamorous floating nightclub moored in Salthouse Dock. Originally a tank-landing craft from the 1944 D-Day landings, in the late sixties it was transformed into a club—people would clamber on board and walk through a hatch down to a bar and an underlit disco dancefloor. It was a fantastic venue, but all kinds of wild parties would happen on that boat. As my mother used to say, "I bet the men all got sore knees the next morning," because people were canoodling on the carpets. John used to stay there after work, drinking late and stumbling back in the early hours. One night I was lying there, sleepless, looking at the clock, and when it got to four in the morning I decided I'd had enough, so I rang the Landfall. When John came to the phone I said, "What are you doing?"

"I'm having a drink with the lads, we have a lock-in."

"Look, if you don't come home now don't come home at all."

Of course he didn't come home, and he stayed out till noon the next day. I told John's father, and Bobby had strong words with him, and after that standoff John would come home a bit earlier. John wasn't a womanizer—if I found out there was anything to do with a woman our relationship would have been over—but he just loved to have a drink with the lads.

John then got offered a job with the Top Rank Suite working in a big band, and in February 1971, when little John was three years old, something amazing happened. Because we had been moving around so much I had temporarily lost contact with the other Liverbirds. I missed them terribly, but I was so busy as a young mother. Then, that night in 1971, John came home from Top Rank and said that he had bumped into Pam.

"God, I didn't know you were here!" she'd exclaimed to him. "D'you think Sylvia would be interested in doing a Liverbirds gig for a reunion event?"

"I'm sure she would."

When John came home and told me, I was delighted. I didn't know that Pam had moved back to Liverpool after the band split up, and was looking forward to seeing her again.

Our friend Allan Williams, the original booking agent for the Beatles, was promoting an event at the Rialto called the Mersey Beat Reunion, with the Merseybeats headlining. "I've done it purely for nostalgic reasons," Williams told the *Daily Mirror*. "Liverpool's dead now, it's like a cemetery. We had 400 groups. Now it's down to 20… but there's a big rock 'n' roll revival." He had asked Pam to perform, so once she knew I was in town she thought it would be great for us to do an impromptu set.

Mary and Val couldn't make it over from Germany, so John took Val's place, playing keyboards instead of guitar, and former Star-Club singer Gaynor Lea was on bass. On the day of the event I brought little John to the Rialto, where the bands were sound-checking and doing rehearsals. It was fantastic to see Pam, looking so cool with her long blond hair, black leather jacket, and green Gretsch guitar. She was still the big diva living for her music; nothing could stop her. I had grown my hair long too, with a center parting, and wore a gray pinstriped jacket. The fashions may have changed but our love of the music was the same. We talked about our past adventures playing rock 'n' roll and touring Europe and agreed, God, we wish we had it back again. It was the first time Pam met little John and she made a big fuss of him. She always loved playing with children.

A journalist from the *Daily Mirror* interviewed us and took our photo. "I'd go back to those days tomorrow," Pam told him. "We were on £100 a week each, and we spent it. Everything we saw, we bought." A hundred pounds a week in 1964 would be the equivalent of £2,000 now. Maybe she was thinking nostalgically about the cream Cadillac she bought on a whim at the Berlin airbase, the Cadillac that took us to the beach on hot summer afternoons before a night playing at the Star-Club. She sold that when she moved back to England. The funny thing was, the article made it sound like we were old codgers, and we were only in our late twenties!

The event started later that afternoon, and my sister Jean looked after little John while we rehearsed. I was frightened about going back onstage, but it was only a few years since we'd been performing, so when we played our set my parts came naturally. Many musicians and all the old Merseybeat fans turned up so the audience was afire, singing along and dancing. The diva in me lapped up the attention.

"Let's keep in touch now," Pam said when we were hugging good-bye after the gig.

"Yes, of course!" I enthused.

But, despite that wish, we wouldn't see each other again for over ten years. It was a time when we were preoccupied with our own lives. Now with smartphones you can get messages to people instantly, but then it was difficult and expensive to phone on a landline. If we'd been able to do Zoom calls and WhatsApp, the Liverbirds would have been chatting with each other all the time.

Even though the Mersey Beat Reunion was a high point, times were hard and we weren't really happy in Liverpool. I never bothered with the Cavern or going into the town; we had moved on, and were trying to survive as a family. Tony Jackson, former lead singer with the Searchers, offered John a job with his Tony Jackson Group—good money playing in the Bahamas. John didn't have any other work at the time so he said, "What do you think?"

"Tour with Tony for a month or two, and see how it goes."

So he did. But when that finished he came back and said, "That's it. I'm not going on the road again. I've just missed you and baby John so much."

John was offered a job in Blackpool opening the 007 Club, an upmarket nightclub created by Brian London, the heavyweight boxer. At that time Blackpool was known as the Las Vegas of the north, a seaside resort town on the Irish Sea coast, which attracted seventeen million visitors a year, with variety shows, casinos, beauty contests, drag acts, and comedians, and the 007 Club was the hottest ticket. Ground-floor booths surrounded a dancefloor that resembled a boxing ring, with ropes as partitions, and photographs of the world's boxing elite adorned the walls. Downstairs in the Gold Room was a VIP area, which became popular with First Division footballers, particularly Manchester United star striker George Best. John teamed up with a drummer as Two's Company, and the night the club opened George Best joined them on drums to signal the start of the party. The atmosphere was fantastic, partly because Brian London was such a great host, known for his dry wit. A former British heavyweight champion, London challenged twenty-four-year-old Muhammad Ali for the world heavyweight title in 1966 and was knocked out in three rounds. London used to say he thought at the start he might catch Ali with a good punch. He said, "But after the first round I knew I had no fucking chance."

It was a good time to be in Blackpool. I was pregnant with our second son, and there was a lot of work on offer. Because he was such a great backing musician John was poached from the 007 by the Brunswick Club, which was one of the biggest working men's clubs in the north. Working men's clubs are a British institution, created as co-operatives in nineteenth-century industrial areas, particularly the north, midlands, Scotland, and north Wales. They were often major venues with a cheap bar, snooker tables, food, and a large stage for live music and comedy—clubs like the Brunswick, right near the seafront and the Central Pier, would attract coachloads of people and big-name stars like the Nolan Sisters. John was in his element, helping to book bands and acting as musical director for artists.

He was much in demand, but working long hours, so he couldn't be there for the arrival of our second son, Steven, who was born in Blackpool on October 4, 1971. Like baby John, he was another difficult job as well. I was in hospital, walking up and down the ward telling the nurses I was in labor, but they didn't believe me.

"You're not in labor," they kept saying.

"I want to push and the pain is terrible."

"But your waters haven't broken."

"I'm in labor. I know." A lady in the next bed said to me, "I know what you're going through, love. You've got what they call back pain labor."

I called out, "I'm going to have this baby now!" and the nurses were trying to fob me off, insisting, "Come on, Mrs. Wiggins, we'll give you something to calm you because you're a bit distressed." When I got onto the bed, suddenly needing to push, the midwife gasped, "Oh my God!"

Steven was delivered right away. Afterward, the nurses had the audacity to write a report and ask me, "Mrs. Wiggins, can you tell us—when did your pains first start?"

"I'm sorry. Sod off. You didn't believe me? I'm not telling you anything for your notes. Put whatever you like."

I was so angry with them but I couldn't remain angry for long, especially when three-year-old John saw his baby brother for the first time. His first comment was, "I can't play football with him!" But later of course they did, and became fervent Liverpool supporters for life.

During the day John could look after the boys, so I got a job in Burton, the high street tailor that specialized in made-to-measure suits. I missed being in a band but that life was incompatible with being a mum—in the 1960s and '70s wives were expected to stay at home with the children. At Burton the old fellas would come in to be measured for a suit, but when they saw me, a female assistant, they'd say in a panic, "You're not doing it!" We used to have a big stick to measure the size of their leg, and we'd say, "Which side do you dress, sir?" Then I'd get the cocky young ones going, "Come on, measure me!" I bought all John's clothes from Burton's. Every time they had a big sale I would buy up cool tailored suits, and shirts for a pound. People used to say to me, "God, your John is always well dressed, the best-dressed musician I've ever seen."

We didn't have much money then so sometimes we had to make do and mend. John frequently used his right foot on the pedals when playing the organ so there was always a hole in his right shoe. We couldn't afford to keep buying new shoes, so we cut out a piece of cardboard and created a makeshift insole. That worked fine until it rained and his feet would squelch.

I was working at Burton's when the news came that John's father, Bobby, had died. His parents were due to come for a visit, and just before they set off Bobby had a massive heart attack. John was at home with the children when the police knocked at the door, and they later came to Burton's to tell me. The police gave me a lift home from the shop and then I never went back. Bobby was so eccentric, with his fart cushions and his Hawaiian guitar, but he was welcoming and loving, and I'll always remember how much he'd admired my Celtic jumper.

I wanted to work again, because I got restless and didn't like being at home all the time, so I found a job at Gus Demmy's bookmakers. I also looked at taking on holiday flats, because Blackpool was a city full of old boardinghouses. For many years factory workers would take their holidays there en masse and the city was very popular with Scots, so in summer it seemed as if the whole of Glasgow was on the seven-mile Pleasure Beach. Soon after I started work at the betting office we were talking to a friend who was an estate agent and he said, "I've got this house that's standing and doing nothing. It's in a terrible state but I'll give you the keys to check it out."

John and I talked it over later. I told him, "We could be making money turning the house into holiday apartments."

"OK, let's have a look."

So we looked and the house was terrible—a crumbling old Victorian three-story terrace on the North Shore, but we could see its potential.

Once we bought the house we had to knock out the chimney breast. There was a lot of brickwork in those Victorian houses—we got an estimate for how much it would be to remove one, and after he had done it the builder said, "God, if I would have known there were that many bricks I would never have done it!" We ended up with rubble all round our feet, and needed to raise more money to finish the conversion. One of the downstairs tenants had left a little electric hob covered in grease and maggots and had nailed his wallpaper to the wall instead of using paste; that room needed a lot of work.

John had a group of friends in Glasgow who would come to Blackpool to see him at the club, and sometimes there would be as many as thirteen mates sleeping on the floor. One guy was in charge of the advertising at the Scottish *Daily Mail*, so he would advertise our holiday flats for nothing. Suddenly we started getting calls. The telephone was in the hallway, and we'd be standing there with rubble on the floors saying, "Yes, the flats are lovely, all modern with quilts, and the kitchen is brand-new. If you just send a deposit that will secure it." I would take the name and address, we'd wait for the postal order to come through the letterbox, and then we would buy more things with which to do the flats up. It was a race against time to get them ready. When the first people arrived for our first summer season, John was still screwing a handle on one of the cupboards. We lived on the ground floor and after a while we were making a regular living from the apartments, but it was a lot of work maintaining and keeping them clean.

At one time we had four jobs between us, with John playing the Central Working Men's Club at night and then a strip club after hours, while I worked at Morgan Stanley's and we did the holiday flats as well. It was like my mum with all her different jobs, when she was steaming clothes in a laundry, working at Appleby Flour Mill, driving a milk float, or cleaning telephone boxes. I have endless admiration for her: working and bringing up small children at the same time is so exhausting. When John came back from the club I'd take the kids to nursery school and let him have a lie-in. Then he would pick them up and have the meal ready when I came home, but he'd have all the pans out and make a mess of the kitchen. He would go off to work for his night shift and I'd clean up, put the kids to bed, and sometimes be ironing at two o'clock in the morning. I thought, *There has to be an easier way to earn a living.* I missed music all the time—it was a wrench going from being in the limelight to being the little housewife trying to swing jobs, making money for the family and keeping a home together. But I couldn't go to the clubs with John because the kids were too little and my parents were over an hour away. It would have been difficult for me to be a touring musician as a mum with young children. John and I would have been in separate bands and we didn't want to do that.

Sometimes John would get a taxi home from Central Working Men's Club. One day a taxi driver said, "You'd make a fortune in Benidorm. Me and the wife go to Spain every year and there's nothing like what you do here."

The moment John got home he said, "Do you fancy it?"

Well, yes. Because I was getting itchy feet again.

26. MARY

Pam Sings for the Shah

When she returned to Liverpool after the band finished Pam was still a big partygoer. She revitalized her school friendships and was always ready to dance, drink, and play music. She lived her life pretty fast, coming home at three in the morning and then going to work at nine, burning the candle at both ends. She worked in Lewis's department store before getting a job as a receptionist for the British School of Motoring shop, working on her own, taking bookings in a small office in town. Sometimes Pam was so tired from the night before she'd be nodding off on the bus. When she got to work she would open the shop, lock the door, clamber onto a shelf under the counter and fall asleep for an hour. It was an absolute scream.

Pam also rekindled her relationship with Lee Curtis in Liverpool. For a short while he supposedly separated from his wife and came to live in the Birch family home for six months. A very handsome man, he responded well to preening and pampering and Pam loved styling his hair. He made himself at home, sometimes asking Pam's eleven-year-old sister Glynne to sit next to him on the couch with a nail file and file his nails. "As a young girl I thought it was so exciting to do this," she says. "In retrospect, I can see why my dad got a bit irritated." She would ease down his cuticles before cleaning, polishing and buffing his nails. Meanwhile Pam would press his trousers with a perfect crease. He was very fastidious and more than a little vain, so when he started getting a little bald patch that was well back-combed over.

Pam enjoyed this phase in their relationship. If she paid me a visit she used to phone Lee up when she flew back from Germany, saying, "Come and get me from the airport." You could have walked to Speke airport from their house, but she liked to be in charge.

Pam's mother, Alma, thought Lee was wonderful, but there was friction between him and Mr. Birch, who mistrusted Lee and thought Pam deserved better. But she was smitten, saying that he was "just everything." In the early stages of their relationship Lee showed a lot of admiration for her musical talent, and that was part of the initial attraction.

Her parents were old-fashioned so Lee was assigned to the spare room while Pam and her sister shared a bedroom. "But I'm fairly sure she didn't stay in the bed that often," recalls Glynne. Mr. Birch tried to warn Pam, but she refused to listen, following her own way. However, it helped her to know that he supported her, and although they fought there was a lot of love between father and daughter.

Lee's family, the Flannerys, were reasonably well known in Liverpool. Pam's father had a job in the Ford car factory and one day at work a man said: "Do you know that your daughter is ruining my sister's marriage?"

"What do you mean? Him and his wife have been separated three years."

"But not as far as his wife knows."

Mr. Birch went home and said to Lee: "Get your things and get out of my house."

*   *   *

Lee wasn't allowed back. People knew that he had a wife and children and that because of their Catholic faith there was no question of divorce. Though not particularly religious, Lee was superstitious about God's reckoning in the afterlife. Pam had heated discussions with her dad, who kept saying: "Lee will never leave his wife," and she would retort, "Yes he will, he loves me. He's gonna stay with me." The off-on relationship continued for a while, and she would have secret contact with him right up until the mid-1970s. Glynne remembers one weekend, when their parents were away, she and Pam had a party and Lee turned up. "She was just immediately with him. It was like he'd never been away." Pam was so independent with all the other men in her life, but not with Lee; maybe because she thought he was the pinnacle. He had everything—the music, the looks, and the attitude—and seemed to be a perfect match.

Lee was like two separate people, with different handwriting for each persona. Peter Flannery was his real name, and Lee Curtis a stage moniker. Once Pam found a letter Lee had written to his wife, and it was in completely different handwriting. It was rumored there was instability and mental problems in the family, and Lee even sang about it onstage with the calypso song "Shame and Scandal in the Family!" When Trinidadian singer Sir Lancelot sang the song in the 1940s it was tongue-in-cheek, but for Lee the family situation made his rendition much more poignant.

Pam drifted for a while, moving from her job at the British School of Motoring to work as a cashier in a garage—any job that would keep her going—until one day she answered an advert for a job singing with a cabaret group in Iran. She went down to London and auditioned, and she got the job, singing for three months with the group in a hotel in the capital, Tehran. When Pam was there the Shah, Mohammad Reza Pahlavi, was still in power—the last Shah of the Imperial State of Iran before its overthrow in the revolution of 1979. The country had been westernized during the 1960s and '70s, with a degree of enfranchisement of women.

Pam seemed to go down well there. In the Liverbirds she never liked showing her legs, but in Iran she let her hair down and wore false eyelashes and short, low-cut dresses. That's the way the group wanted her to be, and she went along with it. She told me that men constantly followed her round the streets in Tehran because, even in those days, Iranian women didn't walk around with such freedom. She mixed a lot with Americans who were presumably in the oil business, and they bought her all sorts of expensive jewelry—gold bracelets, necklaces, and rings. She sang rock 'n' roll pop, and one night even performed for the Shah. Pam had an affair with a musician, and indulged in other liaisons—it didn't bother her if somebody was married or not. If she wanted them, she'd have them, and wives or girlfriends wouldn't confront her, even if they suspected. Most people were too frightened or had too much respect for her to try and make a show of it.

When the Iran job finished Pam returned looking completely different, with long, glamorous blond hair and dramatic eyelashes. Unfortunately, even though she loved the jewelry she'd been given, she pawned some of it for Lee. By then he had a big family to take care of, and she still believed that he would leave his wife. She didn't want to admit to herself that she had made a mistake over so many years, because they were important years for Pam. She could have easily met somebody else and her life would have been completely different, even though it might have been a relationship that didn't last forever, because she had such a strong personality. Who knows, she might have had children and she might have found a way of using her musical talent. That she didn't write more songs is just unbelievable.

*   *   *

When Frank and I got married in 1973, Pam came over to Hamburg to be my maid of honor. While she was there, she realized how much she missed Germany. It was partly nostalgia for the Star-Club days, but also she was disillusioned about her relationship with Lee and needed to escape. By then she and Lee had been off–on lovers for nine years and it was finally dawning on her that he would never leave his wife. She decided to return to Hamburg, and that marked a final break with Lee. She never had a steady relationship after that.

Frank found her a job working for WEA, Warner Records in Hamburg, and she came to stay with us until she found somewhere to live. She was hoping to lead a glamorous life as a PR, accompanying actors and musicians to swanky events, but they put her in the office doing admin work, sorting out photographs and writing press releases. It was about ten minutes away from where we lived but she used to get a taxi to work every morning; otherwise she would have been late. I think she spent more money on taxis than she was earning. She didn't last long there. Even though WEA was based in a beautiful old villa by the lake, she couldn't get used to a nine-to-five job.

Gradually, Pam stopped working at the record company and began working in a pub called Schröder, just around the corner from where we lived. It was a converted shop with two wide rooms that was very popular with students, serving a really good all-day breakfast. She drew a crowd there, and became a local star personality. My daughter Melanie adored Pam. The people who lived in the apartment before us had turned one of the smallest rooms into a dressing room, so we put a bed in there for Pam. She made it a magical place, draping silk and tasseled scarves over the wardrobes and ornate mirrors.

Pam pinned photographs all over the wall of film stars that she adored, like Katharine Hepburn, James Dean, and Marilyn Monroe. And Melanie, who was about four or five at the time, loved going into the room, sitting there and playing with the big gold bracelets and necklaces that had come back from Iran. Pam would talk to her about the film stars as though she knew them. Katharine Hepburn, in particular, was her favorite Hollywood idol. She had loved her since she was a girl, watching old black-and-white movies on the family TV, entranced by Hepburn's feisty role opposite Humphrey Bogart in *The African Queen*, and the comic romance between her and Spencer Tracy's character Adam in *Adam's Rib*. Pam said that Hepburn had such class.

Pam lived with us for about four months before she moved in with Karin and Sebastian, the people who owned the Schröder pub. After a stint working in the bar she started DJ-ing in a popular place called Pick 'n' Pack, which had a well-sprung disco floor. It wasn't like the fancy discos in Munich with all the flashing lights, but you could dance there, and DJ Pam from the Liverbirds played a good rock funk and soul set. At the same time she joined a German band called Full of Juice and for about a year hung out with musicians we had known from the Star-Club.

After she began DJ-ing was when Pam got into cocaine. She never really hid anything; she wasn't ashamed of what she did. The people she became friendly with were all into it as well, so it wasn't a secret. She said, "I have to take a bit of coke to be able to stay awake longer."

27. MARY

Yes Sir, I Can Boogie

One of Frank's luckiest moments was in 1977, writing the lyrics to a song for a little-known Spanish act, two flamenco dancers from the Canary Islands called Baccara.

Frank would always only write lyrics in bed. That was convenient because the phone rang at ten o'clock one night and it was Frank's songwriting partner Rolf Soja.

"I've got these two girls here from Spain. Somebody saw them dancing in a hotel and said you've got to bring them over and take them into the studio," said Soja. He had a song he wanted to record with them and needed lyrics by ten o'clock the following morning.

"Oh my God, that doesn't give me much time."

Frank grimaced, thought for a minute, and then agreed.

Soja lived twenty kilometers from Hamburg so it took half an hour for him to drive to our apartment with the cassette. By then we had moved out of Frank's mother's place into our own apartment in the Isestrasse. Frank ran down four floors to collect it—we had no lift—and then back up before he got into bed, put the cassette on the tape recorder, and, while I was in the bathroom, listened to the song.

First of all he'd play the whole song and write imaginary lyrics to go with the tune. As he was lying there writing, every now and then he would say, "What do you think about this line, Mary?"

In the middle of the night, while I was lying next to him dozing, he was still scribbling away.

"How you're doing?" I murmured.

"I'm stuck…I've written the opening lines but I'm stuck with the second verse."

"Well, what did you write before that?"

He turned on the tape recorder and played back: "*Mister/Your eyes are full of hesitation/Sure makes me wonder/If you know what you're looking for.*"

"OK, I'll think about that."

Soja's music had inspired Frank to think about a little exchange in a club with the girl talking to a guy who fancies her, saying she needs to hear a special song before she feels like dancing. It made me think about the scenario, and how the woman was flirting with the man. She was pretty and she had the power.

"*Baby, I want to keep my reputation/I'm a sensation/You try me once you'll beg for more.*"

So I gave him two little lines for us—which I often did, by the way—and he said to me, "Ten percent." I often got more than that. I wrote poetry when I was younger, so that's why I could help him with lyrics. Smiling to myself, I drifted off to sleep.

Next morning he woke up at nine o'clock and I said, "Did you finish the lyrics?"

"Yeah. I won't do that again. Next time he wants lyrics at short notice I'll tell him to find somebody else."

Once Soja collected the lyrics he recorded with Baccara right away, and they returned to the hotel in Fuerteventura where they were working at the time. Mayte Mateos and Maria Mendiola were dancers, not even proper singers, but that somehow added to their spontaneous charm.

Soja then phoned Frank.

"Do you want to come over? I've already mixed it."

We drove round to Soja's house in the countryside just outside Hamburg, and he played the song—"Yes Sir, I Can Boogie"—over these towering speakers. Everything was big in those days. We listened, nodding our heads and tapping our feet. Afterward as we walked back to the car, I said to Frank, "I think that could be massive."

"Come off it."

"I think it'll even be a hit in England."

"Mary, come off it."

It all turned out right, didn't it?

A lot of people think this song is stupid until they sit down and study it line for line. Great songwriting appears simple, but there's something profound in the lyrics, words that capture a moment without being clichéd. The sparkling strings and mid-tempo Eurodisco beat, combined with the way the girls sang so sweetly in halting English—you could see the whole scene playing out, deceptively simple and seductive. That's why, after it was released in October 1977, it became such a global hit. The lyrics to Baccara's follow-up hit, "Sorry, I'm a Lady" were also really strong. Frank wrote songs like a conversation, often from the viewpoint of two people, and through that creating a story.

The only place where "Yes Sir, I Can Boogie" wasn't a hit was America, but now, forty years later, it is used there in movies, adverts, and TV series. It was adopted by fans of the Scotland national football team and became their anthem for the UEFA Euro 2020 championships, and in 2021 all profits of a cover version by Glasgow band the Fratellis went to Soccer Aid and children's charities. The songwriter

Diane Warren once said when you get a good song it is like a piece of real estate, it has a long life. Not a week passes without something happening—Peer Music is a huge publishing company, and in 2022 it was third on their list. It has been in so many commercials, such as the one for makeup brand Charlotte Tilbury, an advert featuring dancing supermodels Twiggy and Kate Moss. It touches me to know that song continues to move people, even now.

Frank started writing songs when he was with the Rattles, and developed this skill with his band Wonderland. Then of course, like most musicians in the 1970s, he realized: why are we solely dependent on big publishing companies when we can get our own deals? So he and Achim founded Gorilla Music, their first publishing company, and negotiated a lucrative deal with Decca Records. He and Achim worked together until Frank branched off in 1988 with Ja/Nein Music. He came up with the name because he realized that people often start a sentence with the phrase, "Yes, no, but…"

Despite being a full-time mum I put to good use the bookkeeping I had learned at college and made sure things were well organized. I kept the records and brought all the information together, while Frank did the A&R side of the business, working directly with the artists like Axel Zwingenberger, a blues and boogie pianist who toured with Charlie Watts and who often appears with musician and BBC presenter Jools Holland. The latter calls Axel "the best boogie-woogie player ever!" It was Pam who brought Axel to Frank's attention. She and I went to a lot of clubs and gigs together. One night, in the late seventies, we were in a small venue and the place was about to close when a young guy with long hair and a leather coat jumped onstage and started playing boogie-woogie piano. Pam said right away, "He's special. Go and give him Frank's number." I did, and it turned out his name was Axel Zwingenberger. He and Frank worked together for years, and Bill Wyman represented Axel in London. Pam had a good feeling for music and could have been a great A&R person. As for Ja/Nein Music, it still exists, and I'm the owner of it now.

By the 1980s musicians realized how important it was to keep their music publishing, making sure that contracts were properly negotiated and signed, and they're not just shaking hands without a contract like Frank and Achim did for many years. Artists who had a hit in the 1960s and '70s assumed they would have maybe one or two good years out of it. But then compilations started coming out, music was licensed for adverts, and they missed out on potentially huge royalty payments. I'm sure Frank never thought that "Yes Sir, I Can Boogie" would have lasting appeal, but forty years later we still have a good life out of that song.

I once had a conversation with our friend Roy Dyke, who as part of the trio Ashton, Gardner and Dyke had a massive Top Ten hit in 1971 with the song "Resurrection Shuffle." It is one of those tracks that could just take off again so easily, but he says he can't even remember the paperwork. After the 1960s and the end of those really structured days at the Star-Club, some of the musicians we knew were a bit lost and found it hard to settle. It was as though they thought it was going to last forever. But when the music changes, you either adapt or you have to find something else. That must be hard because musicians have to find something to substitute a whole lifestyle. I never felt that music was missing from my life because of working with Frank on his songwriting and running our publishing company. I had a good instinct with money, and that gave me an understanding of the music business.

The post-fame comedown affected even the really big stars. Rattles drummer Dicky Tarrach remembers playing with Chuck Berry in Hamburg in the 1980s, and, unlike that 1964 gig in Berlin where he was such an elemental force, this one was a disaster. Dicky and two other backing musicians got the call to meet with him beforehand

and came expecting to run through some songs, but there was no rehearsal. The only thing Berry said was, "When I do this"—raising his hand—"it's a break." His manager explained: "Mr. Berry never rehearses with the band because you are expected to know his songs."

When it came to the performance there were problems. "I'm a drummer who likes to keep the beat, but Berry slowed up so much I had a hard job following him," recalls Dicky. "I knew all the songs but he was so unprofessional and his Fender Showman guitar sounded awful. I was so disappointed because he was my big hero. He just took the money and ran."

~

The minute the kids got older I became involved in different projects. I was interviewed for *Die Architekt*, a major German architectural magazine, about how Liverpool had regenerated after the 1980s recession, despite prime minister Margaret Thatcher's austere policies. We were friends with one of the editors and he liked doing features on big towns with a special story to tell. "How is Liverpool doing these days?" he asked me.

"It's getting back on its feet..."

"Would you like to help me with an article?"

I organized a trip for them, acting as a location scout for developments in the old docks area and new buildings in the commercial district. I also arranged interviews with important cultural Liverpudlians like post-punk band Echo & the Bunnymen, playwright Willy Russell, who wrote *Educating Rita* and *Shirley Valentine*, and TV writer Carla Lane, who stole our name for her highly successful seventies BBC sitcom *The Liverbirds*. When I met her she admitted it and wasn't in the slightest bit embarrassed. I suppose you could take that as a compliment.

And in 1986 I was offered work as a dialect coach on the film *Brennende Betten*, which translates as *Burning Beds*. Our friend Pia

Frankenberg was the director and star, and she said, "My co-star is a fellow who needs help with the German sections of the script." That person was the musician Ian Dury, who played an ex-punk pyromaniac, a homeless Londoner who has just split up with his wife (played by Frances Tomelty). He ends up in Hamburg, where he meets free spirit Gina (Pia Frankenberg) who is looking to spice up her life.

Everybody said that Ian Dury wasn't easy to get on with, that he was bristly and determined to get his own way. He had grown up in Essex, the son of a single mother, and contracted polio at the age of seven. The illness left him with a withered leg, shoulder, and arm. Despite this he studied at the Royal College of Art under Peter Blake, became an art teacher, and then moved into music as lead singer of Ian Dury and the Blockheads. Along with Blockheads' guitarist Chaz Jankel he co-wrote hit songs like "Hit Me with Your Rhythm Stick" and "Sex & Drugs & Rock & Roll," combining music hall, punk, and sexual innuendo.

Even though Ian could be defensive and difficult, we got on really well together. Chaz Jankel was Ian's best friend and he came over to the studio one day when we were filming. The two of them were amazing, speaking to each other in poetry and riffing lines back and forth. Ian even recorded a track with Frank, adding a spoken-word section to a song he was working on. He was very clever, with a deep, gravelly talking voice.

During the course of filming I became close to some of the cast. Frances Tomelty, who played Ian's wife in the film, was a very successful theater actress from an acting family and musician Sting's first wife. She sat down one day and told me the whole story. She hadn't talked much about how she and Sting split up, and, although they had been divorced for two years, she was still very upset. They had two children before Sting left Frances for her best friend, the actress Trudie Styler. It took Frances a lot of time to get over that.

~

After *Brennende Betten* was released I stayed in touch with Ian Dury and we became good friends. He had a big apartment in Hammersmith, right on the Thames, and fans used to stand outside and shout, "Come out and say hello, Ian!"—which he did willingly, talking to them from his balcony. I'd visit him there, and once he remarked to my daughter Melanie in his strong Cockney accent, "Your mother is a l*ae*dy."

I would go to his gigs and watch him walk up to the stage and step straight off it, diving into the audience. His leg was in cast iron so a bodyguard would pick Ian up and put him back on stage because he couldn't do it by himself. The bodyguard was called Strangler, a muscly man with permed hair, leather, and tons of tattoos. I wouldn't have liked to meet Strangler in the dark, but really, I think he was harmless.

Strangler confided in me: "Mary, I've known Ian for many, many years, and I've only known him to respect one woman in his life. That was his mum. Now you're the second." When Ian brought his mother to the apartment one day to meet me, she said, "My son praises you like mad, and he doesn't do that very often." We shared a sense of humor and enjoyed each other's company until he died of cancer in 2000. I think there was a musical connection between us. He was fascinated with the Liverbirds' story, and thought it was great that we'd done the band so young. He understood why it was so special.

28. SYLVIA

Whisky with Pineapple

As the Liverbirds we had grown and done so much together, which meant that we were always in each other's thoughts through the years that followed, even when we weren't in touch. Mary frequently saw Val and Pam in Hamburg, but as the one who had returned to England, throughout the 1970s I did more of my own thing, concentrating on the family and making a living. By the end of the decade John and I wanted to be independent again, rather than working for other people. Holiday flats provided us with enough income to live a life, but I wanted more. John was the same, keen to build on our Hamburg experience by running a bar or doing something directly connected to playing with bands and creating live music. Benidorm, a warm, sunny town on Spain's Costa Blanca, full of tourists looking for entertainment, seemed like the ideal place.

In the spring of 1981 we put the flats up for sale and flew out to Benidorm to take a look at a bar called the Hawaii Five O. John and I had been warned it was in an awful state but as soon as we saw it, we knew it was the one. The Hawaii Five O was located in Calle Saint Miguel, in a picturesque part of the old town near the beach, with entrances on two side streets. Although it was in a disheveled state, with pipes hanging down from the ceiling, it had nice horse-shoe alcoves and we could visualize where the counter would go and where we could fit John's keyboards. When it came to plastering the walls we wanted a textured effect, but the builders didn't understand what we meant—we couldn't speak Spanish and they had no English. We kept trying to explain, gesturing with our hands. "*No comprendo, no comprendo*," came the reply.

Eventually John and I reached for a nearby bucket of white yeso plaster mix, and lobbed a handful against the wall.

"*Ah!*" said the builders in unison, and threw blobs on the wall as well. To this day the bar still has the same blobs on those textured walls.

We packed up and moved to Benidorm in 1982, but with one snag. Because of customs checks John's keyboards, including his Hammond organ and Leslie amplifier, were held at the Spanish border, so for six months we would be without keyboards. We heard about a piano for sale in a bar at the very top of a headland on a long, steep road. When we got there John played a few chords and said, "Yes, this is all right, it just needs a bit of tuning." Then he went over to the door and looked down the hill.

"How are we going to get it down?"

Our sons, Steven and John, were only ten and fourteen at the time, so we needed more brute force in shifting the piano. Friends who ran a nearby bar called the Magpie's Nest had two strong, older lads and offered to help. "The kids have a skateboard, why not try that?"

So we lifted the piano onto the skateboard and pushed it down the hill. At the bottom John was so pleased he lifted up the lid and started playing, right there in the street with Spanish locals looking at us as if we were mad.

Once we were in Benidorm the boys were enrolled in Sierra Bernia, the international school, and settled in quickly with a great crowd of British, Dutch, and German children. Even today, they've still got their friends from that school. Although they had lessons in English and took British exams, the boys also had Spanish teachers and ended up becoming fluent in Spanish, which was great later on when they became old enough to help in the bar. Our son John would do the lights and we'd pay him to wash glasses, while Steven inherited our musical genes, teaching himself guitar and then singing.

The Hawaii Five O had an apartment above, so when we were working we knew the children were safe upstairs. They would look out the window and notice any activity in the street. When shopkeepers had finished with old stock they would just put it out for the binmen, things like shoes and jewelry. Often when I went to bed I'd find a little trinket under my pillow from Steven, getting there before the binmen. One day I came in from the bar, opened the door to the apartment and couldn't get up the stairs for all these boxes of shoes. Steven had rescued them from the street, and he brought them to the bar the next night. Everybody was saying, "Have you got a size three?" "You got a size five, love?" He was both cheeky and lovable, still wanting to sit on my knee at ten years old.

At Hawaii Five O we started regular open-mic nights for holiday-makers. Word got around that John was playing piano, so all his Scottish friends and their friends would call in until eventually the bar was packed and we had to serve people outside, passing pints out the window into the street. Once our friend Danny asked if he could bring in the acclaimed Irish tenor Josef Locke, known as Mr. X because for tax reasons he couldn't go by his proper name. We told everybody he was going to sing the next night, and the bar was filled with people as he sang all his popular songs, from "I'll Take You Home Again Kathleen" to "Count Your Blessings" and many more. After the set finished Danny came up to John and said, "What do you think?"

"He sang well, but that's not Josef Locke because I've backed him in the UK."

Danny gave a sly wink. "Don't tell anyone, he's got to earn a living."

We got to know local policemen, one in particular, called Pepe, who was really charming. If a policeman visited your bar and took his hat off you were okay, it was just a social call—but if he left his hat on you were in trouble. So Pepe would come and take his hat off and I'd say, "What do you want to drink?" He and his policeman friends never refused a drink.

"Whisky with pineapple."

"You're not! I'm a Scotsman and you are *not* putting pineapple in a whisky," John always replied.

The Scottish people used to get so drunk at the bar that sometimes we had to steer the men (and occasionally women) back to their hotels and put them to bed. By the time he was fifteen, John junior was carrying them home. Because they drank in our bar we had to make sure they were safe, and that's probably partly why people came back again and again, because we looked after them. I used to do all the organizing, ordering beer and food, fixing the televisions, and checking anything electrical. As for John senior, as long as he had a cigarette, a pint, and his music, he was happy.

Late in 1983 we took over a bar in the Rincon de Loix area of Benidorm, calling it John and Sylvia's Cosmopolitan bar. We had room to expand so John brought in four keyboards. Being very particular about sound, he used to play stretching over them like an octopus, a real keyboard enthusiast. He bought a Hohner organ out of a catalog from the only music shop in Alicante, and thank goodness it sounded great—even though Hohner as a model wasn't highly rated amongst musicians, John could make it sing. We developed an act. People didn't know I could play and when John announced, "Sylvia's gonna get up and play the drums," they'd say, "You're kidding!" I'd get up with John to perform a rock version of Bach's "Toccata in D Minor," executing the drum rolls with a flourish. The toccata is a technically complex piece, designed to exhibit the musician's technique. It's such a fierce number, you had to get the breaks and rolls right. People were astonished, standing up to clap and cheer. We were relatively unknown in Britain, and it's only when I played the Bach toccata that people would ask, "Gosh, did you play the drums?" And I'd tell them. Back then I didn't dwell on those days or talk about the band. I didn't have much time to practice. I missed drumming, of course, but I was in charge of a busy bar and that took up so much of my attention.

Artists began to ring us, asking if they could perform. This was before the 1992 EU Freedom of Movement legislation and they couldn't do this without a work permit, so we came to an arrangement where we would provide a holiday flat for their families, along with free drinks and pork pies, which we sold in the bar. Top magicians and comedians appeared at John and Sylvia's, like Terry King, aka the Slipper Man, because he always wore carpet slippers onstage; or Johnny Hackett, a famous Liverpool comedian who was a regular on the 1960s TV series *The Good Old Days* before hosting his own BBC show, *Let's Laugh*. Mary's old boyfriend Billy Howard, the comedian, also came over and did impromptu slots. He had changed his name to Billy Shine and became very well known on the Blackpool circuit, telling funny stories about his life, including the one about having to pee in Mary's garden. Mary told me that later on he looked her up and turned up at her house in Hamburg with his wife, wanting to rekindle their friendship.

The Spanish couldn't understand why our bar was so popular. Back in the northern working men's clubs people would queue up outside to see good artists, and the same thing happened in Benidorm, with British holidaymakers queuing down the street. Spanish bar-owners assumed that people preferred discos to live music, but they soon changed their minds and poached our acts. Of course they didn't secure work permits, and one night police raided all the bars, put the performers in one room at the police station, and then deported them all back to the UK.

~

We were doing so well we bought a Sunseeker speed boat, zipping up and down the bay with friends. John would drive the boat wearing his white cap, sunglasses, and white short-sleeved shirt, looking every inch like James Bond. We bought an apartment, and had money running out of our ears. We adored the sun, the Mediterranean heat, and the laid-back lifestyle. My parents would come to visit and Dad loved rolling his trousers up to paddle in the sea. Mum used to say that John was so laid-back he had different blood in him. The way of life was so relaxing because we could go out at night with our children and eat outside. The only problem was that you could get very fat living in Spain. We would finish work at two in the morning and go for tapas, eating at three o'clock and going to bed on a big stomach of food. Jean and Bob came out to join us for a couple of years, working in the bar and going out with us on the boat or eating with us at night—they were good years.

~

Throughout our time in Benidorm Mary and I would speak on the phone every few months, and in 1985 she and Frank paid us a visit. They brought their sixteen-year-old daughter Melanie and four of her friends, so I suggested, "The girls will want to do their own thing." I was looking after a friend's apartment at the time, so I let them stay there—they certainly lucked out! Frank and Mary came for a night out to our bar, and we were made up seeing each other again.

The 1980s were good years, with me fully focused on life in Benidorm, but for one weekend I was plunged back into the nostalgia of the 1960s. In 1988, nearly twenty years after the Star-Club closed, Frank organized a weekend of Star-Club bands with the Undertakers, the Remo Four, the Liverbirds, and the Zodiacs. I got a phone call from Mary—could John and I go to Hamburg? Apart from the Merseybeat reunion in 1971 with Pam, I hadn't played with the girls in all those years. I was nervous about getting back onstage but I couldn't wait.

By then we were in our early forties with our own families. On one level we thought, *What are we doing?* We thought we were old, even then! John and I flew over but Val couldn't make it because she was looking after Stephan, so John augmented our sound with his keyboards and Tony Coates from the Hi-Fis played guitar with us.

It was great to see the girls again, and we slipped back into old patterns like it was yesterday. Pam, for instance, thought she was in charge as usual. John and Tony went out the evening before rehearsals and stayed out all night drinking, visiting the bars and all the people we knew. Next morning we were rehearsing in Mary's cellar and they were both obviously tired. Tony stood there hungover with his guitar, falling asleep. Pam barked, "Can you not wake up? Are you listening?"

John said, "God, I could be asleep and play that!"

Once we tuned up, John played a little Farfisa keyboard, but for the actual gig he had a proper grand piano and Hammond organ, which created a fuller sound and showed off his musical chops. The following night, when we turned up at the venue, it felt emotional seeing so many old faces and former friends. Manfred Weissleder was there.

As soon as I came in I went up to him and said, "Manfred, I bought you a present." I reached into my bag and pulled out a little ashtray in the shape of a toilet.

"What the hell's that?" he grunted. You could lift the lid up and flick your ash in the minute toilet bowl. A silly trinket I'd brought from Blackpool, I thought it was dead funny.

On the day of the show I was nervous and self-conscious because, aside from my very occasional guest appearances on the drums at the bar, I barely played anymore. I didn't drink, but just before our set Tony poured me a Jack Daniel's. "Here you are," he said. I went onstage, kicked my slippers off, and rolled my sleeves up. I was wearing a black-and-gold glittery top and started shaking my head like I used to, in time to the beat. I began the set wearing big gold earrings, but within five minutes I'd lost them. As we powered through songs like "Johnny Be Goode" and "Why D'You Accuse Me" I stopped worrying and lost myself in the moment. It was just a one-off gig, but it was brilliant, like we were back in the Star-Club again. Everyone was clapping and shouting and afterward wanted autographs. The club had been an underground place for heavy metal and alternative music, and afterward people said that we were the original punks.

29. MARY

What Can We Do for You, Pammy?

At the start of the 1980s Frank and I had bought a lovely family house in Harvestehude, a suburb of Hamburg, and Pam was living in a sought-after apartment near us, working as the star attraction at a gay bar called the Mistral. The place was ideal for Pam because she lived around the corner from the bar and the hours suited her—she didn't start work until eight o'clock in the evening, and the bar would be open until two or three in the morning. Going to work for her was like making an appearance or doing a show. She was queen of the bar, queen bee, bossing everyone around, and even more glamorous than the sparkling drag queens. People flocked to see Pam from the Liverbirds. During this period she became good at saving, and built up quite a healthy bank account.

I remember going there for her fortieth birthday in 1984. Her mum and sisters Dyan and Glynne flew over for a surprise party and we came in disguise wearing big hats and coats. We sauntered up to the bar and once she recognized us there was a lot of delirious screaming and shouting.

Although she was the star of the Mistral, fully in command of the bar, in other parts of her life Pam was out of control. One day, not long after her birthday, she took me aside and said, "I've missed a period."

"Maybe it's the change of life."

"No, I've got a strange feeling about this."

I took her to my gynecologist. He examined her and said she was pregnant.

"Oh God, I'm bloody forty and I'm pregnant, after all this."

"Don't you take any precautions?"

"No, I never have and I never became pregnant. I can't have this baby, it just wouldn't fit into my life at all."

The doctor looked at her, frowning. "This is a big decision you're making, have you spoken to the father about this?"

"There's no use me talking to him because he's only eighteen."

This young fella was a regular at the bar. Pam was a good-looking woman, very talented with cool dress sense, so it was easy for her to attract men and she never seemed to want a long-term relationship. When she confided in her mother, Mrs. Birch said, "Are you sure you're going to get rid of it? Because I'll take care of it for you." But Pam didn't want the baby and in the end she had an abortion. She came to stay at our house for a few days just in case anything went wrong, and one night when we were sitting up late she told me about something that had happened when she was very young.

She was eleven years old when someone close to her family came to the house and sexually assaulted her. Pam had to go into hospital, and after she came out she had her first period. Mr. Birch had caught them, and wouldn't have this boy in the house ever again. Her sister Glynne says, "After it happened nothing else was said and Pam never ever spoke about it. In our parents' generation these things weren't talked about. But probably what she needed was to have some counseling." It's significant that both Val and Pam experienced sexual assault when they were much younger, and in the same way their parents avoided any discussion of emotional trauma, both felt unable to talk about it.

Maybe that's why it was always important for Pam to be sexually powerful, and why it was difficult for her to be intimate or settled with one person. As she grew older she started having bisexual relationships. Sometimes it would be a man, sometimes a woman—she never saw herself as a lesbian; it was more that she just loved sex, and was very experimental in a way that was deliberately challenging to her parents.

Their first and only trip to Hamburg was for her fortieth birthday, and she treated them terribly. There was a rock club in the city called Logo, which every now and then featured cross-dressing shows. In Germany the transvestite performers are skilled professionals and look gorgeous. I knew it was not for my parents, so I would just go there with Frank, but Mr. and Mrs. Birch came along for Pam's sake and sat watching a group of trans artists onstage doing a striptease and impersonating Tina Turner. Pam had fallen in love with one of the trans artists. The trans woman sat flirtatiously on Mr. Birch's knee, with her bust hanging out and something bulging in her knickers. Poor Mr. Birch didn't want to seem like he was old-fashioned, so he was laughing awkwardly. I felt so sorry for them because I could tell that they were really embarrassed. When the show was over, Pam said, "You might as well go home, Mum and Dad, I'm going out with this person."

It was as if she relished the power, deliberately setting out to shock. Mr. Birch was upset at the life she was leading, and worried about the cluster of drinking and partying friends around her. After he got back to Liverpool he said to her, "These people aren't nice. They're using you, Pam." It was hard for her parents to express their fears. As Glynne says, "My mum and dad were of the generation where you didn't talk about your feelings. Although she was extremely loving, my mum didn't give us hugs. Whereas now, with my children, I tell them that I love them. I don't think my mum ever said that. Maybe it's from the war, that's how it affected them."

But despite the friction between them, Pam was devoted to her dad. In 2001 he was dying of prostate cancer and had a phone next to his bed. Pam spoke to him a few days before he died. After he came off the phone Mr. Birch said, "Well, I must be ill. Our Pam just said how much she loves me." It meant a lot to him that she could say that at the end.

Pam would think nothing of phoning me and saying, "I've just told my friends that you can do a great Sunday dinner. You've got loads of room, and you're a good cook. Can we come over?" And she'd arrive sometimes with four people I barely knew, like she had moved into the house. I used to say to her, "Pam, do you realize what you're doing?" I'd be cooking for all her friends, and she'd say, "The flipping salt cellar is nearly empty again, what would you do without me?"

"Fine. Fill the salt cellar up." That was her job.

It didn't annoy me for many years because she was Our Pam, someone so fun to be with, like she had an aura around her. She often arranged to come round with Sabrina, one of the women she absolutely adored, who she really did fall for. Sabrina had a girlfriend called Linda, but it never bothered Pam if somebody had a partner or not. Sabrina was very, very bubbly, with a deep voice and long, shining red hair, like the Italian girl singer Gianni Nannini, who was popular in Germany at the time. She had a chic restaurant just down the road from the Mistral, and we often went there to eat. She would sometimes go on holiday with Pam, leaving poor Linda to run the restaurant on her own. Pam always managed to get a special arrangement like that without annoying people.

There was a Chinese restaurant near her apartment, for instance, and she'd phone and say, "Yes, hello…?"

The staff called her Pammy. "Hello, Pammy. What can we do for you, Pammy?"

"Well, I feel like aromatic duck and plum sauce today."

"Pammy, it'll be ready in ten minutes."

Then she'd go over and get it, and sometimes she wouldn't even pay. Or she'd phone and say, "Can you bring it over to me?" And they weren't a delivery service, it was just a restaurant. Pammy had people who cleaned the windows for her, or made curtains for her, or upholstered her furniture. "I like this. This would fit nice in my place," she would say to a popular interior decorator who lived nearby, and he would be there doing all her decorating. She was a kind of diva, like the Hollywood divas on her bedroom wall.

30. SYLVIA

Back to the Sun

In the late 1980s our good life in Benidorm became more of a challenge. I should have taken it as a sign that our fortunes were changing when my parents came over for a holiday and my dad collapsed in our flat with a heart attack. He was rushed to hospital, where he later died. An eerie thing happened that night—when John, my mum, and I came back, grief-stricken, from the hospital, the boys said that at the exact time he died, the clock fell off their dresser and stopped.

In addition to grieving my dad, I was finding work more of a struggle too. Benidorm was badly affected by the 1990 global recession and things started going downhill. Hotels wanted more money from tour operators, whose response was to move to cheaper places in Turkey and Yugoslavia. To attract more tourists many Benidorm hotels became all-inclusive. So we were getting people staying in their hotels getting drunk out of their heads, before coming down to see the best artists in our bar, and because they were already drunk we didn't sell as much beer. Even with the recession our bar was still busy, but we weren't making the money and the rent was getting expensive.

We had previously started to invest in a new bar, with the hope of one day buying it outright with the help of a bank loan. But we couldn't get the loan, even though the big bosses from companies who supplied us beer and spirits vouched for us. After the loan was declined, we were struggling to keep up on the payments on the new bar, and this is when things became difficult for us. We discovered that Benidorm had a darker side at that time and there were people who could make our lives very difficult, putting us under a lot of pressure. They started telling us to leave and threatening to break John's kneecaps if we didn't.

Then one night, while we were in the bar, our good friend DJ Dave Lane was driving past our apartment block and noticed smoke coming from our floor. He raced to the bar to tell us and then drove back to help to evacuate some elderly residents. He tried to put out the fire himself, and managed to keep the flames away from exposed gas bottles before the fire brigade arrived. Thankfully, the fire was safely extinguished and no one was hurt. But we were unsettled. By then our sons were in their twenties—John had moved to Glasgow with his wife, but Steven still lived in Benidorm with his girlfriend, Nicky, and their baby son. "We've got to be careful here," I said.

We were so scared that eventually we decided to leave altogether. We just had to close up and walk away. The morning we left we packed up our Nissan Prairie and left Benidorm with our remaining cash in a bumbag. I was terrified all the way and didn't stop driving until we crossed the border to France.

As soon as we were over the border, John said, "Let's stop now, it's getting late." We pulled into the next place we saw open, a twenty-four-hour hotel near the roadside. "This will do," I said, parking up. When we got to our room John got into the shower and I turned on the TV. Every single channel was porn, and after a night of doors banging and showers going, we realized we were in a brothel. We didn't care, because it was the first time in months that we finally felt safe.

~

In winter 1993 we found ourselves back in Liverpool, near Aintree racecourse, bidding for a cheap place in a housing auction. Steven and Nicky stayed in Benidorm for eight months while he found work as a singer. Thankfully, they were left alone by the people who were threatening us, because once we left town they got their bar back and that's all those hard-nosed business guys were concerned about.

We found somewhere in Blackpool where I got work as a barmaid, and John had a job in a working men's club on the outskirts of the city, in Kirkham, playing for sequence ballroom dancers. He used to hate it because his tempos had to be dead straight and the dancers would pull faces if he improvised or altered his time signature. "You've got one couple moaning that it's too fast, another saying it's too slow. I can't stand it," he'd say. The weather was dark and cold, so after work I would go and pick him up in the car. One night I collected him, it was snowing and he said, quietly despondent, "Oh, Syl, what are we doing here?"

"We've got to do something else, John."

Thankfully, he was offered a job playing with an act in Los Gigantes, Tenerife, so we packed up again and headed to the Canary Islands and back to the sun. We played six months during the winter, then we went back to Blackpool where we rented the house out and John got a contract with St. Cuthbert's Catholic Club on Queen Street, near the Pleasure Beach. All the Scottish people we knew from Benidorm came to see him in Blackpool, packing the club. When the club invited John back again for the next season, the priest told the promoters, "Pay him what he wants. We've never had so much money for the church, we've even got a new roof." By then John had a growing fan base, so we got into a cycle of playing Blackpool during the summer and Los Gigantes in the winter.

Two years after that, we decided to go to the Costa del Sol, and John had the idea of taking a caravan for us to stay in.

"Look, John, I'm not towing a caravan."

"We can get a twelve-footer, a small one. Let's just have a look."

So we went to a caravan dealer and looked at the smallest they offered. "Oh, God, John, this is like a sardine can, we can't live in that."

"Well, let's look at bigger ones."

So we did, and within weeks I was towing a big caravan all the way to the Costa del Sol. It took a while to master driving and maneuvering and reversing. When I first drove it out of the lot I was halfway up the street when I saw two cars parked opposite each other, so I stopped.

"John, I can't get through there with the caravan."

"You can, love."

"I can't."

"Look, I'll guide you." John got out of the car and made gesticulating motions with his hands. "Come on, you're all right."

"I can't, I can't."

"You can get a fucking train through it!"

A fella working on a building site nearby heard the commotion and came over, saying, "It's all right, love, I'll move me car."

From then on I didn't have a problem, all the way via ferry and motorway and in thunderstorms and rainstorms and blistering heat!

We traveled to a bar called Screwy Hueys in Los Boliches, near Fuengirola, where we played shows and I did daft things like dressing up and belting out "Simply the Best," getting people up to sing. But much as we loved the Costa del Sol, it just wasn't the same as Benidorm. By then enough time had elapsed since we'd left town for us to think about going back, giving it another go. We'd heard from friends that there were opportunities there that sounded appealing. "It's been five years, Syl. It's fine," said John. Because I organized everything people thought I was the baddie and John was the softie, but it was the other way round. Even though he was easygoing, John wouldn't let anyone walk over him, and he was prepared to take the risk. On the Costa del Sol we were working in little pubs and that wasn't us. We needed a proper audience. We needed to get back to Benidorm.

31. MARY

Val in a Lonely Place

Stephan enjoyed reading and books were one of his few pleasures. But in 1978, at the age of thirty, he had been diagnosed with multiple sclerosis (MS) and that affected his eyesight, making it difficult for him to read. As a consequence he wanted to live closer to the center of Munich and his favorite clubs and restaurants. He and Val moved into a massive penthouse with a wide balcony and views of the city. There weren't many high buildings in Munich, but they lived in splendor on the sixth floor. It must have cost a fortune because the rooms were so big, but it was ideal for Stephan because he could wheel right through the apartment without having to open a door.

Around that time they stopped coming to Hamburg, but Frank and I used to go to Munich twice a year for his board meetings with GEMA, the music royalty society of Germany. During the day I would go out with Val and Stephan in their fantastic cars, and at night we'd meet Frank after his meetings were over. During these visits we noticed a change in Stephan—after his MS diagnosis he started getting a bit nasty, becoming cold and critical and sometimes direct-ing it toward Val.

She became quiet, almost robotic. When I came round Stephan would say, "Take Mary out," and he always told her where to go. She had an early mobile phone—one of those big chunky ones—and was always waiting for him to call, checking up on her and making sure she'd be home for a certain time. Sometimes, when we had a moment alone to chat, Val told me that emotionally she was on the edge.

Stephan wasn't an alcoholic but he did like a drink and he pre-ferred champagne, the best Krug or Dom Perignon. I remember one evening Frank and I went out with them to a restaurant. Stephan said something, and when Val didn't jump right away to his orders, he hit her in the face with the back of his hand. He could hardly move, but that was one movement he had mastered.

"Hey, Stephan, that was out of order," exclaimed Frank.

Stephan looked a little ashamed.

"I'm sorry, sometimes I get a bit impatient with Val, I'm in pain."

But I got the impression that happened quite often. Val didn't say anything and didn't even look shocked. I think once Stephan was diagnosed with MS he thought to himself, *What the hell have I done to deserve this life?* and began taking it out on other people.

His mother paid for a top American specialist and he was put on interferon beta, the first disease-modifying therapy available to treat MS patients. At that point it was only available privately, so his mother paid for the treatment for many years. He started to become reclusive and didn't want to go out because he was gradually losing his eyesight. He kept on buying cars, so they had a whole garage full of expensive cars and he would decide each day which one they were going to drive. Other people living in the block complained about how much space his cars took up in the garage, but he continued to buy them. He'd say, "We'll go out in the Jaguar," and Val would get him ready and put him in the car and they'd drive around Munich. They stopped going to restaurants because he couldn't even see what he was eating, so she would feed him in the car. By the early 1990s Stephan's MS had become so bad he had to wear very thick glasses, and after a while that didn't help anymore and he went blind.

Val's life was so restricted by then, and now they had stopped going to clubs she couldn't find consolation in music. After the Liverbirds split up, Val suppressed her musical talent for nearly thirty years. I don't think Stephan went out of his way to tell people about the Liverbirds, and she never would. Part of her life was over with, too painful to think about.

Then, in February 1996, she got the opportunity to pick up the guitar once again. Because our birthdays were so close together, Frank and I had a big celebration for our joint fiftieth with a PA and equipment at a venue near the old Star-Club, calling the party "Celebrating 100 years." Sylvia couldn't make it because she was busy in Benidorm, but Pam was there, and Val came on her own because by then Stephan wasn't up to traveling anymore. She came for four days and I booked her into a cozy hotel round the corner. She looked different, with shorter hair, and she was so happy to see us.

On the night Val borrowed a guitar and we got Dicky from the Rattles to play a few Liverbirds songs with us. It was a special feeling to be onstage again with Pam and Val, even though Val's guitar riffs were a little rough and she didn't attempt any "fiddly bits." That didn't matter, though, because we were caught up in the spontaneous energy. Then after our set Pam jumped back onstage, announcing: "We've got a surprise especially for Mary!" I had no idea. She'd gone to the trouble of getting her sister Dyan and two male singers from Kokomo to do a set of Supremes songs. They shimmied on all glammed up and sounded amazing.

Val enjoyed that night so much. It was the first time she had played the guitar in years. She didn't try solos, but it was obvious that the musician was still there somewhere—she hadn't been able to get rid of it, and I was so proud of her. I think that's what made her realize how much she had given up. She reminisced a lot that night, regretting a few things. Maybe that's what hit her. She started to go downhill so badly afterward.

She was drinking wine at the party, but not out of control. Then, after she went back to Munich, she became ill and started drinking heavily. It was quite obvious when I went to visit her that she was getting more and more shaky. If I was going out with Val, Stephan would say to me, anxiously, "Make sure she doesn't drink too much." It started with one or two glasses of wine a day, then more and more. She became less attentive, so he got a house cleaner and allowed a carer to sometimes take him out in the wheelchair to give Val a break.

I didn't see much of her over the next two years because she would often phone and cancel, saying, "I'm not feeling too good." In that time she made one visit to Hamburg and Stephan rang beforehand to say, "You've got to make sure that you've no alcohol in the house, because she'll find it." His mother, Frau Hausner, kept discovering empty bottles hidden or thrown away in the apartment and started making life hard for Val, openly disapproving of her and encouraging Stephan to divorce her, but he never did. Val became so bad with the drinking that she could barely take care of him, so in the autumn of 1996 Stephan's mother organized a full-time nurse, a Hungarian woman called Maria.

Then, early in 1997, Frau Hausner announced, "Val's got to go," and forced a separation. Stephan rented a little apartment for her on the ninth floor of a block not far from where he lived. Val used to help Maria during the day and give her an hour's break, but the rest of the time she would sit in the apartment or drink in the park with a group of homeless people. Her apartment deteriorated and got into such a bad state that people in the building started complaining about the smell. In one way Val was relieved to have her own private space for drinking, but the alcohol was inducing panic attacks. She became delusional, telling me she was terrified of rolling out of bed and rolling out of the window.

I was so worried about Val during that time, and even though she wouldn't let me visit I tried to keep in touch with her by phone. She could be very elusive. One day I got news that Val's mother had had a stroke and wanted to get in contact, but the phone rang and rang with no answer. I called Stephan's apartment and spoke to Maria.

"I can't reach Val."

"Listen." Maria went into a room where Stephan couldn't hear. "Val's in a place where she shouldn't be. Frau Hausner has got her sectioned in a closed hospital ward."

She gave me the number of a local psychiatric hospital, so I phoned and spoke to the duty nurse.

"I'm looking for my friend, I believe she's there."

"Are you a relative?"

"No, I'm not, but her mum has had a stroke. She's only got her father and he has his hands full looking after his wife."

There was silence for a moment. "I'm only allowed to give this information to family but I just wanted to let you know one thing—Val shouldn't be here. Frau Hausner wants power of attorney over her and a judge is coming to decide if she can do this."

Luckily enough, the judge was a sympathetic woman who said that Val was in a bad state and needed care, but that Frau Hausner had no right to power of attorney. I called Sylvia for help and she put me in touch with Val's auntie. Within a week we managed to get her out of there and set her free.

BOOK FOUR: REUNION

32. MARY

The Big Beat Party

When we rescued Val from the psychiatric hospital in Munich she returned to Liverpool and moved back in with her parents. Val's auntie paved the way by telling Val's dad, "Whatever state her mother is in, Val needs to come home." After she had been home for a month, Sylvia and I arranged to go for a visit. It was the first time Sylvia had seen her since the band split up in 1968, and she was shocked. She told me afterward she thought Val looked really sad. "It was lovely seeing her but I felt sorry for her, she was so thin and haggard."

Val's mum was also in a bad state, crippled on one side and unable to talk very well, but something was clearly agitating her. Whenever Val went out of the room, Mrs. Gell banged on the chair—I don't know what she was trying to communicate because we couldn't understand her. We found out later that Mrs. Gell was worried that if Sylvia and I went out with Val we might have let her drink alcohol. We had dinner together and Val said, exasperated, "My mum's killing me. She doesn't trust me and she's terrified I'll start drinking again."

Val didn't even want a drink; she was determined to dry out. When she set her mind to something she had incredible willpower.

Despite the friction with her mum, Val stayed at home for three months, rested and got sober. Being at home with her parents, away from the heartache of her situation with Stephan, was an important part of her recovery. When she felt stronger she moved back to Hamburg and she stayed at our place for a while until she found herself an apartment.

We knew Val was on the mend when she agreed to join us for a full Liverbirds reunion at the Big Beat Party, a special festival organized by Frank and our promoter friend Karsten Jahnke in the Congress Centre, a concert hall right in the heart of Hamburg. The lineup was impressive, featuring so many bands from our days at the Cavern and the Star-Club: Gerry and the Pacemakers, the Troggs, Dave Dee, Dozy, Beaky, Mick & Tich, Ian and the Zodiacs, and Lee Curtis. Also on the bill that day were the Pirates (minus Johnny Kidd, RIP) and Screamin' Lord Sutch—who despite struggling with various issues that year managed to get a band together for the gig, and the promoters hired a coffin. The band was like a tribute act impersonating Screamin' Lord Sutch, but he guested onstage and started screaming from the coffin.

Val spent some time preparing for the show. For years she didn't allow herself to think about the band because she was caring for Stephan or too ill herself, but she felt ready now. She had deliberately ruined her guitar thirty years before, when she couldn't go with the Liverbirds to Japan, so she finally got it repaired and started practicing again. After a few weeks she announced, "There's no way I can play lead guitar and sing, not anymore." She started having lessons again but her sound wasn't as strong; it was not the way it used to be. At that time Frank was producing a girl group called Die Braut Haut Ins Auge (The Bride Hits You in the Eye), and they were big fans of ours, especially their lead guitarist, Barbara Hass. She was a fantastic guitarist and a good-looking woman, and she adored Val, so I asked her to join us on vocals and guitar. Barbara said it would be a privilege.

We rehearsed two afternoons. Sylvia had bought some electronic syn drums because for her it was a good way to practice. It's harder to drum as you get older because your wrists lose strength, and she thought she wouldn't be able to get the right atmosphere on a real drum kit. The first day we practiced in my house, and the second day it was in a proper rehearsal room near the Hotel Pacific. We were rusty for the first few takes. Because of not having that much time to rehearse, we had to stick to the songs we knew everybody wanted, like "Johnny Be Goode," "Got My Mojo Workin'," and "Before You Accuse Me." Pam tried to boss us around, but then she always did. At the previous reunion in 1988, when I had brought out a sparkly top, she said, "You're not gonna wear that are ya, Mary? Don't wear that golden thing!" She wanted us to wear the white frills we had in the sixties. So, for the 1998 reunion, we did. She made them; she was a handy seamstress. Whenever we appear now we always wear frilly shirts with trousers. Frills belong to the Liverbirds!

My parents came over for the show because they had never seen us play in the Star-Club days. They arrived with two of my sisters and I got them all backstage passes. My dad was made up with his VIP lanyard.

By the time it came to the show, our set flowed easily. We went on at nine because that was the time we always went on at the Star-Club. It was great to look over and see Val, cool and composed on guitar, Pam at the mike, and Sylvia on drums shaking her head to the beat. Barbara was on guitar to help Val with the solos. There was such a buzz onstage. All the other bands had been playing on the cabaret scene and changed their style but because we hadn't played much in the intervening years, our sound was original sixties. And that's what everybody enjoyed—it was as if we hadn't stopped. We'd started something together and been through it together, an important part of our lives that changed everything for us.

It says a lot about our close friendship that even though we were now in our early fifties the musical connection was still there. Pam would have liked the band to get back together—that would have made her very happy. Reunion gigs were complicated, though, because we were all living in different places and it was hard to get together for rehearsals. Pam didn't have any dependents or commitments. To her it was like, "Let's just do it!" She didn't think about me and Sylvia both having children. Her sister Glynne says: "Pam was very good at totally ignoring anybody else's commitments. She didn't do empathy particularly well. She was in her own world, Pam's world."

~

After the reunion gig Val's mood picked up and she seemed happier, feeling grounded by sobriety. She never drank again, but somehow after the alcoholic stage she lost her sparky sense of humor. One day she sat down and admitted, "Mary, it was bad." She told me about drinking with the gang of street people and how it got to a stage where all her hair fell out. She drank everything, anything going.

Val had always been very reserved, but when she came back to Hamburg it took a while for her to come out of her shell, because of what she'd been through. She never got back to being the old Val, but she was a good friend, and reliable. I remember a few weeks after she'd come back to live in Hamburg, I said to her, "I'm going to England, why don't you come with me?" And she said, "You'd really do that? You'd really take me with you?" as though she couldn't believe it. Her self-esteem at that point had gotten so low.

Stephan was still alive then, very unwell with the MS, but he refused to sign a divorce paper that Frau Hausner had drawn up in the early 2000s. He never divorced her, even though his mother was obsessed about Val taking the family money. Frau Hausner made sure that everything officially went to him, but he took care of Val, even after he died in 2014 at the age of sixty-six. He and Val had put money into a few apartments in Munich, so he added a clause in his will that if anything happened to him, the apartments would go to his brother, but Val was to receive rent from one for the rest of her life. Two thousand euro a month was a lot of money.

When Stephan died he was buried in a grave by himself, even though there was only his father in a family plot that had enough room for eight. It is very expensive to buy a grave in Germany. Frau Hausner bought a plot next to their family one, and made Val pay the full eight thousand euro for it—because she was still married to him.

When we were in the band people used to think the four of us were lesbians, and they would always say that about Val. We never thought for one minute it might have been true. One night, when she was staying at my place, Val sat me down and said, "I've got something to tell you."

"OK."

"I don't know how you're gonna take this, but I'm really more interested in women than men."

Everybody used to speculate about Val, but we didn't believe it, we had no reason to suspect she was gay.

"I've fallen in love with a woman," she said.

For a moment I panicked, thinking, *Please don't let it be me!* I wouldn't know what to say. But it was actually a woman she had met at the reunion gig. Val was fascinated by her and the two of them fell in love. They had a passionate but brief relationship for about four weeks, and after it finished, Val met Suzann Nilson, a care worker who was fifteen years younger, and they soon developed a relationship. Suzann had a little house close to where her parents lived in

Bad Oldesloe, a convalescent resort in a quiet, pretty town thirty miles from Hamburg, and she and Val would often go there. Suzann worked in a home for people with disabilities and got Val a job there too because she'd had the experience being a full-time carer for Stephan. Val worked there part-time because, understandably, after years of lifting and carrying, she didn't want to do this all the time.

Suzann didn't drink so that was ideal for Val. They liked going out for walks, listening to music, or watching films, and when they went out for dinner they would just have juice. In a way they were very much alike, appreciating the calmness of routine, and because they were perfect for each other that made it easier for Val to accept the new life that she had and to stay clean. They were a devoted couple— they had the same hairstyle, the same kind of clothes, and often they would sit quietly on the sofa just looking at each other. Val said that she didn't have a happy childhood or good memories of Liverpool, but Suzann encouraged her to go back to the city to visit family. They used to enjoy going to Crosby, the windy seaside town close to the River Mersey. They would stay in a hotel on the waterfront and go for meals. Val never told her father they were a couple, but I'm sure he guessed. He said to her once, "Just remember, the main thing for me is that you're happy."

33. MARY

Pam Said, "I'll Buy a Little Scooter..."

It was some time during the 1990s I realized that the people around Pam weren't really her friends. They were people who were leading her astray, who just wanted to hang out with her to take cocaine and get high.

It got to the point where she was saying, "I'll bring Sabrina and her girlfriend Linda." She would do her usual trick of telling me that she was bringing round lots of people for Sunday dinner, and I would sit there waiting, having prepared the whole lunch, and they wouldn't show up. Frank would say, "Mary, when are you going to learn? When?" I'd say to him, "She wouldn't have done this again, Frank, she wouldn't have just let me down. Something must have happened." And I'd go around to her little flat because she lived on the ground floor and I could look through the window. I'd peek through the window and there she would be, fast asleep. She was just asleep and didn't even bother to call, and that's when I just stopped. "Oh, no, Pam. This is it now. That's enough."

The last few years of Pam's life were sad. She really went downhill. The Mistral changed ownership in the late 1990s. A gay couple, Bernd and Uwe, had owned the Mistral and the ten apartments above the club, but when Bernd died in the late 1990s Uwe lost interest, so a woman named Margaret took over the bar. She got on very well with the customers, but she wouldn't put up with Pam coming in late or going early, the way Bernd had.

"Either you take this job more seriously, or you have to leave," said Margaret.

Pam didn't like being answerable to another woman, so she stopped working there. She helped a few nights in Sabrina's restaurant, ironing the tablecloths. They had white antique ones that were very delicate, and she managed them really well. When Pam pressed her shirt, you would think a professional had done it for her. She always was good at ironing, and she earned a bit of money that way. But behind the scenes, her life was falling apart.

Pam lived off social security and was drinking a lot by then. Her favorite drink was sambuca and white wine, followed by a Jack Daniel's or cognac, and she was regularly taking cocaine. She wasn't dealing, but her apartment became a safe house for dealers, and she would receive some coke as a "thank you"—that's how she managed to pay for it, stashing the drugs in a spare corner of the attic. Sabrina was an addict as well, so every day she would do the shopping for the restaurant before hanging out in Pam's house for hours, leaving Linda to do everything else. Pam used to phone me, saying, "Sabrina's here at the moment, she's been on shopping. She's bought... What have you bought today, Sabrina?" And Sabrina would say, "Half a salad." That was their excuse to get out of the place and go to Pam's attic.

Dealers would bring coke to her house, about four hundred orders a month. I never saw the drugs because she always said to me, "Mary, this is my life and you wouldn't stand for it, so just keep out of it." Frank said to her so often, "Pam, write a few songs, I'll find somebody to record them." She did have a try because she was good at writing songs when she was unlucky in love. That's how she wrote "Why Do You Hang Around Me," "Leave All Your Loves in the Past," and "It's Got to Be You" when she was pining about Lee. So, at the time when she was mad about Sabrina, she began composing a few lyrics like "Why do you bother coming in every day?" but never completed any songs. Frank bought her a guitar, and she would sit and play, working on chords and melodies. The sections she played for me sounded good; they would have been strong songs if she had finished them, but after a while she pawned her guitar and didn't even try to write songs anymore.

Pam would have loved for the Liverbirds to get back together but, in her mind, how could we top the experience we had had at the Star-Club? She was drifting, the substance issues distracting her from proper creative work. Making music needs a certain discipline, and you can't have that structure when an artificial substance is ruling your life. Even though she loved the songwriting process once she got going, it took effort and organization to kick-start herself. And everything got in the way of Pam doing that, a sort of self-sabotage.

By then Val was back in Hamburg and they would fight like cats and dogs, trying to get my attention. Val just didn't understand Pam letting herself go the way she did. Even though Val became an alcoholic in the Munich years, when she realized how bad she was getting, she stopped. She wouldn't even have a chocolate with a bit of alcohol. Val didn't have much sympathy for Pam because of everything she had been through with Stephan, irritated that Pam could not appreciate the fact that she had a good life. Tension between them flared up once when we paid an overnight visit to Val's apartment. In the morning we were organizing breakfast and before going to the shops Val said to Pam, "Don't touch that television because I've just set all the programs and the aspect ratio." After we came back Pam was sitting there, looking sheepish. Pam was like a child—she'd been told not to do something, so she did it to provoke a reaction.

"I haven't touched it."

"Why can't you admit it? Why can't you tell the truth?"

Of course she had to admit she had fiddled with the TV. They had a blazing argument and Pam started to cry. She couldn't wait to get out of the place.

After that, the three of us still went out together for meals, but toward the end, we were always paying for Pam. She thought nothing of borrowing money and not paying you back, saying, "You're OK. You can pay for this, can't you?" I did get frustrated with her. "This is my little bass player," she used to say to people. "This is my little bass player, she's loaded."

Pam kept in touch with her sisters, particularly Glynne, who remembers going on holiday with her to sunny places like Greece, Spain, and Italy. "We had some good times, but she would sometimes put me in an awkward position, like when she came home for Christmas, and she didn't have any money. I paid for a flight and then discovered that she brought lots of drugs with her. 'I'm a bloody teacher,' I'd say to her. 'You can't do this! If you get caught I'll lose my job.' She never saw the consequences of things like that."

Pam's addiction had started way back in the early days of the Liverbirds, when we first went to Hamburg and she was doing pills to keep herself awake. But as the years went on, it progressed to cocaine. If we asked her what she was doing, she would say airily, "I'm only doing a little bit. Don't worry about me, I'll be fine." Things came to a head with Glynne one weekend when Pam was over on a visit and staying in the family home. By then their mother was in a nursing home. The care manager told Glynne that Pam persuaded her to release money from their mother's bank account, saying, "Mum wants me to have this." Glynne remembers going ballistic, angry she put their mother and the home in that position.

"You're overreacting. Mum wouldn't mind me having that money."

"Well, that's not the point. She's not in good health. You can't be doing that. For God's sake, if you're that desperate you could have asked me!"

But she wouldn't, because she knew that Glynne would say, "What's it for?"

When Pam came back to Germany she was like a little girl, bewildered by her sister's anger. She confided in me, saying, "Glynne shouted at me—I've never known her to do that!"

Even though Pam tested us to the limit, there were times when she was still so endearing. Her love for iconic film stars was undiminished, and she liked to feel she was part of their world. One afternoon I was doing my shopping and I called in about four o'clock for a cup of coffee. Pam was sitting there in her tiny apartment in her Japanese morning coat with her hair flowing and golden.

"You'll never guess who I slept with last night," she said.

"No idea, but I'm sure you'll tell me."

"Jean-Paul Belmondo." The swoony French actor was the hero of 1960s new-wave cinema and a huge star in Europe.

"It must've been someone who looked like him."

"No, Mary, it was him. I know it was him."

The next day there was a newspaper report saying that Belmondo had been in Hamburg, so knowing Pam, her fling with him was probably true.

Pam reserved her most enduring admiration for Katharine Hepburn, and she used to send cards and presents to the movie star every Christmas and birthday. She would get letters back from

Ms. Hepburn's secretary, saying, "Thank you very much for the handkerchiefs, they were much appreciated." Pam vaguely knew her address and one time, when Glynne was traveling to New York, she said, "Go and look at the apartment for me, it's somewhere near Central Park."

"I can't go and wander around Central Park looking for a random apartment."

"Just go and take a picture of something and pretend it's her place."

When Pam sent cards she always asked if she could have an autograph, but always got the answer: "Ms. Hepburn does not sign autographs." Then one year she received a handwritten card, which read: "Miss Birch I thank you for all the cards that you have sent me over the years—but as you know I don't sign autographs. Signed: Katharine Hepburn." Pam framed the card and treasured it, giving it pride of place on her wall.

When Ms. Hepburn died in 2003 Glynne read about it in the newspaper and rang Pam. She said, "You're the only one who has rung me because Katharine has died." Pam fixated on her Hollywood idol partly because she saw parallels with Lee in the relationship between Spencer Tracy and Katharine Hepburn, because he wouldn't leave his wife. She was a woman who had a love in her life that she was never allowed to have; an elegant actress with remarkable poise and strength. Ms. Hepburn would have never played a simpering woman, and to Pam she was the perfect role model.

Our last gig together was 2006 in Liverpool, a big party for my sixtieth birthday held at the Pirrie, my brother Joseph's social club. By then he had become a successful entrepreneur, running clubs and venues and organizing music nights all over Liverpool. For my birthday lots of friends came and played, including Lee Curtis, the Undertakers, and Ian and the Zodiacs. Val was there too, with Suzann, both sitting there, heads and backs very straight, looking around and taking it all in. Val had brought her guitar and was keen to play. Although the Liverbirds weren't officially back together, we liked to jam or do reunion gigs when we could. We had rehearsed a couple of days beforehand and didn't know at that point it would be the last time. Pam didn't have much longer to live.

On the night, Lee came with his wife, Beryl. Pam thought nothing of going up to Beryl and saying, "C'mon, Beryl, let bygones be bygones and have a dance." And they did. Beryl was OK with that because she was the one who kept Lee, not Pam, so she'd won the battle. We all sat there, stunned—we couldn't believe it when we saw them dancing together.

The Liverbirds got up and had a jam session, and once we started playing, Ian from the Zodiacs and Tony Coates joined us on guitar, all charging through Liverbirds' songs. Everybody in the audience was shouting, "Look at Mary McGlory with her group!" The Pirrie is at the end of Ternhall Road where I used to live, so all the neighbors were there, finally coming to see the Liverbirds. All these years later, this was the first time they saw us onstage, and they were cheering and shouting. After we played, Sylvia got up with Lee Curtis's band to jam, and Pam was sitting on Ian's knee. It was like a big happy family got back together for the night.

My mum was there, and she died a few months after that. She was already very sick with myeloma, but she looked so happy. It was one of those nights I wish I had on video. I'd watch it over and over again.

~

In 2009 Pam went to stay with Glynne, who lives by the sea in Lincolnshire. They decided to have a walk on the beach and sit in the sun, which she always liked to do. But she couldn't walk the five hundred yards from the car park to the beach because she was getting out of breath. Not long after that their mother died, and Glynne, Dyan, Pam, and Jenn were planning the funeral. While they walked to the florist to arrange flowers, Pam had to sit down halfway, and that's when the sisters realized there was something badly wrong. But she refused to talk about it. "I'm out of breath, that's all," she said.

A few months later when they diagnosed her with lung cancer, she was like a child, saying, "Mary, they said it's cancer, what should we do? Will you come with me to the examinations?" I was the one, not Sabrina, who would be asked to go with her to these appointments. After her diagnosis Pam cut down on the coke, but she carried on smoking forty a day. Dunhill cigarettes were the strongest and most expensive, yet she was unrepentant. "I just enjoy this, my life is the way I want it to be," she said. As her health was failing she would get breathless and couldn't walk far. "Wait a minute, I'll just have a little sit-down," she would say. She never walked far, anyway, and just going from her apartment to Sabrina's restaurant, she had to keep resting on the wall.

Even when she was very ill, Pam had a flimsy grasp of what was happening. The hospital consultant told her that because of the cancer they needed to remove a lung, and she would need to have an oxygen bottle with her whenever she went. Pam was convinced that after this operation, which would take away two-thirds of her lungs, she'd be all right. "I'll buy a little scooter and I'll be fine. I'll just get around town." She was making jokes on the Saturday before her operation, sitting on the hospital bed with her hair immaculate, saying, "The doctor's just in, I think he's after me. Otherwise he wouldn't come on a Saturday."

Maybe in her private moments Pam did know how ill she was, but she would never convey that to anybody. Sylvia and I said to her sisters, "Pam's got this idea that she's going to come out and everybody's going to look after her. We can't do that." The operation was the following Thursday, and on the Friday she was recovering, but very quiet. The next day Dyan and I walked into her room to find it empty and Pam's slippers on the floor next to the bed. Dyan rushed out to find a nurse.

"Where's Ms. Birch?"

"Oh, she had to be taken down for an emergency operation."

The other lung had collapsed so they put Pam in a coma.

Pam was in a coma for ten days before the doctors said, "We've done everything we can now…we're going to turn the machines off."

I was there at the end. Dyan was holding one hand and I was holding the other when they turned off the machines. For a while we sat there waiting, expecting to hear a noise. And then the nurse said quietly, "She's passed away. We've turned it off, she's passed away."

We know so much more about addiction now, but in 2009 there was less awareness about intervention, and how to look after people or help people look after themselves. Pam was always in denial, which made things very difficult, and sadly her sister Dyan had an addictive personality as well. Dyan was fortunate in that she had supportive people around her, so she was still productive and still had a musical career in the band Kokomo until she died of chronic pulmonary disease (COPD) in 2020. Pam felt she had nurtured her younger sister into the business and in a way, Dyan was Pam's protégée, so she was very proud of that.

After Pam was cremated, Frank, Dyan, and I went to pick up her ashes, which were kept in an urn in a fine black-and-gold velvet bag. As we drove to Pam's old apartment, Frank said, "Shall we go and have a coffee?"

"I'll just bring Pam home first," said Dyan, and went to the apartment.

When she came back to the car she said, "I've put her in her armchair."

Pam was taken to the cemetery in Liverpool where her parents are, and she is scattered on the same plot. We had a farewell ceremony in Hamburg, putting a picture and a few of her belongings in one of her favorite pubs, one she liked to hang out in until four or five o'clock in the morning. Sabrina and Linda were there, and it was very touching. So, that was my farewell.

People used to say to me, "How do you put up with her, Mary?" She could really get on your nerves, yet nobody bore a grudge against her for doing what she did, because she was so lovable. A few months after she died, Glynne was going through Pam's belongings and found a bundle of love letters from Dave Brown, her teenage boyfriend from Speke Comprehensive. She had kept them all those years. Despite hanging on to the love letters I don't think she would have changed anything, or felt regret—she would see hers as a life well lived.

There is a hard-living side of the music industry that is attractive when you're young, but over time it really takes its toll. Pam was aware of all the adoration from the fans, and the fact that it disappeared after the band split up. The problem was, she couldn't handle being ordinary, and having tasted the high life she never really wanted to settle down. Apart from the group in Iran and our reunion gigs, she didn't play again with other musicians. Where she was happiest was with the Liverbirds; any other band just wasn't the same. When Pam wanted to do things we were happy to go along with it. We went through so much together. We were almost like sisters.

34. SYLVIA

Our Special Place

Pam's death was so quick. Mary phoned me and said Pam was in a bad way, that she was dying. I don't like to look at photos in the year before her death, it saddens me. I like to remember Pam as she was. What stays in my mind is that gig in Frodsham in 1964 when the Kinks said, "There's this girl." She was standing there and we were little girls. Pam was so tall, looking so fabulous and way out. That's my enduring memory of Pam.

~

John and I returned to Benidorm in 2001 and from the moment we set foot in the town again I looked across the sea and thought, *God, this is our place*. Without the financial difficulties we had got into in the past, we could enjoy life again, working in the Hotel Regente and Shooters bar in Calle Ibiza, which we loved, before being offered work at the Payma bar near Levante Beach.

The first time we walked into the Payma there was a large television blaring out live football. The owner said, "You won't be able to play music if the dominoes people come in. There's two lads who like to play dominoes."

We thought, *Bloody hell.*

The owner had a massive, full-size snooker table in one half of the room.

"Is there any way you can get that snooker table out?" we said. "We're not being funny, but once people know we're here you are going to be full, I promise you."

"I'm not taking the snooker table out."

"OK."

Within weeks word got round that Sylvia and John were at the Payma getting comedians and musicians up out of the audience to perform live, professionals on holiday doing a turn—and the place was absolutely rammed. The owner ordered a wide wooden board to cover the snooker table at night so people had somewhere to put their drinks, and we dotted chairs all the way around the improvised bar. The Payma became so successful that the owner didn't question us booking live acts again.

We got into a cycle where we were playing St. Cuthbert's in Blackpool during the summer season and coming back to Benidorm for the winter, where we had a static caravan. Even though it was fun, the constant moving back and forth was tiring. But thankfully our friend Benny—the boss at Traffic Lights, a busy Benidorm bar in the Rincon de Loix area—had a new opportunity for us. He needed a new keyboard player. The pay he offered was so fantastic that there was no point in us running our own bar. People see cash going into the till and presume you are making a lot of money, but the overheads are high and the payouts astronomical. In this new arrangement Benny ran the bar, took his money, and paid us, and we were in charge of the entertainment.

As well as featured singers and musicians, we had themed nights, like a Valentine's Day *Mr. & Mrs.* quiz, based on the popular TV show of the time, or a special event for Christmas Eve with a buffet, port, balloons, fancy dress, and Father Christmas. All the women wanted to be photographed sitting on his knee. We used to do Burns night every January 25, our most popular night of the year, when everybody would wear kilts and we'd bring out the haggis on a big silver plate while another friend, John, from Falkirk, would address it—that is, he'd recite Burns's famous poem "Address to a Haggis."

We loved it so much we stayed there for the next ten years until we retired.

In 2007 John and I celebrated our fortieth wedding anniversary—our ruby wedding—by going to New York. I'd only been to America once before, to Disney World in Florida, and the closest the Liverbirds got was the offer, by Chuck Berry's manager, to play topless in Las Vegas. So it was a thrill to be in New York, taking photos in Times Square, walking around Manhattan, eating delicious hamburgers and going to a bar where you could try all kinds of beers.

We went up Trump Tower on Fifth Avenue, the fifty-eight-story building that Donald Trump had, apparently, envisioned since childhood. Trump had just started his political career and was nowhere near the presidency—at that point he was just a notorious hotel- and casino-owner with his series of wives. The top floors of the building had glass all the way round and I'd never seen anything like the public toilet downstairs in the atrium—all marble, gold taps, and perfumes. There were jewelry shops at the bottom, and John bought me beautiful pearl earrings and a pearl bracelet.

Next door to the tower was Tiffany's flagship store filled with gleaming, high-end jewelry. John said, "Let's go in."

"Nah."

"We can."

The hefty doorman nodded his head to us and we went in. We

were looking in glass boxes at glittering necklaces, elegant gold brace-lets, and rings when an assistant appeared.

"Hello, can I help you?"

"Just looking…"

John said, "Actually we're looking for a nice ring, it's our ruby wedding."

"Come with me."

I snatched a look at John as if to say, *What are you doing?*

"Oh dear," said the assistant. "We haven't got a ruby ring but we've got some beautiful ruby bracelets."

"All right, let's have a look."

The one she showed us was astonishing, gold inlaid with gorgeous rubies and diamonds. John was always a man just happy with his drink, his cigarettes, and his music. I thought, *Has he been getting money from somewhere and not telling me?*

"Try it on," the assistant said.

I tried it on, admiring its beauty. Then I looked at the price—$57,000.

"It's lovely, but no," I bluffed. "I really wanted a ruby ring."

Without batting an eyelid John said, "Oh gosh, what a pity you don't have the ring."

He had such a dry sense of humor; he thought it would be fun to see what was there and to indulge our imagination. As for me, I couldn't get out of there quick enough.

As we walked away toward the door I suddenly noticed I was still wearing the bracelet. I went back to the assistant. "I've still got it on."

"Oh. Oh dear!" She took it off me before we set the alarms off, and John and I went giggling into the street.

We stayed four nights in a hotel before going on a cruise from New York to the Virgin Islands, where we went on a helicopter ride. There were just six of us on the helicopter and because of the distribution of weight the pilot seated John up front. He was delighted—he had a new video camera, there was a big glass bottom at the front where he could film the sea below, and headphones so you could talk to each other. Shortly after takeoff John said to everyone, "It's all right, the pilot has given me permission. I'm taking over now." It was so funny to see other people's faces. The flight was spectacular, gliding over a turquoise-blue Caribbean sea that was so clear you could almost see the coral on the seabed below. Then we returned to New York for another four days before flying home.

It was such a special holiday—even though we were constantly busy working at the Traffic Lights bar in Benidorm, it was so important to have a break and to take that time together. You need to make the most of loved ones while they are here. It was just a couple of years later that we would all be reminded of this, when we suddenly lost Pam.

～

In 2011, when John was seventy and I was sixty-five, we decided to retire. We went on cruises round the Mediterranean and, best of all, we could go home for Christmas. For so many years we never had a Christmas and New Year off because we were always at work, entertaining people. Finally we could spend time with family, seeing our children and grandchildren, and enjoy seeing them forge their own way in life.

Our oldest son, John, met his wife, Patricia, in the Cosmopolitan, the bar we ran in the new town in Benidorm. She came with her parents from Glasgow and hit it off with John, and by 1988 they were married. John wanted to join the Royal Navy but a motorbike accident in Benidorm left him with a dodgy knee so instead he worked for his father-in-law who owned McCormack's, the legendary music shop in Glasgow where all the local musicians bought their instruments. The Rolling Stones even cut the ribbon on the opening day in 1963 for their store on Bath Road; so many crowds turned up that they had to barricade the doors and lock up the band inside. John became manager of the shop after his father-in-law retired, keeping the business going. The shop was a Glasgow institution, but badly affected by online competition—it closed down in 2011. Over the years, though, McCormack's sold thousands of guitars and was visited by everyone from the Beatles (who used their amps for a show) to Status Quo, the Eagles, and Slipknot.

Our younger boy, Steven, meanwhile, made a good living as a singer and met his partner, Nicky, while she was working for us in Benidorm. He had an agent but found it lonely being on the road as a solo artist, missing family weddings and parties because he was always working, so he decided to pack it in, settling with Nicky in her hometown of Barnoldswick, Yorkshire—near where I now live.

One of my biggest delights is our grandchildren—Rachel and Victoria, who were born in Scotland; Jake, who lives in Barnoldswick; and his sister Bethany, who now lives in the Isle of Man. They're lovely children, hard workers who have never got into trouble. I've got two sons and two great daughters-in-law, so I feel blessed.

35. MARY

Val Went to the Baltic Sea

In the 2000s many sixties artists were struggling financially, even though the work they created was famous around the world. Getting rights back for musicians and artists is ongoing, because most of the contracts in those days were a joke. Our friend Astrid Kirchherr, for instance, was cheated for years—her pictures were used everywhere and she didn't get a penny out of it. She became friends with Ulf Kruger, a German musician who then made a deal for her with Getty Images. The pair of them started K & K, a Hamburg shop that sold vintage photography and books, and she made appearances at Beatles conventions, signing and selling prints. The 1994 film *Backbeat*, about her relationship with the band and with Stu Sutcliffe, also led to a re-evaluation of her as an artist.

"I'm a very silly girl," Kirchherr said later. "I just had the joy of taking pictures, and I never cared about my negatives. I just gave them away whenever anybody asked for them. I never cared about the money so much, because it was such a joy meeting the Beatles and becoming very close friends with them." In 2011 she sold the rights to her work to a private collector and retired. Like many musicians and artists from the sixties scene, she had to fight for the money, copyright, and recognition she deserved.

Frank was on the board for German record society GEMA for twenty years, ending up vice president in 2015. Since 2005 GEMA has been involved in a long fight with YouTube, Spotify, and other platforms over artists' rights. The big tech streaming giants thought they didn't have to pay musicians for using their music. Frank worked tirelessly for years, engaged in countless meetings with important U.S. lawyers. When he did something, he really did it thoroughly, but he was getting himself so involved I think he just overestimated his own strength.

After our reunion gig Val started having jazz guitar lessons and her playing improved again. She just needed time to get back into music. She bought herself a new guitar and when I went to visit she would show me the jazz pieces she was playing. I was amazed by how good she was, and it reminded me of how fantastic she was as a musician. Val admitted to me, "Mary, to be quite honest I'm very autistic. I've got a barrier up when I'm out socially, but with the music I've learned to get through to people." I noticed that in playing music she was a different person, communicating through her guitar.

Val had a settled existence, getting a wage, the money from Stephan's apartment, and a pension as well. She bought herself a Mini and another car for Suzann, and as often as possible they went away to places, to quiet seaside resorts. They had been together for fourteen years and were enjoying their lives when in 2012, Val was diagnosed with the blood cancer multiple myeloma—strangely, the same thing that my mother had died of a few years earlier. That was when Suzann suggested Val move from Hamburg to her house in the rural town of Bad Oldesloe.

Doctors told Val that the cancer was incurable but they could pro-
long her life with a serious blast of chemotherapy. She decided she'd
take this, even though it meant just a few more years. The six-week
treatment was in Lübeck, close to Bad Oldesloe, and while Val was
in the hospital all her hair fell out: I remember the first day I went into
the room and she said, "Mary, I don't want you to see me like this."

"Val, of course I've got to see you like that. It doesn't matter, you're
my friend." The treatment was so savage that Val was hallucinating.
But it cleared away the cancer and after six weeks she was allowed
to go home. She went back to work while in remission, and for the
next four years she had good days and bad days. Every now and then
she came to Hamburg to see me and sometimes she would bring her
guitar.

The illness affected Val's appearance—her hair had been cut very
short, she was bloated by the chemotherapy, and she no longer looked
quite herself. During this period Sylvia and John came to stay for a
few days along with our old Liverpool friend Beryl Marsden, and Val
drove an hour and a half from Bad Oldesloe especially to see them.
When I answered the door Sylvia thought Val was another guest and
gave a casual hello.

"All right," she responded, in her typically low-key way.

I took Sylvia aside and whispered, "That's Val."

"You're kidding me!"

Sylvia was mortified that she hadn't recognized Val, and it hit her
how much the cancer had taken its toll. But we all sat around the big
table in my kitchen and were soon laughing and catching up on news.

By the autumn of 2016 the cancer had returned—it got so bad that
Val finally realized she was dying. She went back into that hospital in
Lübeck, where she had first had the treatment. I went to see her and
we would go and sit in the corridor and chat. As we walked slowly
around the grounds she reminisced about being in the studio with

the Kinks and talked about the Star-Club days—playing with Chuck Berry in Berlin and her affair with Shay from the Crickets, how he wasn't a big man but he had the biggest thing she'd ever seen. She said how much she appreciated the Liverbirds and being able to do what we did.

By then both Val's parents had passed away, and she spoke about how she and her mum had never got on well, but that she'd always had a very close relationship with her dad. I know that he used to feel sorry for Val, for the way her mum treated her after that horrible rape. He wasn't a strong enough person to stand up to his wife and say, *Do you realize what's just happened to her? Don't be shouting at her!* Val was sure that she and Stephan would have stayed together even if there hadn't been the accident, and that if they'd had a normal marriage she would like to have had children.

My son Benny was living in Stuttgart at the time, and I was down there in early December when I got a phone call from Suzann.

"They reckon she will probably pass away tonight."

"Well, let me know the minute anything happens."

A few days later, on December 11, when I was back to Hamburg, Suzann rang to say that Val had passed away.

It's so sad. I couldn't help but think of what a fantastic, talented person she was and how a lot of her life had been quite terrible. But I also thought of the lucky years Val had had with Suzann. One of the places that they loved was a little peninsula called Fehmarn, in the Baltic Sea, near Denmark. Val had decided she wanted a sea burial, and she wanted her ashes to be scattered. The ceremony was very touching. Frank, Benny, and I were there, along with Suzann and her father and a gay couple who were friends, but nobody from Liverpool. Her father and aunt had already died.

Val did say that one of the reasons why her mum didn't want a big family was that she wanted a good life with the one she had. Val had worn good-quality clothes compared to other children—it was important for Mrs. Gell that they had holidays and smart outfits. When Val was a child they went every year to the Isle of Man and one year they took Sylvia with them, going to see the Ivy Benson orchestra and a hypnotist. Mrs. Gell always made Sylvia welcome at the house and got on with our parents, which made her treatment of Val so strange and bewildering. It was important to Mrs. Gell that nobody knew about the rape, that nothing disrupted the perfect picture.

But even before Val was born there was the shadow of dark memories in her family. Val's father was a thoughtful man. He was one of the British soldiers who liberated Bergen-Belsen concentration camp, and he spent some time in Hamburg after World War Two. He told Val that what he had seen there haunted him for the rest of his life. And when he went to Hamburg years later to visit her, it brought back a lot of memories.

It's testament to Val's strength that, despite the terrible trauma she experienced as a girl, she became such an inspiring musician. Sylvia told me later how it was Val who got her into rock 'n' roll. "I'll always remember when I was fifteen, sitting in her bedroom, and she got her guitar out. I couldn't believe she could play an instrument," she said. I think about Val doing the Liverbirds 1998 reunion after drying out, and I could see how determined she was. I'm proud of the fact that I knew Val—somebody who achieved what she did, and who changed our lives for the better.

36. SYLVIA

Do You Like That, Dad?

John and I wanted to stay active in our retirement, so we volunteered for a Benidorm charity called HELP International, which offers assistance to holidaymakers in trouble—if they have their money stolen or flights canceled or they're ill and can't get back home. We would never give them money, but we might buy their flight and take them to the airport and make sure they got home, or visit them in hospital. As well as helping people, I would go to meetings and write reports. Eventually I became president of HELP and found myself organizing a charity event for Valentine's night, February 14, 2017. John was going to play the keyboards and we had a raffle and singers booked.

About two weeks before, at the end of January, he said to me, "Syl, have you got a paracetamol?"

John had never taken a tablet in his life.

"You want a paracetamol?"

"Yeah, my back's killing me."

"OK."

Then a few hours later he said, "Syl, give us another paracetamol, I need two, that's no good."

"My God, John, that's not like you." He couldn't walk properly, his back was hurting so much.

"Oh, John, we're gonna have to cancel. Love, you're not going to be able to do it."

"No, no. Don't cancel it. Get Tim." Tim Prince was a friend of ours who used to play keyboards in Shooters bar three nights a week after we retired.

"Ask him if he'll do it with you, because you've got it all arranged. The tickets are sold and everything."

Over the next two weeks John's pain came and went. He lost his appetite, sat in a chair all day and couldn't eat. He loved home cooking and often cooked himself, so I knew something was up. When it came to the day of the charity gig I said, "Right, John, I'm not doing this unless you get up to the hospital."

I ran the event with Tim as stand-in, and the next morning, February 15, I took John up to the hospital in Benidorm. The doctor got ready to do blood tests, saying, "You wait in the other room and we'll keep Johnny just for a while. Then we'll find out what's going on."

The doctors kept John in hospital for three weeks while they did MRI scans, a biopsy, and a full series of tests, and they discovered that he had cancer everywhere. Large tumors had spread out from his lungs so they wanted him to do radiotherapy. He came home and four days later had an oncology appointment, with radiotherapy booked the following week. My sons took it in turns to help me, with John junior flying over from Glasgow with his wife one week, and Steven the next. Steven left the night before his father was due to go back to hospital for radiotherapy, but in the early hours of the morning John awoke, saying, "Syl, I can't feel my legs. I can't get up."

"Come on, try and get up."

"I can't, Syl, I can't. My legs have gone."

I phoned John Junior and he said, "Get him to the hospital."

The moment I rang they sent an ambulance right away. The surgeons and the specialists at the hospital were absolutely fantastic but the aftercare was terrible. There are only two patients to a room, but there is pressure on the families to look after them, feed them when the food comes, and help them to the toilet. Nurses administered the medicines and changed the beds but were awful with him. They would send me out while they were changing him and I heard him cry, "Syl, Syl!" I could tell they were just throwing him on one side, then on the other. I said to the doctor, "He's not staying here. I'd like to take him home. Would you provide an ambulance for me to the airport if I get the flight?" She agreed, and gave me all his reports along with DVDs of the scans showing the tumors. My son John got in touch with the doctor at home in Glasgow and said, "I'm bringing me dad. He's not got long to live. But he's not with a doctor."

"As soon as he sets foot on soil here in Britain, in Glasgow, register him," they said.

Steven came over to Benidorm to help me get John out of the ambulance and into the wheelchair at Alicante airport. As soon as he was in the wheelchair the first thing he said was, "Give us a ciggie." And Steven looked at me as if to say, *Don't you dare refuse him.* I knew it was too late anyway. He hadn't been able to smoke in the hospital, so Steven gave him a cigarette. Then we went through Departures and just before we got on the flight he said to me, "Syl, I've got a pain. I'm in terrible pain." We had morphine sprays to put up his nose so Steven said, "Right, just give him what he wants."

"I might overdose him."

"You can't overdose it. Just give him some to get him home." So I did. He was completely out of it, and he didn't bother about anything.

We got him home on the Monday, and in the last few days while he was on the morphine we were playing all his Big Six music on CDs. We'd see him grin. My sons would say, "Do you like that, Dad?" and a smile would spread across his face.

John died at home in Glasgow on Sunday, April 2, 2017, within six weeks of being diagnosed. It was just before our fiftieth wedding anniversary. When he died all the boys got the whisky out and we had an Irish wake, talking to him and remembering him. Steven was a heavy smoker—he never told me this until a year later—and went out that night for a cigarette. When you die you have your mouth open, so when he came back in he blew the smoke into his dad's mouth and said, "Here you are, Dad, here's your last fag."

People might say that's terrible, but it was great—that's how much they thought of him. And you know, from that day, Steven stopped smoking. After he saw what happened to his father, he never smoked again. So that was his last cigarette, too.

John had a fantastic funeral, and so many people came. When we got to the crematorium I said to the boys in the car, "We're too early, there's all these people coming out from the other one."

"Mum, look who's there. Look at the people."

It was all our friends; I just couldn't believe it. I said, "Oh my God, how many?"

John didn't believe in religion, so before he was cremated we had a humanist celebrant talking about his life, and people were saying afterward, God I didn't know he'd done that much! We had a reception in the Station Hotel pub, put on food, and everyone was laughing and telling stories about John's life. The Grand National was on in the pub so we all had a bet and hours later we were still there at midnight and they had to throw us out.

*   *   *

John was a good man. My life wasn't all roses, but he looked after his children, the money was there, and he was happy. I know he loved me and I loved him, and that bond was there right from the start. There was something very romantic about that meeting at the Star-Club—it started with music and continued to be about music, and it lasted half a century.

37. MARY

That Was a Lovely Walk

I look back to when I was forty years old and feel that was a perfect part of our lives. "Yes Sir, I Can Boogie" had happened, we had moved into our house, the kids were teenagers, becoming independent, and Frank and I had enough money to do what we wanted. I was so content with life, and that continued as we watched the kids grow up and make their own way.

Melanie studied jewelry design, moved to London, and had a small shop in Portobello Road for ten years. Her partner was a gardener who traveled around with all his equipment in his van. She became pregnant and our grandson Auryn was born in 2004. On the day of his birth Melanie's contractions were coming fast, so they drove, with her still in pajamas, to St. Mary's Hospital in Paddington and parked the van in front of the building. While her partner was buying a parking ticket, baby Auryn fell out into Melanie's pajama leg. That reminded me of how quickly Melanie herself had been born, back in 1969, when the midwife and I had been taken by surprise. My granddaughter Lillyan arrived four years after her brother. Now

Melanie works in Tate Britain, showing around parties of German visitors and organizing special events in the family room.

Our son Benny works as a music promoter for a big event agency. He married Michelle, a nursery teacher and writer of children's books. They live in Hamburg with our two teenage granddaughters, Eva and Marlena—the latter is already involved in music, singing in the school band. It's wonderful to see them all thrive.

In 2017 Melanie and the children came over from London for the Easter break, and on Easter Monday we went out for a meal with them and Benny to an Italian restaurant just down the road. The next morning we drove Melanie to the airport and said goodbye, waiting until she and the children had gone through security. They waved at us, then we went home and Frank walked the dog while I made us something to eat. It was April 17, a lovely spring day that wasn't too hot, and when he came back after a couple of hours Frank said, "God, Mary, that was a lovely walk. I really enjoyed it."

We ate a roast dinner, turkey with roast potatoes and cabbage. He always said my gravies were the best gravies in the world.

"That was good, that meal, I really enjoyed it."

Frank didn't often say things like that. After dinner we watched a film on TV and he fell asleep. It was about midnight when I said, yawning, "Oh, Frank, I'm going to bed. Good night."

"Good night," he said. On nights like that he'd end up watching the TV till three or four o'clock and sleep in the guest room so he wouldn't disturb me because he was a terrible snorer.

The next morning I got up, had breakfast, and noticed it was ten o'clock and he still wasn't awake. *I'd better wake him up*, I thought, *otherwise he won't be able to sleep tonight*. So I went and opened the door of the guest room, and he was lying there, dead.

*   *   *

For the first second I thought he was pretending, but then I realized, *He wouldn't do that*. He was sprawled half in and half out of bed.

"Frank, Frank!" I cried, and ran downstairs to phone Benny at work.

"Benny, I think Frank's dead."

"What did you just say?"

"You better come. And you'd better phone an ambulance."

I couldn't even remember how to phone the hospital. Then I phoned Sybil, who was one of my best friends, and she and Benny were there within minutes. When the ambulance came, the paramedics said he had died of a heart attack. "He's been dead for hours," they said, in a way that was so impersonal.

Frank didn't have pajamas, so he wasn't wearing anything when I found him. He was always a hippie at heart. He used to walk around naked, and if Sylvia came to stay she would be at the top of the stairs saying, "Oh, Frank."

"What's the matter, sexy Sylvia?"

When I touched him, he was like ice. He was like marble. He was just seventy-one.

I had to get someone to tell Melanie because we'd only taken her to the airport the day before, and the rest of the family came over as soon as they could. The two young paramedics got Frank ready, brought him down, laid him in the hallway and said, "Would you like to say goodbye to him?" We looked at my Frank for a few minutes before they zipped up the sack and carted him away. I didn't want this to be the last time I saw him—so I later went with the family to the funeral parlor to say a proper goodbye.

Frank had done so much for musicians in securing them royalties that the owner of a very popular club in Hamburg offered to host a memorial service. A few weeks later, Frank had a really good farewell.

The club was completely crowded and a lot of young people came up to me to tell me how kind Frank had been to them. One said, "Frank helped me so much. When I asked how I could repay him, all he wanted was a Diet Coke!" This happened often, and when Frank told me about it, I used to say to him, "Can't you ask for a bottle of champagne and I will buy you the Coke!" When the speaker at a funeral service talked about Frank's life it made me realize how many different things he had done. He had even written and produced two *Sesame Street* musicals and one *Bear in the Big Blue House*. They toured all over Germany, Austria, and Switzerland, and children loved them.

Frank is buried in Ohlsdorf Cemetery. We found out later that the captain who torpedoed my uncle's ship during the Second World War is buried in the same place as Frank. Even though it was horrible to lose my uncle, without that torpedo I wouldn't have existed.

Sylvia couldn't come to the funeral because her mother had also just died, aged 103, eleven days after her husband. John died on April 2, Sylvia's mother on April 13, and Frank on April 18. April 2017 was a month of huge loss for us both.

38. SYLVIA

Green Shoots

Just before Frank died, a Liverpool writer called Paul Fitzgerald phoned their house and got through to Frank in the office downstairs in the cellar.

"I don't know if this is the right number, but I'm trying to reach Mary from the Liverbirds."

"What do you want with my beautiful wife?"

"Well, I've got this idea and I'd like to get in touch with Mary and Sylvia. Is it possible to speak to her?"

"Well, you are the luckiest man in the world because I only allow my beautiful wife to talk to other men once a year and that's today."

Paul wanted Mary to write a short version of our story for a magazine he was working for at the time. So she did, and he got back in touch saying, "Gosh, this isn't just a short story, this needs to be a play or a musical."

He and his friend the award-winning playwright Ian Salmon got in touch with us after Frank and John died, but it was a bit too soon.

"Can we leave it for a little while?"

A few months later we came to Liverpool and made arrangements to meet them in a restaurant. Mary and I got together beforehand. We had no idea who we were seeing, so I said, "We're going on a blind date, Mary."

It was the first time we had seen each other after Frank and John died. We put our arms round each other, and you could tell we both knew what the other one was thinking. *There's two people missing at this little meeting, but they'd be made up that this show is happening.* When we went for dinner with Ian and Paul it helped to know the private pain that Mary was going through and vice versa. I'm glad we had each other. We were bonded not just because our husbands had died so close together but because we'd met them in the same place, at the Star-Club. John and Frank always got on and admired each other. It was like they were with us that night.

Ian and Paul were so charming and enthusiastic that they took our mind off things, talking to us about their plans for a Liverbirds musical. They even had a working title that cleverly echoed John Lennon's comment to us: *Girls Don't Play Guitars.*

It took two years to formulate the show, but once the idea was conceived it captured everyone's imagination. *Girls Don't Play Guitars* chronicles those heady five years, from the day in the studio with the Kinks and Mick Jagger, to meeting Brian Epstein, to getting the audition with Henry Henroid and all that frenzied Star-Club period culminating with the tour of Japan. Along the way characters like Klaus Voorman, Chuck Berry, Jimi Hendrix, and even Jimmy Savile put in appearances. Bob Eaton, an acclaimed theater director who has written over twenty musicals including *Lennon, Soul Sister* (about Ike and Tina Turner), and *Our Day Out*, with Willy Russell, came on board early on, along with musical director Howard Gray. The musical was cast and a four-week run was booked at the Liverpool Royal Court Theatre through October 2019.

Over the summer we went to rehearsals, thrilled to see the production taking shape with four young actor musicians who researched us so well that it was like seeing younger versions of ourselves. Lisa Wright played Pam, belting out the songs with a feisty strength, and Molly Grace Cutler was uncannily like Val—right down to her long mane of brown hair and the way she played complicated riffs on guitar. With its vivid primary colors and banks of amplifiers and TV screens, the stage set echoed the style of sixties German TV program *Beat Club*, the perfect backdrop to our story.

During rehearsals Howard said, "If there's anything we can add, just tell us." When the band started playing, Mary and I got up and started dancing together.

"What's that?"

"Well, that's the Stomp, that's what we used to do in the Cavern." So they incorporated that into the musical.

Then just before the show opened on October 3, Howard asked us if we'd like to get up on stage with the backline and perform a song. We had done some small Liverbirds gigs the previous year in Hamburg and Berlin with musician Stefanie Hempel and Bernadette La Hengst, the lead singer/guitarist with Die Braut Haut Ins Auge. We were getting back into a groove, but felt nervous about taking part in the musical.

"We haven't played for ages."

"Just do 'Peanut Butter.' "

"OK."

We started, Mary on bass and me on the drums. They all jumped back.

"Could you do that in the show?"

When it came to the opening night the audience was transfixed throughout the show, and at the end, just when they thought it was over, we walked onstage to join the band. Mary picked up the bass, I sat at the drums, and we launched into "Peanut Butter." People were cheering us and shouting, "Come on, girls!" Even though it was a different version of the Liverbirds, Molly and Lisa replaced Val and Pam in a way that was seamless, and it felt great to be performing again. Mary said later that, while she was playing her bass, she turned around to see me shaking my head and banging the drums just like I used to, as if it were yesterday.

All our children and grandchildren were there, and at the end of the show everyone cried. All the girls from Littlewoods came along, the gang that I used to chat with in the canteen when I was fifteen. They were so delighted to see our story brought to life. How that lifted us—after John and Frank dying, *Girls Don't Play Guitars* really helped us deal with the loss.

I still think about that meeting backstage at the Cavern Club with John Lennon and Paul McCartney in their earlier years before they became really famous. That remark from John made us more determined to have a go. A few days after the show opened we played a promotional gig at the Cavern, and that was a real high point for me. Afterward I got on the mic and said, "Fantastic to be here after fifty-six years. I bet you thought we'd all be on Zimmer frames!" It was like we had come full circle.

Reviews of the show were sparkling: "It crests along on a wave of energy…one of the strongest shows the Royal Court has produced," wrote the *Liverpool Echo*, and *Liverpool Underlined* called it "unmissable." We were interviewed on national breakfast TV and featured in the press. After it closed in November there were plans to tour the show but the COVID pandemic hit and lockdown postponed everything. When they finish a show at the Royal Court they usually get rid of the props and scenery, but over lockdown they kept ours in storage. It was the most expensive stage design they've ever had. At the time of writing, we are excited to hear the show will be back at the

Royal Court once again in 2024, with plans for a tour after that. And in October we went into the studio with Hamburg producer Alexander Seidl to record an album with Molly and Lisa from the Royal Court show. It'll be a mix of old hits plus some new tracks written by Sylvia's son Steven, her grandson Jake, and my brother Joseph. It's great that the band continues to grow.

When I'm asked what I learned from my time in the Liverbirds I'd say it opened my eyes to the world. I was seventeen when we first went to Hamburg, and in those days we were more protected and controlled by our parents; we didn't have the same freedom that teenagers do now. Being in the band and traveling through different countries gave me the confidence to start a business in Spain. It was nothing for John and me to say, "Let's go and do it." Our sons thanked us for what we did because taking them to Spain has given them a fantastic, broad outlook on life.

I have wonderful memories, but I also feel sad about Pam and Val and wish they were here, going on this new journey with us. Another thing I have learned is the strength of female friendship and how Mary and I were able to support each other, both losing our husbands within sixteen days. There were three funerals in close succession. When my mum died I accepted it more because she was 103, but at her funeral my legs went, and my daughter-in-law had to come over and help me. I think that was when it really hit me about John. We had been married for fifty years, which is exceptional for musicians. After we moved to Spain we were together twenty-four hours a day, but we understood and supported each other through difficult times, and we got back up and carried on. The band taught me resourcefulness, working with different people, and adapting to many situations— that's why my back's gone, with arthritis and neck pains; that's all from carrying John's keyboards and amplifiers for years.

*   *   *

Val, Pam, and Mary and I are friends for life. When I think about what endures, it's about being kind and understanding and being there for one another. Sometimes that's easier said than done, so if there is conflict you have your say, have your argument and then forget it. Never fall out. I hate it when I see families where sons and daughters are not talking to each other. I always said to the boys, if ever in life you quarrel, please forget about it the next day. Don't hold onto resentment, and promise me you'll never fall out.

Friendship is the glue that keeps you together, and that's what propelled us into making music in the first place. If I could give advice to any young girl wanting to start a band I'd say, whatever your dream is in life, you can achieve it. Go for it, and if it doesn't work out, at least you can say you tried.

39. MARY

The Cavern Family

In 2019, while the musical was in rehearsal, I was back in Hamburg one evening and there was a message on the answering machine. "Hello, my name is Gabe, I'm phoning from Los Angeles and looking for Mary McGlory from the Liverbirds. I work for a film company called Breakwater. Could you please get in touch if this is the correct number?" I put the phone down and thought, *Somebody's having a joke, this can't be true*, but when I called back I realized what a big opportunity this was. Producer/screenwriter Gabe Godoi works with Academy Award–winning filmmaker Ben Proudfoot, the creative force behind Breakwater Studios. Specializing in short documentaries, they had seen the promotion for *Girls Don't Play Guitars* and wanted to shoot a film about the Liverbirds for the *New York Times* website. I called him back. "I'm off to Liverpool in two weeks to see final rehearsals and meeting Sylvia. Would it be a good idea if you came there?" I said.

Two weeks later Breakwater showed up at the Royal Court Theatre with a full production crew and the most amazing amount of equipment. They shot some of the show and then filmed interviews with us at Sylvia's sister Jean's house in Litherland. I've done many interviews over the years, but this was unusual. Another producer/editor, Ben, set up a tent with special lighting in Jean's front room and asked me questions via video from another room while I talked to the computer screen. With no obvious camera pointing at me I was relaxed and didn't feel nervous, so I found I could talk freely. He interviewed me for four hours. Meanwhile, Sylvia was upstairs getting impatient and wondering how long it would take before it was her turn. Then he spoke to her for four hours.

After the shoot we went with the crew around Liverpool. By chance the house they had rented for five days was on Menlove Avenue, just a few doors down from where John Lennon lived with his auntie, so they filmed us walking by his house.

Shortly afterward the Liverbirds documentary went up on the *New York Times* website and got millions of views. Feature-film offers started to come in, and then snowballed, with over seven different companies interested. One woman even came over to Hamburg to meet me and Sylvia. We've kept in touch with Ben, however, because he was there from the beginning and he really understands our story. We now have a very successful writer from Liverpool working on the screenplay, and in 2024 the film is going into production. There have been other opportunities too, with our cover of "Peanut Butter" ending up in a Coen brothers film, *Drive-Away Dolls*. Pam and Val would have been so proud to know that four decades on, their voices have endured in that way.

I'm amazed at the interest in the Liverbirds, but in doing this memoir I've realized how much our story is part of the time, the sixties era. I'm sometimes asked if I have any regrets. Maybe for a second, years ago, we might have thought, *What would have happened if we had gone with Brian Epstein?* On the other hand, not everybody who went with Brian was a success. Remo Four are still for me one of the best bands that existed and Brian more or less used them as a backing group. In 1967 they played on George Harrison's first solo album, the soundtrack to the movie *Wonderwall*, yet never got royalties. I'm still so impressed by them and think they'd have been more successful with somebody else.

Writing this book has also made me reevaluate my family and my life. I realize what a hardworking woman my grandma was, and how difficult it must have been for my mother and yet she still got it all together, settling down with my father and having all those children. I realized the support I was given when Frank was going through a lot with the Star-Club finances, and when I decided to stay in Germany after the Liverbirds finished. I don't think I could have done it without my friend Erica, Achim's wife, who took me out dancing when I was feeling low, and even though she and Achim later divorced she has always stayed in touch. It's made me appreciate the importance of friendship.

I think the secret of the Liverbirds' friendship was the fact that we shared rooms together and that gave us the opportunity to get to know each other and become like sisters. We knew we could rely on each other and if anyone was in a bad state or in need, one of us would be there to help. There are good friendships between men as well—Dicky Tarrach and Frank stayed friends for life, and they were the two in the Rattles who shared a room together on tour. Sylvia and I still think nothing of staying in the same room and sometimes even share a bed. We laugh and say, "This is just like the olden days!" When I think back, one of our best moments was seeing the Beatles at the Cavern, going on to play there as a band, and realizing we'd achieved something. When we went onstage and girls started cheering and doing the Stomp, we knew we were part of the Cavern family.

~

Everything happening with the Liverbirds has enabled me to cope with loss and to occupy my mind. I was absolutely devastated when

Frank died. I always thought, because of my asthma and my chest problems, that I'd be the one to go first. Frank always seemed so healthy. After the first night of the musical it was lovely to see my grandchildren all sitting there together, saying, "That's our grand-mother!" They were so proud. It's really sad that Frank didn't see it because he always wanted this to happen—he used to say, "If nobody writes a play about your band, I'll do it."

It would have also been such a big help to Val and Pam, because they would've realized they are appreciated for their part in musical history. We all played our part. We were young girls having the cour-age to make a go of something; it's an easygoing story that wasn't easy to do. Once we did the Liverbirds it made everything possible and gave us the confidence to do more. It happened as we wanted it to happen, and we wouldn't have had it any other way.

The Liverbirds:
Select Discography

Albums

All on Star-Club Records unless otherwise indicated.

1965

Star-Club Show 4: "Johnny B. Goode," "You Can't Judge a Book by Looking at the Cover," "Love Hurts," "Talking about You," "Mona," "Money," "Too Much Monkey Business," "Road Runner," "Diddley Daddy," "Hands Off," "Before You Accuse Me," "Leave All Your Old Loves in the Past," "Got My Mojo Working"

1966

More of the Liverbirds: "Peanut Butter," "It's So Exciting," "He Hardly Ever Calls Me Honey Anymore," "For Your Love," "Oh No Not My Baby," "Around and Around," "Down Home Girl," "He's Something Else," "Heatwave," "Why Do You Hang Around Me," "He's About a Mover," "Long Tall Shorty"

Singles & EPs

1964

"Shop Around"/"It's Got to Be You"

1965

"Peanut Butter"/"Why Do You Hang Around Me"
"Diddley Daddy"/"Leave All Your Old Loves in the Past" (Fontana)

1966

"Loop De Loop"/"Bo Diddley Is a Lover"

Compilations

1965

On *The Star-Club Singles Complete Vol. 2*: Various
The Liverbirds: "Shop Around," "It's Got to Be You"

2009

On *Destroy That Boy! More Girls With Guitars*: Various (Ace)
The Liverbirds: "He's Something Else," "Talking About You," "He's About a Mover"

2010

From Merseyside to Hamburg—The Complete Star-Club Recordings: "Talking About You," "Bo Diddley Is a Lover," "He's Something Else," "Long Tall Shorty," "He's About a Mover,"

"You Can't Judge a Book by Looking at the Cover," "Johnny B. Goode," "Mona," "Road Runner," "Diddley Daddy," "Money (That's What I Want)," "Got My Mojo Working," "Hands Off," "Too Much Monkey Business," "Before You Accuse Me," "Leave All Your Old Loves in the Past," "Shop Around," "It's Got to Be You," "Peanut Butter," "Oh No Not My Baby," "It's So Exciting," "He Hardly Ever Calls Me Honey Anymore," "Loop De Loop," "Love Hurts," "For Your Love," "Around and Around," "Down Home Girl," "Heatwave," "Why Do You Hang Around Me" (Big Beat Records)

2019

On *She Came From Liverpool! (Merseyside Girl-Pop 1962–1968)*: Various (Ace)
The Liverbirds: "Long Tall Shorty," "Why Do You Hang Around Me"

2023

On *Let's Stop! Merseybeat And Beyond 1962–1969*: Various (Strawberry)
The Liverbirds: "Talking About You"

Acknowledgments

Mary

We'd like to thank all the people who contributed to this book, including interviewees Glynne Bulman, Tony and Irene Coates, Lee Curtis, Roy Dyke, Gibson and Tina Kemp, Oskar Machelet, Beryl Marsden, Joseph McGlory, Jean Ramsey, Chris Saunders, Rosi Sheridan, and Dicky Tarrach.

And we want to thank Lucy O'Brien—where would we be without you—your help, patience, and knowledge.

Huge thanks go to Paul Fitzgerald and Ian Salmon, Gabe Godoi and Ben Proudfoot at Breakwater, and Fred Dostal.

We'd also like to thank Jenny Hewson and Alexa von Hirschberg, along with our editors, Fiona Crosby at Faber and Karen Kosztolnyik at Grand Central, for their enthusiasm and belief in the book. Also Christine Feldman-Barrett for context on the Liverbirds in Germany. We would like to thank agent Susan Golomb for finding us to tell our story in the USA.

I have to thank my children and grandchildren for being proud of their Nana, and encouraging us to do it. And our soul mates Pam and Val. Doing this book has brought back so many memories—the four of us were like a jigsaw puzzle. They were two amazing people (even though Pam could be a bit of a headache!), and Val—despite her struggles she still had the willpower to not give up, and she made a new life for herself. I am full of admiration for my friend.

And of course Frank, who helped me to be the person I am today—always making sure that I realized how much he needed my opinions and that we were a team—we were equals. He always said we should write a book, I wish he had been able to see this become reality. Yes, Sylvia and I married our biggest fans.

Sylvia

We are eternally grateful to Lucy O'Brien for capturing our story exactly as it happened and exactly how we wanted. Mary and I have had mainly happy but also some sad memories when recalling our lives in the Liverbirds. We wish Val and Pam could have shared in the journey Mary and I have had writing the book and hope we've done them proud and retold their parts how they would have wished.

I'm also so happy my siblings, my sons, and my grandchildren can read about how we conquered prejudices of the 1960s with our music and friendship. They will hopefully be as proud of us as we are of them.

And of course, my John. We had our own journey, after the Liverbirds. An adventure that was equally wonderful.

John and Mary's Frank were always proud of us and always wished our story could be told.

About the Authors

Sylvia Saunders and Mary McGlory—The Liverbirds was one of the world's first all-female rock 'n' roll bands. Consisting of bassist and vocalist Mary McGlory, drummer Sylvia Saunders, vocalist and guitarist Valerie Gell, and guitarist and songwriter Pamela Birch, the band started on the Merseybeat music scene in 1962. They achieved success in the UK and Europe, particularly in Germany, where they were a top attraction at the Star-Club in Hamburg and reached number 5 in the German charts. The group was active for five years and in that time recorded two hit albums, toured stadiums, and played with the Kinks, the Rolling Stones, and Chuck Berry. Pamela died in 2009 and Valerie in 2016. Mary lives in Hamburg and Sylvia in Lancashire.

Photo Credits